DATE		
MAY 7 '86	NO 18 '99	
NOV 26 '86	JUN 03 '02	
FEB 9 1990	MAR 31 '04	
SEP 11 '92	AG 28 '07	
FEB 28 '94	SE 22 '10	
NOV 14 '94	AP 28 11	
NOV 21 '96		
DE 11 '97		
OC 15 '98		
DE 18 '98		

the ABC of
PSYCHOLOGY

the ABC of PSYCHOLOGY

Leonard Kristal

General Editor

Facts On File Publications
460 Park Avenue South
New York, N.Y. 10016

The ABC of Psychology

Published in the United States by
Facts On File, Inc.
460 Park Avenue South
New York, NY 10016

Library of Congress Cataloging in Publication Data
Main entry under title:

The ABC of psychology.

1. Psychology. I. Kristal, Leonard. II. Argyle,
Michael. III. Title: A.B.C. of psychology.
BF121.A22   1982   150   82-1524
ISBN 0-87196-678-6   AACR2

Printed in The United States of America
10 9 8 7 6 5 4 3 2 1

Foreword

"In regard to human knowledge, there are two questions that may be asked: first, what do we know? and second, how do we know it? The first of these questions is answered by science, which tries to be as impersonal and dehumanised as possible ... but in relation to our second question, namely how do we come by our knowledge, psychology is the most important of the sciences. Not only is it necessary to study psychologically the processes by which we draw inferences, but it turns out that all the data upon which our inferences should be based are psychological in character ... The apparent reality of our world is in part delusive and in part inferential: all the raw material of our knowledge consists of mental events in the lives of separate people. In this region, therefore, psychology is supreme." Bertrand Russell, *Human Knowledge, Its Scope and Limits.*

The study of psychology covers virtually every aspect of our lives. It examines our behaviour, our motives, our thoughts, our feelings, our perceptions, and how we think about our behaviour, motives, thoughts ... In a rapidly changing and complex world, psychology has become a major problem-solving discipline. Since the problems are legion the questions to which psychologists seek answers are legion. The science of psychology has travelled far since Wilhelm Wundt set up the first experimental laboratory at Leipzig University in 1879. Today the American Psychological Association alone has 50,000 members, most of whom hold doctoral degrees. Thousands of other psychologists work in universities, hospitals and research establishments in virtually every country in the developed world.

There is probably no culture that does not have its storehouse of psychological knowledge, its theories about how the mind works. We are all psychologists of a kind. In our everyday lives we do what the psychologist does in the laboratory. We observe people. We listen to what they say: We watch how they react. And on the basis of this information we form theories. We then test our theories by making predictions and seeing if they come true, or we search around for evidence to support them.

It is almost impossible to watch television or read a newspaper today without having pseudo-psychological interpretations thrust at us. In an era when life's options are wider than ever before and when, for that very reason, we are more vulnerable to confusion and manipulation than ever before, there is a great need for clear self-understanding and an awareness of the psychological forces acting on us. We can, if we understand them accurately, use the ideas of the great men and women of psychology to make sense of social and political change, spot the occasions in our personal lives when we have the choice between passivity and positive growth, and come to appreciate more fully the people around us.

The ABC of Psychology contains up to date and often topical summaries of all the major concepts, movements and applications of psychology today. Brevity is a virtue we decided to abandon when writing about issues of great social concern – aggression, drug addiction, alcoholism, mental illness – or topics of special interest to the general reader – phobias, hypnosis, sex therapy, parapsychology. Accounts of fascinating experiments often take the place of dry definitions. Descriptions of psychological disorders are accompanied by information about treatment. Ideas are set firmly in the perspective of the 1980s and related to common experience. We trace the often mysterious associations between psychology and physiology. We sketch in the lives and ideas of famous psychologists – in choosing which names to include we decided that it was more important to choose those whose concepts relate to the contemporary psychological scene, even though others may be just as important historically.

Though entries are arranged in alphabetical order, this is emphatically not a dictionary of definitions, nor is it exhaustive. The wide-awake reader will soon realise that the length of entries is a fairly reliable guide to their relative importance in psychology today. When planning this book I decided that it should be a mosaic of many of the most forward-looking ideas in psychology. Each of the major contributors has completed significant research which has in some measure changed the course of thought and enquiry in his or her special discipline.

Most readers will, I am sure, be surprised to learn just how many aspects of their 'private' lives have been looked into by psychologists. As well as working in hospitals and clinics, many psychologists today are engaged in far-reaching research, seeking answers in controversial and sometimes very intimate areas of human experience. Psychology has made enormous strides in the last two decades, but it still has a vast contribution to make to education, industry, penal reform, crime prevention. It is now recognised that it has a mighty contribution to make to health, traditionally the preserve of the medical profession – psychologists have proved beyond a doubt that the mind reigns over the body. Indeed the mind has always been the physician's greatest ally when treating patients.

Psychology today is one of the most dynamic of all the sciences and the one most accessible to every man and woman of common sense and average curiosity. In the sense that psychological truths can be absorbed and acted on with the speed of thought, it is also the most instantly useful. I speak for all those who have contributed to this book when I say that psychology should be 'given away', because it is a potent force for improving the quality of human existence.

Which brings me to the pleasant task of saying thank you to everyone who helped in the preparation of this book, in particular to my eminent associate editors, Michael Argyle, Gerald Davison, Hans Eysenck and Charles Spielberger, and to a very distinguished international cast of contributing editors. I am also indebted to at least a dozen other people for their expert help with research and checking. And finally my thanks go to Anne Cope who wielded her creative and rigorous editorial skills to put this alphabetical jig-saw puzzle neatly together.

Leonard Kristal
General Editor

General editor

Leonard Kristal, Ph.D., is Lecturer in the Department of Psychology at the University of Maryland (European Division), London, and General Editor of the *Life Cycle* series, which has sold over 2 million copies worldwide. He studied psychology and sociology in South Africa and Israel, and clinical psychology at Cambridge University. As a Post-doctoral Fellow at Oxford University and later as Senior Clinical Psychologist at Shalvata Psychiatric Centre, Tel Aviv University Medical School, his ideas about making the findings of psychological research available to the general public began to crystallise. In 1977 he launched a specialised publishing and audio-visual enterprise to put these ideas into practice. He lectures regularly and has made a number of appearances on television and radio. His latest book *Understanding Psychology* is one of the titles in the *Life Cycle* series.

Associate editors

Michael Argyle, D.Sc., is Reader in Social Psychology and Fellow of Wolfson College at the University of Oxford. He is the author of 11 books, including *The Psychology of Interpersonal Behaviour*, *Social Interaction* and *Bodily Communication*, and co-founder of the *British Journal of Social and Clinical Psychology*. He is a Fellow of the British Psychological Society, and a past chairman of its Social Psychology Division, and also an affiliate member of the European and American Societies for Experimental Social Psychology. He is a visiting professor of universities in the USA, Canada, Australia, Europe, Israel and Africa. Michael Argyle's ruling interest, for which he is internationally acknowledged, is the experimental study of social interaction and its application to social skills training as well as to wider social problems.

Gerald C. Davison, Ph.D., is Professor of Psychology and Director of Clinical Training at the University of Southern California. He divides his time equally between teaching and clinical work, and is a leading authority on behaviour modification techniques and on the clinical training of behaviour therapists. His special area of interest has been sexual and homosexual problems, and the legal and ethical issues of treating such problems by behavioural techniques. He also has extensive experience of applying behavioural techniques to phobias, autism and certain compulsive behaviours. He is consultant editor and reviewer for some two dozen American and Canadian psychological journals and a regular contributor to many more. He is a past president of the Association for Advancement of Behavior Therapy and Fellow of the American Psychological Association.

Hans J. Eysenck, Ph.D., D.Sc., is professor of Psychology at the Institute of Psychiatry, University of London, and one of today's best known and most quoted psychologists. He pioneered experimental research into individual differences in personality and intelligence, and the behavioural approach to psychotherapy. He is the author of some three dozen books including *The Biological Basis of Personality*, *Sex and Personality*, *Uses and Abuses of Psychology*, *The Inequality of Man*, *Sense and Nonsense in Psychology* and *Know your own IQ*. He is a Fellow of the British Psychological Society and the American Psychological Association, serves on the boards of at least a dozen British, American and German journals of psychology, has lectured in universities worldwide and has been Visiting Professor at the Universities of Pennsylvania and Berkeley, California.

Charles D. Spielberger, Ph.D., is Professor of Psychology and Director of the Center for Research in Community Psychology at the University of South Florida, Tampa. A leading international authority on stress and anxiety, he has contributed extensively to the literature in his field of study both as author and editor. His *State-Trait Anxiety Inventory* is rapidly becoming the international standard for measurement of anxiety. Professor Spielberger is a Diplomate in clinical psychology of the American Board of Professional Psychology, and a Fellow of the American Psychological Association, of the American Association for the Advancement of Science and of the Society for Personality Assessment. He is a past president of the Community Psychology division of the American Psychological Association and also founding editor of the *American Journal of Community Psychology*.

Contributing editors We are pleased to acknowledge the special contributions of the following, all of whom are listed in greater detail on pages 251 and 252: Alan D. Baddeley, Judith M. Bardwick, Leonard Berkowitz, Irving Binik, Shlomo Breznitz, John J. Conger, Brian S. Everitt, Frank Falkner, Marjorie Fiske, Donald W. Goodwin, Jerome Jaffe, Robert Kastenbaum, Christopher Macy, Kevin M. McConkey, Donald Meichenbaum, Martin T. Orne, Rhona Rapoport, Robert Rapoport, Martin P. M. Richards, Judith M. Rodin, A. John Rush, Thomas S. Szasz, Leonore Tiefer, Sheldon White, Robert T. Wilkinson.

Abnormal A greater or lesser degree of deviation from whatever norm one has in mind; because of its judgemental overtones the word is sparingly used by modern psychologists. *Abnormal psychology* is the study of the nature and treatment of mental and behavioural anomalies.

Abreaction Literally 'a reaction away from'; the discharge of pent-up emotion by *working through* (recalling and verbalising) repressed memories, in the presence of a psychoanalyst or psychotherapist.

Absurdity Something which appears incomprehensibly silly, meaningless, devoid of all relevance. *Absurdities tests* are diagnostic of a person's ability to think logically. Intentional absurdity, representing 'time-off' from logical thought, can be side-splittingly funny.

Accident-proneness A tendency towards self-injury motivated, according to Freudians, by unconscious masochism. A simpler explanation might be lack of co-ordination or absent-mindedness. Some personality theorists have even suggested an accident-prone personality type.

Accommodation Changes in the lens and ciliary muscles of the eye which alter depth of focus; cessation in the transmission of nerve impulses when stimulation is continuous or unchanging (e.g one accommodates to tickling very quickly).

Normal or abnormal?

Acetylcholine Neurotransmitter substance which ensures that nerve impulses cross synapses in the parasympathetic part of the autonomic nervous system, and also synapses between motor nerves and skeletal muscles.

Murray

Motivation

Achievement Supposedly one of the most potent motives in human behaviour, and entirely socially based. Social psychologists have devised various tests which measure *achievement motivation* as well as the equally pervasive motivation to avoid failure, the 'fear of success' motive. Low achievement motivation and/or a fear of failure can inhibit academic and occupational success even in persons of good ability. Many feminists argue that the study of achievement-motivation has been biased by the male sex-role stereotype.

Acting out Unconsciously expressing buried memories and conflicts in one's actions. You hide your resentment of your boss, but you 'take it out' on your workmates! The opposite of 'working through'.

A

Nervous system

Psychoanalysis

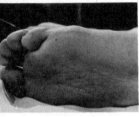

You won't feel a thing

Drug dependence

Action potential The extremely short-lived reversal of the different electrical potentials on the inside and outside of an axon membrane when a nerve impulse travels along it.

Active therapy A psychoanalytic technique designed to shorten treatment time. The analyst actively intervenes in the patient's mental life, injecting interpretations, advice or suggestions from his or her clinical experience, rather than concentrating solely on material offered by the patient.

Acupuncture Blocking pain, and more lately diagnosing dysfunction, by sticking fine needles into certain sites on the skin remote from the organ requiring treatment or diagnosis; a method of pain relief tried and tested in China for thousands of years, though Western interest has centred on its anaesthetic uses.

Addiction Compulsive use or abuse of any substance, sometimes producing withdrawal symptoms (anxiety, craving, sleep difficulties, aches and pains) when use is discontinued. The line between physical dependence and psychological dependence is very hazy.

When a habit like smoking becomes unbreakable, or only breakable with difficulty, it can fairly be called an addiction. The word 'addiction' comes from the Latin meaning 'given over to a master'. An addict is a slave to his addiction.

Alfred Adler, 1870–1937

Adler, Alfred Alfred Adler was born in Vienna in 1870, into a prosperous middle-class family, and received his doctor's training at the University of Vienna, specialising first in ophthalmology and then in psychiatry. Like Jung he was an early disciple of Freud but later broke with him and all forms of psychoanalysis in the belief that man is primarily a social rather than a sexual being. His own approach to psychology, known as *individual psychology*, attracted a large following in the 1920s and 1930s. In 1935 he moved to the United States where he continued his practice as a psychiatrist. However his life in the New World was shortlived – he died in 1937.

Adler's major contribution to personality theory was the concept of the *creative self* – a personal, subjective power which interprets and translates our experiences into a coherent system, and which seeks (and even creates) experiences which lead to a unique lifestyle. Unlike Freud he believed that people are motivated more by their expectations of the future than by the shadow of their past. He also developed the concept of the *inferiority complex*, for which he is commonly best remembered. Feelings of inferiority, he theorised, are due to a sense of incompletion in any sphere of life.

Adolescence *John Conger*

Adolescence can be a time of irrepressible joy and seemingly inconsolable sadness, gregariousness and loneliness, altruism and self-centredness, of confidence and self-doubt. But above all adolescence is a period of rapid inner change – physical, sexual and intellectual.

In contemporary industrialised societies the adolescent is expected to master many complex developmental tasks in a very short period of time – independence from parents, social and working relationships, adult sexual roles. He or she is also under pressure to decide on personal and vocational goals.

'Who am I?' To meet these challenges, the adolescent must develop a sense of his or her own identity, a view of the world and a set of standards that are 'non-negotiable'. Many adolescents find themselves playing roles that change from one situation or one moment to another. They worry about which, if any, is the 'real me', and self-consciously try out different roles in the hope of finding one which 'clicks'.

Auditioning for a role in life

I doubt whether anyone can have survived the past couple of decades, except possibly on a desert island, without hearing the term 'adolescent identity crisis'. So widespread has the term become that its 'inventor' Erik Erikson was recently prompted to wonder if so many young people would be having 'identity crises' if they didn't think they were supposed to!

Identity: positive and negative The process of identity formation starts in infancy and continues through all the partial identifications that a growing child forms with parents, peers, and others, well into mature life.

The process of identity formation can be relatively simple or agonising, depending on many factors. Contemporary society offers great opportunities for personal growth and development, but there is little unanimity as to appropriate values and life-styles. Youngsters are increasingly left to their own resources. The lucky ones have parents with well-defined identities of their own, who can serve as sound role models. But for some youngsters the struggle to achieve a rich, full and unique identity is 'prematurely foreclosed', to use Erikson's term: instead of finding themselves when they leave school, get married and go out to work, they become like everybody else.

Unfortunately, the only protection that some adolescents have against identity confusion is development of a negative identity: they adopt a negative, deviant identity, becoming delinquents or dropouts. For them, socialisation has missed its mark. Successful adjustment to society is the process of achieving one's unique potential without infringing the liberties of others.

Emotions

Adrenaline (Epinephrine, USA) A hormone secreted by the adrenal glands which readies the sympathetic nervous system for fight or flight by increasing heart rate and metabolism, constricting non-vital arteries, releasing sugar into the bloodstream, etc.

Affect Any feeling or emotion temporarily attached to an idea; hence 'incongruity of affect', feelings inappropriate to a specific idea, like laughing on hearing of a serious accident. The adjective *affective* is used in phrases like *affective tone* (the general hue of one's feelings), *affective deficiency* (lack of feeling) and *affective association* (any feeling fairly consistently connected with an idea).

Afferent Literally 'carrying towards'; nerves which convey incoming sensory information into the central nervous system are afferent.

Murray

Affiliation need Our need to associate with others, preferably those with similar concerns; increases with increased anxiety and uncertainty, but decreases in extreme emotional states (grief, end of a love affair); most psychologists regard affiliation as essential to psychological well-being.

Ageing   *Robert Kastenbaum*

During a recent conversation with a woman who was close to her 100th birthday, I asked her what she made of her life in general. She promptly replied: "Can't tell yet! I'm still making my life!"

The prejudice that old age is a worthless, miserable state is virtually guaranteed to poison us throughout our life span. Of

Hard lessons worth listening to

what value is adulthood if it leads to such a valueless state?

Old age in perspective In many parts of the world it is the old who are responsible for transmitting history, value, culture. Only a real person can make the past live and help us understand our place in the ancient procession of life. Among our elders today are many who have overcome adversity. Their accomplishments are real, and deserve respect.

The old do not have to look exclusively to the past. Relieved of some of life's responsibilities and fortified by many years of experience and knowledge, they may have a much better idea of how to spend their time enjoyably than they did in their youth. And not all enjoyment is restricted to the philosophical or creative. Healthy physical activity remains quite possible for most of us well into our later years.

Old people sometimes display surprising freedom and forthrightness in the expression of their thoughts and feelings, and an ability to transmit affection. It is as though some of the rituals which constrict us in earlier life fall away.

But - there is always a but - a higher percentage of people suffer from emotional distress in old age than at any other time in adult life, and the gap between need and care is often filled by dubious measures, such as heavy-handed prescription of drugs. For many years it was assumed that old people were not appropriate candidates for psychotherapy. But a few clinicians have risen to the challenge and discovered that individual and group psychotherapy is just as effective with the old as with the young.

It is easy to understand why an earthquake causes terror. Yet in old age there may be terror of a very private nature, a sense of disintegration sometimes stemming from inner conflicts, sometimes from a premonition of death or the fear of becoming dependent.

The spectre of dependence Dependency is a grim choice: insecurity and deprivation must be weighed against loss of autonomy and integrity. But, as biologists and social gerontologists point out, if there is nothing shameful about the dependency of a baby or a young child, there should be nothing shameful about the dependencies natural with old age and diminishing physical resources.

The complexity and impersonality of the bureaucratic establishments which have the means to provide help is often threatening to old people. The younger generation today, on the other hand, will have had many decades to interact with 'the system' by the time they reach old age.

The end of life Many of us (including health care-providers) assume that we know what old people and dying people want, but our assumptions are often a projection of our own thoughts and feelings, and often based on personal interpretations of very scanty bits of observation. Such assumptions are really an excuse to avoid close contact with the terminally ill. Assuming we 'know' what they want, we absolve ourselves from being with them, and sharing their thoughts about the end of life.

Senility

We sometimes assume, wrongly, that the old person is too confused or senile to be aware of the nearness of death. In consequence, communication between a dying person and others is subject to extraordinary omissions and distortions. 'Protecting' the dying from knowledge of their condition often serves to protect *us* from the uncomfortable prospect of talking about dying and death. Evasions like this only lead to increasing isolation at a time when emotional honesty and understanding are most needed.

Physical violence: essentially different from the violence of social, political and financial institutions?

Aggression   *Leonard Berkowitz*

The term 'aggression' means different things to different people. Consider the many different behaviours that are lumped together as 'aggression': forceful or assertive actions (we sometimes hear of an 'aggressive salesman'); attempts to overcome difficulties (we talk of 'attacking' or 'tackling' a problem); any form of behaviour that hurts someone, whether the injury is deliberate or not (American football is often called an 'aggressive sport', but players rarely set out to hurt each other). Some authorities believe it is valid to call all such actions 'aggression' on the grounds that same underlying drive motivates them all, but this view is disputed. Aggression is now increasingly defined as any action, verbal or physical, that is intended to hurt its target. It is injurious or destructive intent which marks a behaviour as 'aggression' and not its outward form, however rough or forceful it might be.

Instrumental and hostile aggression However, it is useful to distinguish between different types of aggression. Even when we employ the relatively narrow definition given above, it is fairly obvious that the kind of aggression displayed by carnivores hunting for food, and even by hired human killers, is very different in origin from aggression as an act of self-defence, malice or cruelty. In all of these instances the aggressor is trying to hurt or destroy the victim. But the first sort of aggression is *instrumental aggression*, in the sense that its main aim is to obtain food or money, not to inflict pain. Aggression prompted by hate or cruelty is called *hostile aggression* by some authorities since its main aim clearly is injury of some kind. Hostile aggression is not uniquely linked to the motive of malice or cruelty, however. Anger can also cause people to want to harm others, whatever other aims they have. There is even evidence that we are inclined to show hostile aggression simply as a result of being exposed to unpleasant events. *Defensive aggression* may be yet another type of aggression, in which the aim is to escape an unpleasant stimulus or end a particular danger.

Where does aggression come from? No matter how many categories of aggression are eventually identified by students of human and animal behaviour, it is now clear that aggression does not always arise in the same manner. Sigmund Freud, Konrad Lorenz and their followers argue that one driving force powers every form of aggression (and other kinds of behaviour as well, such as assertiveness, the striving for mastery, and even attempts to achieve independence) and that this force or 'aggressive energy' constantly builds up by itself inside the body and constantly seeks expression. According to this notion, aggressive energy must be 'discharged' safely, in make-believe aggression or in games, or the result will be a sudden, explosive outburst of violence.

However, besides demolishing the idea of a single aggressive drive, recent research has seriously brought into question the idea that people are pent-up depots of aggressive energy. Some people attack others because they have learned that aggression is enjoyable, or because they find that aggressive behaviour 'pays off'. Except when we are angry, it is highly unlikely that we have an aggressive force churning inside us that impels us to hurt others.

Most serious students of aggression rule out the existence of an 'aggressive instinct'. Neither animals nor humans have an inborn urge to hurt or destroy others. What we all possess is a number of physiological and psychological mechanisms that have to be appropriately stimulated by some outside happening before they begin to operate. Some of these mechanisms we are born with, others we acquire through learning.

Reward and punishment Aggression of the instrumental kind is obviously greatly affected by past learning. We tend to repeat those actions that are rewarded; if we find aggression pays, by bringing approval or social status or even money, we will probably continue to be aggressive. Bullies become bullies because they learn that they can get what they want by threatening people smaller and weaker than themselves. Members of violent groups learn to be tough because toughness wins high status in the group. Hostile aggression, in which the primary aim is to inflict pain, is more of a mixture.

Some people are aggressive because they have learned that it can be pleasurable to hurt others; they lash out when they want this form of pleasure, even when they are not angry. However, most of us engage in hostile aggression in a more emotional fashion, mostly when we are angry as the result of an unpleasant experience. This reaction is probably partly 'built into' us by our biological inheritance, but here too learning is undoubtedly important. If we attack someone when we are angry and feel gratified rather than remorseful that our attack has hurt them, we are more rather than less likely to indulge in anger-induced hostile aggression again.

Research has repeatedly shown that the opportunity to aggress, and successfully inflict pain or injury, encourages still more aggression. Clearly, aggression does not work on the catharsis principle.

Finding answers Aggression is a phenomenon of huge importance in the world today. And it is one of psychology's major challenges to understand it, and reduce and control it if possible. One way to lessen the likelihood of aggression, of course, is to try to reduce the number of decidedly unpleasant happenings that provoke anger and aggression. More realistically perhaps, we can also teach people to restrain themselves when they are angry; people can learn to solve their problems constructively when they are emotionally aroused instead of engaging in destructive violence. And most important of all, we can avoid encouraging or rewarding aggressive behaviour.

Agoraphobia Not, as is so commonly thought, dread of open spaces, but fear of being in public or in crowded places (*agora* means 'market place'); an agoraphobic might be far happier in an open field than in a department store on a Saturday afternoon; a phobia much commoner in women than men.

Alcoholism

What is alcoholic dependence? The exact definition of alcoholism is still debated. Agreement is fairly general when dependence on alcohol is severe, in other words when most of the components of the alcohol dependence syndrome are clearly present. The syndrome includes: subjective awareness of a compulsion to drink; drinking taking precedence over family, job, friends, and health; narrowing of the drinking repertoire so that drinking behaviour becomes more and more stereotyped; increasing tolerance to alcohol; withdrawal symptoms

Reinforcement

Catharsis

Phobias

17

A

such as shakiness, sweating and depression; frequent drinking to escape and avoid withdrawal symptoms, which typically disappear after a few drinks; bottles hidden away at home or at work in readiness for the sudden onset of withdrawal symptoms; inability to remain abstinent for long.

There is no particular point at which a heavy drinker suddenly becomes an alcoholic. Alcoholic dependence is not an all-or-none phenomenon but, like deafness or fatness, manifests itself by degrees.

Genetic factors and conditioning in alcoholic dependence Donald W. Goodwin

There is evidence that a tendency towards alcoholism is inherited. There is also evidence that conditioning is a powerful influence on addictive behaviour. So how do these two factors, inherited tendency and conditioning, interact?

Euphoria

Some people experience more euphoria from alcohol than others. This is a physiological reaction, and so there is good reason to suppose that it is genetically determined. Because euphoria is a 'positive reinforcer', in other words pleasant and something one would like to repeat, presumably people who experience the most euphoria are the ones most likely to drink heavily.

Now, like most drugs of abuse, alcohol is quickly absorbed and eliminated. Its effects appear and disappear rapidly. Euphoria appears and disappears equally rapidly, to be replaced by the opposite sensation of 'dysphoria'. Presumably those individuals who experience the most euphoria also experience the most dysphoria. And the most immediate and available cure for dysphoria is more alcohol. After a few drinks, they drink more to relieve the dysphoria than to restore the euphoria. So drink begins to have a double reinforcing effect: it produces a high, and reduces a low. Thus, in genetically susceptible individuals, drinking is massively reinforcing.

After abstaining for a while, binge drinkers often relapse. Why should a binge drinker start drinking again after experiencing the truly ghastly effects of a binge? Some alcoholics are psychopaths, in which case relapse may be a genuine inability to 'learn' from experience, but most alcoholics learn from *most* experiences as well as the next person. So why do they relapse? A phenomenon known as 'stimulus generalisation' may be the answer.

Generalisation

A stimulus becomes 'generalised' when the ups and downs produced by a specific stimulus, in this case alcohol, become associated with a wide variety of internal states and external circumstances. Even heavy drinkers drink more heavily on certain occasions and in certain settings. Their drinking highs and lows then become associated with those occasions and settings. All euphoriant stimuli become the cue for a drink, and all dysphoriant stimuli call for a drink too. A wide variety of internal feelings and external events become 'conditioned

Pavlov

stimuli', encouraging the 'conditioned response' of drinking.

Relapse can therefore be seen as a conditioned response to a combination of internal and external conditioned stimuli. Probably the exact combination is different for different people at different times.

Host or hostage? There are two ways in which genetic factors may operate to increase or decrease the possibility of an individual becoming dependent on alcohol and on other rapidly-acting psychotropic drugs.

Fortunately many of us are 'protected' because we experience unpleasant physiological and subjective effects when we try taking even a small quantity of such drugs. There are individuals who simply cannot indulge in cigarettes, alcohol, sleeping pills, amphetamines or opiates because they make them ill.

Behavioural genetics

The alcoholic often has a desperately lonely fight to retain self respect. In the last 20 years alone the ratio of female to male alcoholics has jumped from one in eight to one in four or five.

Stress

Genetic 'protection' probably operates in another way too. Some individuals just do not experience enough euphoria or positive reinforcement from drinking or smoking or pill-popping to want to make it a habit. Nor, by the same token, do they experience the adverse effects which makes them feel they must re-establish euphoria with another drink, cigarette or pill. Their constitution is such that the vicious circle of euphoria-dysphoria is never established.

Environment There is no question that availability, in the broadest sense, hugely influences drug use. During Prohibition in the United States, hospitalisation rates for cirrhosis and other drink problems dropped precipitously. This was also true in France and England during World War II when wine and beer were scarce, expensive and even rationed.

Cultural attitudes obviously are important. Many fundamentalist religious groups condemn alcohol and their members often abstain on religious grounds. Interestingly, lower rates of use in these groups do not necessarily correspond to a low rate of *abuse*. For example, only about 40 per cent of southern Baptist men in the United States drink, but alcoholism is relatively common among those who do. On the other hand, almost all Jews drink on occasion but Jewish alcoholics are uncommon. The reason for this is not known, but most experts favour cultural explanations over biological ones.

Climate may even be important. For example, there appears to be more alcoholism in northern countries than in southern countries; alcoholism is more of a problem in Northern France, say, than in Southern France. City people drink more than small town or rural people, a fact which is sometimes attributed to the 'stress' of city living. It is rarely clear what stress refers to in this context, but cities, with their anonymity and cosmopolitan values, do seem to bring out the drinker in many of us.

Alienation In the Marxist sense, a state of affairs in which one is denied the fruit of one's labours; as used by Fromm,

19

Erikson and others, the feeling that one's life has no meaning, that the human and natural world around one is impersonal, mechanistic and unsympathetic.

Allergy An unpleasant physiological reaction to substances eaten, breathed in, etc.; sometimes has a psychological component, as in one famous case in which an allergic response to pollen became generalised to paper flowers!

Gordon Allport, 1897–1967

Allport, Gordon Gordon Willard Allport is chiefly remembered for his work concerning *personality traits, functional autonomy* and the *mature personality*. He distinguished between traits which are common to large numbers of people, such as shyness or aggression, and those that are unique to particular individuals, which he defined as *personal dispositions*. Allport argued that traits cause people to react to a variety of situations in a consistent way; for example, people with the trait of aggression consistently need to express this trait in their behaviour. He also believed that the expression of a trait was a goal in itself. This is what he meant by functional autonomy; a child who is forced to do dancing lessons may eventually enjoy them for their own sake. In other words, the behaviour of dancing has become functionally independent of the original motive.

The mature personality, Allport believed, possessed an *extension of self*, or a diversity of interests and activities. He also defined maturity as including the ability to project ideas into the future, and make realistic judgements about oneself and about others.

In addition to receiving virtually every accolade the psychological profession could bestow, Allport was a prolific writer, his two most important books being *Personality: A Psychological Interpretation* (1937), and *Pattern and Growth in Personality* (1961). Almost all his academic life was spent at Harvard University. He died in 1967 at the age of 70.

Meditation

Alpha (α) rhythm The pattern of electrical activity in the brain typical of relaxed, meditative states, characterised by waves of greater amplitude and lower frequency (8–12 Hertz) than those seen in attentive wakefulness.

Brain waves

Altered state of consciousness (ASC) Up to 20 different states of consciousness have been identified by psychologists. All of them occur quite naturally, but most can be induced by an appropriate drug. 'Normal' consciousness, characterised by beta (β) brain waves, is defined as thinking, planning and feeling in control of one's mental processes. Other states are: *dreaming and sleeping; hypnagogic* (just before sleeping) and *hypnopompic* (just before waking); *hyperalert* (extreme alertness or wakefulness due to prolonged concentration, or amphetamines); *lethargic* (due to lack of sleep, depression, malnutrition); *rapturous* (induced by frenzied dancing, religious rituals, sex); *hysterical* (intense emotions aroused by terror, anxiety, being part of a mob); *fragmented* (as in schizophrenia – can be due to brain trauma, sensory deprivation, hypnosis); *stuporous* (as in some psychoses – can be due to opiates, alcohol); *trance* (induced by rituals, hypnosis, long-distance driving); *daydreaming* (reverie, fantasising); *meditative* (clear, relaxed, unfocused state achieved through meditation); *'expanded'* (through use of psychedelic drugs).

Altzheimer's disease A very rare nervous disease, a form of pre-senile dementia (causing premature senility) marked by impaired speech and movement and gradual loss of intellectual capacity.

Projective tests

Ambiguous figures A standardised set of 'unstructured' or ambiguous stimuli used in projective diagnostic tests; testees are encouraged to interpret freely what they 'see'. With no right or wrong answers, interpretation of responses has to be particularly skilful.

Defence mechanism

Ambivalence A defence mechanism; the co-existence in consciousness of opposite feelings about another person; *ambivalent oscillation* is the alternation of such feelings. Simultaneous love-hate, annoyance-amusement, etc., are defensive because they cancel each other out.

Brain damage

Dissociative reaction

Amnesia Partial or total loss of certain areas of memory for a short or long period as the result of brain damage (due to ECT, injury or senile dementia) or a dissociative reaction. Amnesia following injury wipes out events immediately preceding the injury; in senility long-term memory may be occasionally unreliable but memory for recent events is very shaky. Sensory memory is rarely affected, though; amnesics remember how to walk, talk and generally look after themselves. Loss of identity (though not of talents, abilities and general knowledge) is more typical of dissociative amnesia; it is as if the person has taken psychological flight from his or her problems; memory usually returns when the flight proves unsuccessful. Selective forgetting (repression) of unpleasant events is not amnesia.

Amphetamines A group of stimulant drugs, including Benzedrine and Dexedrine, at one time widely used to treat mild depression, combat fatigue and suppress appetite. They are assumed to act by facilitating the release of neurotransmitter substances from nerve endings. Their effect is to increase concentration, alertness, activity level, elevate mood and reduce appetite. 'Speed freaks', amphetamine abusers, quickly develop tolerance, requiring higher and higher doses to produce the desired effect. Sustained abuse produces symptoms akin to those of schizophrenia.

Anal stage The second of Freud's five stages of psycho-sexual development, occurring between the ages of one and three when toilet-training starts. The anus becomes the focus of sexual gratification. Over-emphasis on bowel control, Freud theorised, may lead to a stubborn, stingy or obsessively orderly adult personality.

Androgyny   *Judith M. Bardwick*

Androgyny (from two Greek words, *andros*, man and *gune*, woman) is a very old concept. It has occurred to people of many cultures that the ideal being would be one who was both masculine and feminine. Though sexual bi-formity is a power-ful myth, seen in representations of gods and heroes, it is not a physically realisable state. Hermaphroditism, the condition in which female and male genitalia are both present, is a sex anomaly found exceedingly rarely in humans.

But as a concept of personality, androgyny is highly rele-vant to the individualistic age we live in. Psychologists now hold the view that people function best if they have both feminine and masculine characteristics. Most of us are fairly well aware that we are more complicated and more variable than the traditional stereotypes 'feminine' and 'masculine'. Many aspects of ourselves, many of the things we do, are unrelated to our gender.

Femininity

The androgynous concept of psychological health is that people should have a blend of interests, abilities and traits which are both 'expressive' (traditionally female) and 'instru-mental' (traditionally male). We are not saying, however, that 'androgynous' equals 'asexual'. Our identity must include our body; we must find pleasure in our body, in its sexuality and in its reproductive capacity, because our body is an intrinsic part of our self-concept. We can certainly transcend the sex roles imposed on us, but we cannot transcend the fact of being male or female. While there are other components of our identity, our gender is still critical to our self-concept.

So, provided we do not seek to deny the physical fact of being male or female, androgyny is a very positive concept. By highlighting our complexity it shows us how our lives have been unnecessarily constricted, and how simplistic the terms 'masculine' and 'feminine' really are. We are now more aware that our self-worth is not based primarily on our reproductive capacity but on our capacity to experience life in the broadest imaginable range.

Anger   *Leonard Berkowitz*

Anger is not a synonym for aggression. It is a mixture of feelings and physiological reactions, rather than an observ-able action like aggression (though that does not mean that angry feelings are not sometimes revealed in open behaviour). Researchers are virtually unanimous in saying that anger is an experience and aggression a behaviour. So one can be angry without being aggressive and sometimes aggressive without being angry.

However, there is no such consensus about how anger arises. Anger is undoubtedly one of the primary emotions, and it usually has a specific cause. But what kinds of events produce anger, and what mechanisms, psychological and physiological, are involved?

Emotions

Why do we get angry? All emotional sequences begin with the awareness of some significant external happening. According to one school of thought, people get angry when they feel threatened. Other authorities believe a far wider variety of occurrences can provoke anger. Some writers point to frustration, unexpected failure to reach a desired goal, as a source of anger. A more generally held view is that anger is caused by events we usually attempt to avoid – how *angry* we get depends on how unpleasant these events are. Therefore extremely unpleasant happenings would produce anger, whereas mildly unpleasant ones would cause irritation or annoyance. Of course, if the unpleasant event is thought to be dangerous, the emotion of fear might be dominant and mask the emotion of anger.

Theories also differ as to exactly what happens once we become aware of unpleasant, or frustrating, events. One of psychology's classic formulations, the James-Lange theory of emotion, maintained that we experience emotion because of 'gut' reactions to stimuli. So, if someone insults us, we feel angry because our innards automatically react in a certain way. This theory fell into disfavour in the 1920s and 1930s for several reasons, including the fact that the viscera are too insensitive and too slow to react to produce the differentiated rush of emotions we experience as anger, fear, and so on.

A process of interpretation Recent years have seen several interesting variations on the James-Lange theme. A number of writers have pointed out that our muscular reactions, and especially our facial expressions, help to determine just what we feel when we are aroused. These reactions apparently 'feed back' into the central nervous system and affect the nature of our emotional experience. According to this view, an Englishman who has learned to keep a 'stiff upper lip' may have the same basic inclination to get angry as a volatile Italian when things go awry, but English and Italian differences in facial and postural expressiveness seem to give rise to somewhat differently experienced feelings.

Another contemporary variation on the James-Lange theory maintains that our thoughts at the moment of arousal shape the nature of our emotional experience. Stanley Schachter has taken this position, arguing that what we feel and do in response to a crucial happening depends on how we

Physiological arousal

interpret our physical sensations. The initial stimulus supposedly creates only a general, diffuse arousal state – indeed, researchers have found it very difficult to detect any physiological difference between fear and anger – so we use cues in our immediate external environment to interpret or label our arousal. The feelings we then experience accord with our interpretation: someone has insulted me, I feel upset inside, the insult should make me angry, I therefore *feel* angry.

Although Schachter's hypothesis has been very influential, it is incomplete. The way we interpret a situation undoubtedly affects our emotional experience, but it is not only our interpretation which determines the quality of what we feel. Some events are inherently or unambiguously unpleasant and cause annoyance or anger even if we do not believe we have been attacked or insulted. This point is very important. Contrary to Schachter's ideas, we do not always have to place a particular interpretation on an emotion-arousing event in order to feel angry. It is perfectly possible to feel anger without going through the interpretation process.

Anima   Jung's term for the inner part of the personality as opposed to the *persona*, the mask concealing it.

Animism   The belief, found in many primitive and not-so-primitive societies, that certain natural or man-made objects are temporarily or permanently inhabited by spirits with benign, neutral or evil powers.

Body image

Anorexia nervosa   Almost entirely confined to girls and younger women, and medically diagnosed when at least 10 per cent of body weight has been lost due to persistent fasting or food abuse. Amenorrhea is common, as are other disturbances (hallucinations, apathy) typical of malnutrition. Anorexia can be *primary*, occurring between the age of 11 and 18 and brought on by a crisis reaction to the bodily and emotional changes which come with puberty and adolescence, or *secondary*, occurring between the age of 19 and 35, when it is more likely to be the result of a weight phobia, social inadequacy, neurotic depression or general inability to cope.

Adolescent anorexics tend to come from middle and upper class homes. Many are of above average intelligence and trying to live up to high parental expectations or some personal model of perfection. Anorexics in their 20s and 30s more typically come into the fast-and-binge category, inducing vomiting after eating and abusing laxatives. Treatment usually involves hospitalisation and voluntary eating, accompanied by psychotherapy appropriate to the underlying causes. Intravenous feeding is a last resort.

Antidepressants (see Drugs and mental disorder)

Anxiety *Charles S. ielberger*

Anxiety is a unique mix of subjective and physiological events. The subjective or emotional reactiors associated with an anxiety state include apprehension, tension, worry, and nervousness. The physiological events include rapid and shallow breathing, increased heart rate (palpitations, tachychardia), sweating, dryness of the mouth, nausea, and muscular-skeletal disturbances which cause trembling, restlessness, and feelings of weakness.

Threat

Any situation that is perceived as threatening will evoke an anxiety state, and the intensity and duration of that state will be in proportion to the amount of threat perceived and its timespan. The objective or real characteristics of the situation, the thoughts and memories it conjures up or revives, and one's previous experience of similar situations will all contribute to one's reaction.

The enemy without and within An anxiety state may be triggered by external or internal stimuli. The prospect of having a tooth out or leaping out of a plane in a parachute represent two sorts of external stimuli. Other sorts of external stimuli are not physical in their implications; their threat is mental. Being criticised or ignored, having to meet deadlines, having to compete - these all involve other people and potential damage to self-esteem, and most people find them worrying to some degree.

Internal stimuli can also switch on the anxiety. The memory of a serious accident may continue to evoke an anxiety reaction long after it happened. When one meets an especially critical person a second time, or goes to the doctor about a complaint one suspects is getting worse, one is also likely to experience a sudden flood of anxiety.

Well-founded or vague? Sigmund Freud undoubtedly contributed more to our understanding of anxiety than any other person. He emphasised that anxiety is a danger signal, a warning that some form of adjustment is necessary. Freud made the distinction between threats in the external world and threats coming from the inside. Outside threats resulted in *objective anxiety*. For Freud, objective anxiety and fear were synonymous. Internally caused anxiety he labelled *neurotic anxiety*. At the same time he recognised that objective anxiety can be converted into neurotic anxiety. Suppose a child has

Repression

been consistently punished for normal sexual and aggressive impulses; in later life, when he meets cues associated with

Neurosis

the behaviours he was punished for, he becomes objectively anxious, an unpleasant experience; if, in consequence, he represses or banishes from awareness all thoughts and memories associated with his 'naughty' behaviours, the stage is set for neurotic anxiety. If the repression process were complete and final he would have nothing to worry about. But it isn't. Fragments of symbolic representations or derivatives of repressed events occasionally erupt into awareness, and he experiences *free floating anxiety*. The actual memory of the repressed event remains submerged in the unconscious. Only ripples come to the surface, ripples which he cannot consciously attribute to anything in particular, hence the term 'free floating'.

Always or only sometimes? Another distinction one cannot escape when discussing anxiety is that between *trait anxiety* and *state anxiety*, often abbreviated to A-trait and A-state. Trait anxiety is 'anxiety proneness'. We all differ in our predisposition to perceive our environment as dangerous or threatening. Our anxiety states also differ in their frequency and intensity. By contrast, state anxiety refers to one's feelings here and now, at a precise moment. A person low in trait anxiety may occasionally experience high state anxiety, but someone who is highly trait anxious will experience more and intenser moments of anxiety. This is because he or she perceives more situations as dangerous or threatening, especially situations which pose some threat to self-esteem.

People suffering from psychoneuroses or depression are very high in trait anxiety, and also likely to be prey to neurotic anxiety. The connection between neurotic and trait anxiety is a fairly intimate one, since both involve internal stimuli. Fortunately, most neurotic and depressed persons develop defences which give them occasional relief from their anxiety, enabling them to relax. They can be helped by being diverted from the internal stimuli which keep on triggering state anxiety reactions.

Aphrodisiacs Substances reputed to arouse sexual desire or enhance sexual performance. Their effect, if any, is psychological rather than physiological, as established in double-blind tests. If you believe oysters will make you randy, they probably will.

Applied psychology That branch of psychology which seeks to apply the findings and methods of experimental psychology to everyday life; industrial and consumer psychology are disciplines within applied psychology.

Approach-avoidance An unpleasant state of conflict in which one both wants and doesn't want something - a 'love-hate' relationship, being shy but wanting to socialise, loving cakes and ice creams but scared stiff of getting fat. Conflicts of this kind can be resolved by behavioural therapy, specifically by bolstering the approach motivation or trying to reduce the avoidance motivation.

Approach-approach and avoidance-avoidance are easier to live with; one simply has to reconcile oneself to getting one of two desirable alternatives, or to evading one of two unpleasant alternatives (income tax rather than alimony).

Cognitive dissonance

Behaviour therapy

Assertion training A technique in social skills training which aims to resolve the anxiety, resentment and self-disparagement which come from knowing one is being downtrodden, ignored or denied one's rights. Between them, therapist and client draw up a list of exercises called 'graded assignments' designed to give the client practice and confidence in situations he or she finds difficult, such as standing up for his or her rights when taken unfair advantage of, or taking the initiative in social encounters. Assertive behaviour is sometimes taught through modelling or through rehearsal between client and therapist. Graded assignments are reported on in therapy sessions but undertaken outside them.

Association Any idea, mental image, memory or subjective experience which sparks off another. Associations are assumed to be the result of experience and learning, but the number of bizarre associations most of us can make when we try begs the question. Association undoubtedly enriches all forms of human experience and expression, and is the source of much creativity and humour. *Word association tests* were once commonly used to diagnose various schizophrenic, neurotic and depressive conditions. *Free association*, as used by psychoanalysts, is the free flow of thoughts which may or may not give clues to hidden conflict.

A summary of attitudes: faith, strength, persistence ...

Social psychology

Attitude A tendency to react in a certain way towards specific events, people, ideas or objects. Attitude has three components: thoughts or beliefs (cognitive), feelings (emotional), and behaviour. *Attitude scales* consist of questions to which one answers yes or no or agrees/disagrees on a five-point scale. The answers to an *attitude survey*, on the other hand can be as open-ended as respondents choose. The *semantic differential* developed by Osgood measures attitudes to words or the concepts they represent. The lost-letter technique is an ingenious method of investigating attitudes without resorting to questionnaires or interviews.

Attribution theory Why does he drink heavily? Why is she anxious? We are constantly trying to explain and predict our own and others' behaviour: attribution theory is the study of this process. Attribution theorists are particularly interested in the biases which influence our judgements of behaviour. We may, for example, give too much weight to personality and too little to situational factors; in explaining our own behaviour we often give more weight to the situation. And we attribute our own success to our own efforts, but our failure to chance or to other people.

Ideology

Authoritarian personality A concept developed by American social psychologists after World War II. Their concern was to identify which personality traits are predictive of fascist tendencies, or of obedience to fascist propaganda. Authoritarianism represents a combination of the following: repression of unacceptable impulses in oneself; projection of those impulses onto others; avoidance of self-questioning or self-criticism; a high degree of conformity to bolster one's ideas about right and wrong; a search for power rather than for love or affection; rigidity of attitudes. The authoritarian personality often tends to have a natural affinity towards undemocratic ideologies.

Childhood

Schizophrenia

Autism A childhood psychosis not dissimilar to childhood schizophrenia; distinguished by extreme inability to respond to other people but obsessive involvement with things. Most autistic children are boys, though it is not clear why. Symptoms can include extreme food fads, body rocking and head banging, apathy, fear of change, failure to imitate or react to parents and others, and often a total inability to use language for ordinary communication. Autistic children are perfectly normal in their co-ordination and appearance. Behaviourists blame autism on faulty conditioning, on inconsistent reinforcement. Child psychologist Bruno Bettelheim, however, suggests lack of parental affection as the cause (parents of autistic children tend to be extremely cold and negative in their feelings). Other psychologists suggest an organic cause, such as malfunction of the reticular activating system in the brain. Though there are brilliant exceptions, many autistic children are so psychologically handicapped that they end up in institutions.

Autonomic Functioning independently or involuntarily.

The autonomic nervous system controls the body's involuntary activities (heartbeat, gut contractions, sweat secretion, etc.). For Erikson *autonomy drive* is the urge to exploit, master and generally impose oneself on one's environment.

Aversion therapy   Counter-conditioning techniques used, with mixed success, to eliminate compulsions like drinking, smoking, gambling, shoplifting, taking drugs, etc. The principle of aversion training is that the urge to smoke, to drink, and so on, becomes associated with an unpleasant stimulus and therefore decreases and disappears. Some patients report that aversive conditioning is so anxiety-making that their compulsion becomes a positive relief!

Avoidance (see Approach-avoidance)

Axon   The long, thin, insulated main extension of a nerve cell specialised for the transmission of nerve impulses.

Albert Bandura, b. 1925

Bandura, Albert Albert Bandura, born in Canada in 1925 and presently on the faculty of psychology at Stanford University, is generally regarded as the high priest of *social learning theory*, which states that one of the basic ways in which we learn new behaviour is by watching and imitating others. Bandura was chiefly responsible for giving the theory an experimental foundation, mainly through his work on the role of modelling (imitation) in learning. One of his special interests has been the acquisition and alteration of personality traits in children.

The concept of *modelling* has been expanded by Bandura in many ways. He showed, for instance, that new behaviours can be learned by watching other people perform apparently unrelated behaviours; nor does behaviour have to be imitated at the time it is being modelled in order to be learnt successfully. Though he agrees that rewards and punishments are important shapers of behaviour, he nevertheless insists that neither are always or absolutely necessary. Like most social learning theorists, he is more interested in the effects of indirect rather than direct reward and punishment. In his studies of aggressive behaviour in children, he demonstrated that models of behaviour which are rewarded are far more likely to be imitated than models which are punished.

Barbiturates A large family of sedative-hypnotic drugs ('downers', tranquillisers) derived from barbituric acid and prescribed to produce sedation and relaxation, lower anxiety and induce sleep. High doses produce effects similar to alcohol. Abuse leads to tolerance, abrupt withdrawal to convulsions, delirium resembling the DTs seen in alcoholic withdrawal, fever, hallucinations and occasionally death.

Basic anxiety Anxiety which develops in childhood and fuels various neurotic (non-rational) needs in adulthood; a concept developed by neo-Freudian Karen Horney; she describes it as "the feeling a child has of being isolated and helpless in a potentially hostile world".

Basic trust To quote Erik Erikson: "The infant's first social achievement is willingness to let the mother out of sight without undue anxiety or rage because she has become an inner certainty as well as an outer predictability." This is basic trust, the rudimentary identity on which selfhood is built.

Bedwetting A widespread problem for parents, not alleviated by the medical tag 'nocturnal enuresis'. At age five around one in two children wets the bed occasionally, with boys presenting the problem about twice as often as girls. By the age of 12, however, only about 1 in 50 children bedwets. A very few children continue to bedwet well into their teens, at which point intensive specialist help, psychological and psychiatric, is usually sought. Most children get over the problem much earlier, many without professional help, although most parents consult their general practitioner at some stage.

Traditional remedies for bedwetting are fairly ineffective because it is possible to wet the bed even when only minute amounts of urine are present in the bladder. This is why the 'urine alarm' or bell-and-pad apparatus was developed. As soon as the pad begins to get damp, an electrical circuit is completed and the bell rings, waking the child. Use of the bell-and-pad comes under the heading of behaviour therapy, the idea being that the child gradually learns to associate waking with internal body cues. Results are very good at first, but the relapse rate (when the therapy is discontinued) has been shown to be very high.

There appear to be no specific causes of bedwetting beyond general unfocused anxiety as a reaction to stress or pressure. Sometimes bedwetting is accompanied by other temporary 'behaviour disorders' like night-terrors and temper tantrums. On its own, however, bedwetting is not serious; it is best reacted to by lessening the pressures on the child and attending to overt signals of distress.

Nightmares
Temper tantrum

Eager to start walking on his own. Trust in a parent is the beginning of self-confidence.

Behaviour One's total motor and glandular response to a situation, as distinct from one's intellectual or emotional response. *Behaviourism* is the doctrine that behaviour is the only valid area of psychological investigation, it being the only one observable and measurable.

Behavioural assessment Very detailed evaluation of a client's problems in order to pinpoint the therapy to which he will respond best. The behavioural clinician examines: the client's physical and mental state; the environmental factors which cause difficulties; the client's overt behaviour; and events which reinforce the difficulties. Information about the client is gained by direct observation, role-playing, questioning, asking the client to monitor himself and taking physiological measurements.

Behavioural genetics *Hans Eysenck*

Genes

The science of genetics has traditionally concerned itself with investigating single genes and their effects, but human behaviour is far too complex to be explained by the operation of single genes. Qualities like intelligence, extraversion or neuroticism are 'polygenic' in origin, the result of the interaction of sets of genes, as few as 40 or as many as 100 in each set. Behavioural genetics, therefore, is the special branch of genetics which investigates multiple gene action.

The sort of questions behavioural geneticists ask are: how much are differences in intelligence due to genetic factors and how much to environmental factors? To what extent, and in what way, do genetic and environmental factors interact? Are the particular genes involved dominant, and if so in what direction does this dominance lie? Is there assortative mating (the tendency for like to marry like) in respect of certain abilities or traits? How many genes are involved in determining a particular ability or trait? The answers to these and a host of other questions can be obtained by using various experimental paradigms and applying some rather complex statistical rules.

Ready-made experimental material The behavioural geneticist has two major sources of information at his disposal; he can look very closely at biological accidents (twins) or he can scrutinise social accidents (adopted children or orphans). Roughly speaking, therefore, if heredity is an important determiner of trait or ability differences, identical twins should be more alike than fraternal twins; this is indeed the case. In fact the difference between identical and fraternal twins constitutes an index of the degree of heritability of the trait or ability in question. For intelligence and for most personality traits, identical twins are much more alike than the fraternal twins. Identical twins brought up entirely separately in different families are an especially vital source of information, since any differences between them must be due entirely to environmental factors; usually it is found that identical twins brought up apart are very similar in intelligence and personality.

Adopted children receive their hereditary component from their true parents, and their environmental component mainly from their adoptive parents. As many studies have shown, children tend to be more like their true parents than their adoptive parents with respect to intelligence, personality, and even such complex behaviours as criminality.

'Regression to the mean' is another important source of information for the behavioural geneticist. It is well known, and can be deduced from genetic theory, that the children of very tall parents will be tall, but less so than their parents; in like manner the children of very bright (or very dull) parents will be bright (or dull), but to a less extreme degree than their parents. This is just what one would expect from genetic principles – they act to preserve balance and stability in the population at large.

Just what do we inherit? However, the heritability of abilities or traits, determined by applying statistical methods to genetic data, must not be over-interpreted. Statistics on heritability apply to particular populations studied at particular moments in time. When one says that the heritability of intelligence is 80 per cent, one is really only speaking of the present-day populations of America, England and Western societies generally. Neither does the estimate apply to individuals; it is strictly an estimate of the importance of genetic factors across an entire population.

Statistics

It would also be wrong to think of intelligence or any other heritable ability as 'fixed' by heredity in an unbreakable mould. Differences in height in Japanese men and women are largely determined by genetic causes, but when many of them emigrated to the USA their children grew up to be much taller, presumably because of better nutrition. So the height of Japanese people is not 'fixed', even though variations around the mean are strongly determined by genetic causes.

To return to the questions asked in our first paragraph, the genes which code for intelligence are dominant over those which code for dullness. And, yes, assortative mating does go on – bright men do marry bright women. When it comes to personality, however, there appears to be no dominance and no assortative mating, even though personality is almost as strongly inherited as intelligence. Environmental factors like socio-economic status are important for intelligence, but much less so for personality; however environmental factors within the family have much more bearing on personality than on intelligence. Behavioural genetics is still a young discipline, but some of its findings have already given valuable insights into the foundations of human ability and behaviour.

Personality
Intelligence

Behavioural medicine *Irving Binik*

Behavioural medicine is a new discipline in which knowledge and techniques drawn from the social sciences (psychology, sociology, anthropology) are applied to the study of physical health and illness. This new branch of medicine formally came into being at the Yale University Conference on Behavioral Medicine, 4–6 February 1977. This meeting and a later one at the National Academy of Sciences, USA, defined behavioural medicine as: "The *interdisciplinary* field concerned with the development and *integration* of behavioral and biomedical science knowledge and techniques relevant to health and illness and the application of this knowledge and these techniques to prevention, diagnosis, treatment and rehabilitation."

Breaking new ground Behavioural medicine is an extension of an existing discipline, namely psychosomatic medicine, but it differs from it in several important ways. First, behavioural medicine doesn't just focus on the 'classic' psychosomatic illnesses (e.g. ulcers, hypertension); it investigates the psychosocial factors in all illness and, just as importantly, the psychosocial factors associated with health. Second, research in behavioural medicine has been more influenced by models and paradigms drawn from behavioural psychology than from Freudian psychiatry. Third, it plays down the role of psychiatry as the major mediator between medicine and social science in favour of direct interaction between them.

Psychosomatic

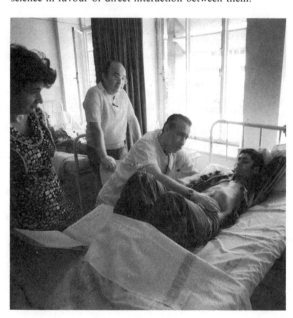

New definitions of health and unhealth, and new cooperation between doctors, social workers and psychologists

Pain

Biofeedback

The sort of research which comes under the heading of behavioural medicine ranges very widely indeed. High on the list come socio-cultural and cross-cultural studies of illness and health, psychophysiological studies of stress, studies of cognitive factors (e.g. placebos) in recovery from illness, and work on the assessment and treatment of pain. One branch of behavioural medicine particularly well known to the general public is biofeedback, now used for the treatment of headaches and for learning to relax to reduce stress.

Another area of research which has hit the headlines recently concerns the role of a specific syndrome of behaviours and attitudes, called Type A, in the development of coronary heart disease. Type A individuals are described as aggressive and ambitious workoholics, constantly striving for self-imposed goals in unrealistically short periods of time. Recent research indicates that such individuals are at a significantly higher risk than others of developing coronary heart disease. Interestingly a Type A behaviour pattern is a better predictor of coronary heart disease than traditional physical factors such as cholesterol levels or obesity.

Out of these and other areas of research have come mass advertising campaigns to promote healthy living, campaigns to encourage people to cut down or cut out smoking, change unhealthy eating habits, increase the amount of exercise they take and so on. This type of approach underlines a preventive rather than a curative approach to illness.

A prognosis So far most of the enthusiasm and organising energy on behalf of behavioural medicine has come from North America. Many of the major universities and medical schools including Harvard, Yale, University of Pennsylvania, Stanford and Johns Hopkins, have set up research and training programmes in behavioural medicine. A multi-disciplinary group called the Society of Behavioral Medicine and a journal entitled the *Journal of Behavioral Medicine* have already been founded. The American Psychological Association has also formed a new division, Health Psychology, and government agencies are giving grants for research.

It is hard to predict the course which behavioural medicine will take. The current flurry of activity and interest is probably something of a fad. At the moment psychologists dominate both clinical and research activities – as yet there has been little direct participation by other social scientists – and among the psychological fraternity there is increasing evidence and influence of non-behavioural ideas. If this trend continues, the field may have to be renamed 'psychological medicine' or 'health psychology'. On the other hand, the new emphases and applications of research in behavioural medicine may lead to the establishment of a truly new field devoted to modifying the somewhat ailing medical model of illness and to humanising our present health care system.

Behavioural psychology *Hans Eysenck*

Psychology used to be considered the science of the soul (psyche), or of consciousness, and much investigation of the nature of consciousness was done using *introspection*, (trying to look into one's own mind and catch it on the wing, so to speak). This proved to be an impossible undertaking, and so, around the time of World War 1, another approach to psychology began to stir, *behavioural* psychology, the subject matter of which was human (and animal!) behaviour. The virtue of basing psychological theory on behaviour is that behaviour can be observed and measured accurately and objectively; the scientific study of psychology is inevitably tied to behaviour. The prophet of the new doctrine, known as *behaviourism*, was J. B. Watson, a young animal psychologist who tried to introduce into human psychology methods found useful for studying animals.

Watson

The term 'behaviour' in this context is much more inclusive than one might think. Brain waves, changes in the electrical conductivity of the skin, nerve impulses preceding muscular contraction, the effects of hormones like androgen and oestrogen (the sex hormones) or adrenaline and noradrenaline, the action of various neurotransmitters ... all of these body functions come into the category of 'behaviour' because they can be objectively recorded and analysed. Speech too is now considered behaviour, and on similar grounds.

Neo-behaviourists (a much later generation of behavioural psychologists) try to have their cake and eat it by allowing into the scientific arena 'hypothetical constructs' and 'intervening variables' which look suspiciously like the forbidden artefacts of the introspectionists. Thus mental images are admissible, provided they can be tied down to some measurable and observable kind of behaviour. I may ask you to try throwing darts at a target 'in your mind's eye'; I can then ask you to throw real darts at a real target and show that your aim has improved thanks to the 'mind's eye' exercise! Some fundamentalists reject such apparent casuistry, but most behavioural psychologists are quite happy to admit such 'mediational' concepts into their psychology.

Behaviour therapy *Gerald C. Davison*

Initially, in the 1950s, when behaviour therapy was first talked about as a new approach to psychotherapy, it was equated with conditioning therapy. At the time it was believed that new methods of treatment could be derived from what laboratory psychologists knew about classical and operant conditioning. However, behaviour therapy today is much broader in scope.

Conditioning

The tools of the behaviour therapist Let us take as an example a client who is seeking therapy for a number of avoidances and anxieties which are grossly handicapping her. She is fearful about leaving her home, about talking to people she

Anxiety

doesn't know well, even about approaching small animals. To alleviate her anxieties the behavioural therapist might well employ to *systematic desensitisation*. First he constructs, with the help of his client, a 'hierarchy' or graded list of anxiety-provoking situations which reflect her fear(s). Each item on the list describes a specific encounter, actual or potential, liable to cause distress in real life. Two such items might be: "Your are introducing yourself to a new employee at your firm's Christmas party" and "Your daughter brings home a guinea-pig from school to look after it for the weekend". The therapist also teaches his client one of several relaxation techniques, so that she will be able to remain calm while imagining, and later actually experiencing, an anxiety-provoking situation. Initially the therapist asks the client to relax and picture a scene low in the hierarchy they have constructed together. If the client becomes anxious, the therapist distracts her attention, encourages her to relax again, and re-presents the scene. In another widely used variation of this technique, the client is urged to relax away the anxiety, coping with the discomfort in imagination.

Over a number of therapy sessions, most clients are able to climb the hierarchy in imagination. As clients learn to tolerate more and more anxiety-provoking situations in imagination, they gradually become less anxious about similar situations in real life, even to the point of becoming quite nonchalant about events that used to cause extreme upset.

Operant conditioning, or the shaping of behaviour by judicious rewarding and punishing, has been used to lessen childhood problems like bedwetting, misbehaving at school, reading difficulties and temper tantrums. It has been used for a range of adult problems too. If an individual's behaviour is susceptible to change by a system of rewards and punishments, an operant treatment regimen makes sense. Clearly operant conditioning, which is nothing more nor less than the manipulation of the behaviour of another human being, must be tempered by an awareness of the values one is imposing.

In recent years behaviour therapists have addressed themselves to the cognitive or thought processes of their clients as a way to help them change how they feel and behave. One approach, known as *rational–emotive therapy*, assumes that emotional suffering is primarily due to the unrealistic demands people make on themselves and others. It is, for example, unrealistic to feel miserable because not everyone has a high opinion of you. In rational-emotive therapy the client is persuaded to change self-defeating and self-deprecating patterns of thought.

Modelling is another approach extensively used by contemporary behaviour therapists. It is an efficient way of teaching complex patterns of behaviour and reducing groundless fears - it has long been a part of folk wisdom that people can learn by watching others. Some dentists, for example, show their

Rational-emotive therapy

young trainees a film of an initially fearful youngster undergoing various dental procedures with increasing composure.

An evaluative role While behaviour therapy is primarily a clinical enterprise - some of the techniques we mention are even used by therapists who prefer to call themselves psychoanalysts or client-centred therapists - it also has a strong commitment to research and to the constant reappraisal of current principles and practices. In ten or twenty years from now the practices of behaviour therapy may be rather different from those just described - it is a commonplace of science that prevalent ideas are continually assaulted and challenged. To conclude, behaviour therapy is rather more than an arsenal of techniques used in clinical psychology and psychiatry. It represents overall an abiding faith in the use of scientific methods for the further development and evaluation of therapy.

Bereavement Loss of someone deeply loved, followed by a 'grief reaction' and a period of mourning. Grief is distinct from mourning, which ordinarily lasts for anything up to six months and does not upset normal functioning. Grief is the relatively short-lived state of shock and disbelief which immediately follows bereavement; the individual temporarily withdraws, is pre-occupied with thoughts of the dead person and may be unable to cope normally. Mourning is, it seems, a necessary period of acceptance of one's loss; unresolved grief is often implicated in declining physical and mental health.

Survivors of the 1980 earthquake in Southern Italy - the double burden of loss and trauma

Binet–Simon scale A series of graded intelligence tests devised by French psychologist Alfred Binet and physician Theodore Simon in 1911.

Biofeedback

Physiologists and psychologists have for many years assumed that it is not possible for most of us to voluntarily alter our heart rate, raise or lower our blood pressure, cause our palms to sweat or our stomach to contract in quite the same way as we are able to nod our head or raise an arm. Unlike the muscles surrounding our bones, which we can control at will, our visceral organs (heart, gut, urethra) only react, or so it was thought, as part of a reflex response (an increase in heart rate in response to a sudden loud noise, for example). Yet some special individuals, yogis for example, are known to be able to exert an unusual amount of voluntary control over their physiological responses. Why can't all of us perform such feats?

How am I doing? It is well known that all learning requires feedback. If I want to learn to throw a ball into a basketball net, I need to see where the ball lands after each throw, so that I can aim nearer and nearer the net. But imagine a basketball player who is blindfold. No matter how many attempts he

Polygraph

makes he will get no nearer the basket. With no feedback from his performance there will be no learning. Similarly we have no feedback from our gut or heart, no knowledge of what these organs are doing. But if feedback is provided with the aid of complex electrophysiological equipment, we can modify our physiological responses.

The subjects of biofeedback experiments are provided with visual or auditory signals which tell them about the activity level of the organ concerned. Their heart rate might be displayed on a dial, or their skin temperature represented as a tone of variable pitch becoming higher as skin temperature rises. The subjects in such an experiment might be requested to move the needle on the dial or raise the pitch of the tone without even knowing which particular physiological changes they are aiming to achieve. Quite amazing results have been achieved in such circumstances. To take a few examples, subjects were able to increase or decrease their heart rate by between 10 and 30 per cent, increase the blood flow in particular fingers relative to others, and even increase the activity level in one half of the brain only!

Biofeedback evaluated Physiological control using biofeedback is by now a fairly well-established phenomenon, but its usefulness is less clear. Some studies have demonstrated that feedback of blood pressure levels can help hypertensive patients to lower their blood pressure, although the effects are no greater, and considerably slower, than those achievable with drugs. Feedback about heart rate has been used in attempts to iron out cardiac irregularities, but here again the evidence is unreliable. Many attempts have been made to help subjects learn to relax in order to combat anxiety or tension headaches – this can be done by giving feedback on levels of muscular activity. Despite very significant reductions in muscle tension, subjects do not always experience equivalent decreases in emotional tension. Furthermore, biofeedback has not been shown to be superior to other methods of achieving relaxation (meditation, doing exercises). Feedback of brain waves has been used to train epileptics to develop brainwave patterns resistant to epileptic fits, but again the results of clinical research have been equivocal.

Placebo effect

Could some of the successes attributed to biofeedback be due to that most amazing of medical practitioners the 'placebo effect'? Does the impressive and complicated electronic gadgetry of biofeedback induce self-fulfilling expectations of improvement? Only time and further research will tell.

Childbirth

Birth trauma At birth the warmth, comfort and protective darkness of the womb is suddenly exchanged for the cold, noisy instability of the outside world. At one stage Freud suggested that all later experiences of anxiety and fear are modelled upon this first physiological and psychological shock. Otto Rank further claimed that the sudden separation

Primal therapy

from the womb leaves everyone with a burden of primal anxiety, a 'life fear', the fear of separation. The normal individual, Rank claimed, is able to overcome the birth trauma by asserting his separateness and individuality. Conversely a neurotic - an agoraphobic who remains emotionally tied to his mother for example - has never overcome the trauma of birth, and is therefore dominated by feelings of dependence and an inability to achieve self-assertiveness. In primal therapy the neurotic patient is forced to develop self-assertiveness by re-experiencing the anxieties of the dramatic moments of birth and separation from mother.

Bisexual This term sometimes refers to persons who possess both female and male sex organs, but more commonly it refers to individuals who, during sustained periods of their lives, engage in both homosexual and heterosexual activity.

Homosexuality

About one homosexual male in five describes himself as being significantly heterosexual as well. In fact it is very likely that an individual's arousability to same-sex erotic stimuli is to some extent separate from his or her response to other-sex stimuli. A normally heterosexual person may or may not be sexually excited by persons of his or her own sex. In line with this view is the high frequency of limited homosexual experiences in the general population. Thirty-seven per cent of male and thirteen per cent of female interviewees in Alfred Kinsey's famous study claimed to have experienced homosexual orgasm (usually through mutual masturbation as teenagers). Bisexuality is also very common in primitive cultures. In a large-scale anthropological study 49 out of 76 primitive societies were shown to find bisexual behaviour in males reasonably acceptable.

A significant number of premature babies and babies subjected to difficult delivery show some degree of intellectual impairment.

Hormones

Some differences however have been shown to exist between exclusively homosexual males and bisexual ones. The latter tend to have a weaker identification with the gay community and to experience more guilt and anxiety about their homosexual activities. Contrary to previous assumptions, though, bisexuals do not seem especially confused about their sexual identity or unable to adjust to their bisexual lifestyle. In view of this, psychiatrists and psychologists are becoming increasingly reluctant to treat bisexuality, or indeed homosexuality, as if it were some form of illness.

Theories of bisexuality, like those of homosexuality, span the full spectrum of psychological thinking. One biochemical theory suggests that bisexual orientation is the result of inadequate hormone production during critical periods of foetal development. The learning theory approach stresses the consequences of positively reinforcing (rewarding) early homosexual experiences and negatively reinforcing (punishing) heterosexual encounters early in life. By contrast psychoanalytic theory emphasises the role of unusual parental behaviour in the family history of bisexuals, drawing particular attention to the frequent presence of a dominant mother or a weak father.

Blushing A form of non-verbal communication? Increased blood flow to the face, ears and neck causing reddening; typically accompanies feelings of shame and embarrassment. Charles Darwin noted that blushing is limited to normally visible parts of the anatomy - scantily clothed primitives blush over the abdomen and arms. The psychological complexity of blushing is not well understood. Neither infants nor severely sub-normal adults blush. The reaction clearly requires considerable intellectual capacity on the part of the blusher. In psychoanalytic theory blushing represents the displacement of forbidden sexual excitement from the genitals to the face.

Non-verbal communication

Body image None of us sees our body as others see it - to that extent we all have a distorted image of our own bodies. Anorexia is perhaps the most drastic manifestation of distorted thinking about body image; anorexics, even when skeletal, see themselves as fat. Altered body image (feeling separate from one's body, or sensing parts of one's body as bigger, smaller, lighter or heavier than usual) can also be induced by hallucinogens like LSD and mescalin; localised brain damage can also lead to body image disorders.

Anorexia nervosa

Out-of-body experience

Body language Graphic synonym for non-verbal communication, and in some ways preferable, since it implies a flexible reportoire of mutually understood postures, gestures, etc., rather than a mechanistic process. For example, Italians use

Hands and body used for emphasis and denial.

rather different gestures from Anglo-Saxons, Arabs from Americans, though their facial expressions are the same.

Brain   *John Boddy*

The brain is the organ of the body which generates mental life and behaviour. As the central executive organ of the nervous system, its primary function is to evaluate stimuli from inside and outside the body and orchestrate behaviour in the interests of personal and species survival.

The volume of the human brain is very similar to that of most car engines, around 1500 cc; its average weight is 1440 grams in males and 1230 grams in females. However, there is no systematic relationship between brain weight and intelligence; the huge 2012 gram brain of Russian novelist Turgenev was no more imaginative than the modest 1017 gram brain of distinguished French writer Anatole France.

Neurons or nerve cells are the basic units which give the brain its capacity for receiving, processing and transmitting information. The human brain contains between 10 and 14 thousand million neurons, each one making thousands of connections with other neurons. Thus the number of alternative pathways along which nerve impulses can theoretically travel is incalculable.

In appearance the brain is unprepossessing. It is clearly divided into two hemispheres, the *cerebral hemispheres*, two large fistfuls of pinkish-grey tissue whose surface is broken by

Inside the human computer
1 Cortex   2 Subcortex
3 Corpus callosum
4 Thalamus
5 Hypothalamus
6 Pituitary
7 Midbrain
8 Hindbrain
Geography of the cortex
9 Main area controlling body movements
10 Main area receiving messages from body and sense organs
11 Main area concerned with hearing
12 Main area concerned with seeing

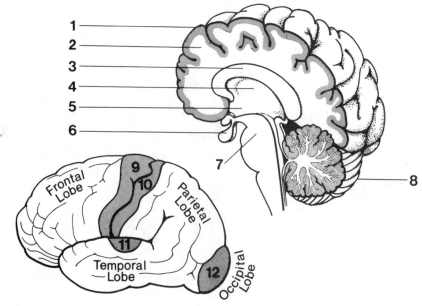

many *folds* separated by deep *fissures*. The hemispheres communicate via a bundle of nerve fibres, the *corpus callosum*.

Forebrain The much-folded surface of the brain, the *cerebral cortex*, is grey-pink in colour because of the dense concentrations of nerve cell bodies it contains; this surface position gives them access to oxygen and nutrients from the network of blood vessels threading over the cortical surface. The greater the surface area of the cortex – multiple fissures and folds are one way of increasing surface area within the narrow confines of the cranium – the more nerve cell bodies can be accommodated. Man is distinguished from his nearest living relatives, the apes, by the relatively vast cortical surface of his brain, which correlates with superior intelligence.

The cerebral cortex represents the most recently evolved part of the human brain. Its major landmarks are the oblique Fissure of Sylvius dividing the *temporal lobe* from the *frontal and parietal lobes* above it and the vertical Fissure of Rolando (or central fissure) separating the frontal from the parietal lobe. The rear part of the cortex is called the *occipital lobe*.

Certain areas of the cerebral cortex carry out specific functions (see diagram). However, there are large areas of the cortex whose functions are less clear. These relate to foresight, hindsight and perceptual, intellectual and learning abilities and are only slowly being mapped.

Beneath the cerebral cortex lies the *subcortex*, composed of less recently evolved structures concerned with more fundamental aspects of behaviour. Certain deeply buried clumps of nerve cell bodies called the *basal ganglia* are concerned with fine control and co-ordination of movement. The centrally sited *thalamus* relays sensory information to appropriate areas of the cortex, and is also implicated in our ability to focus attention on one thing at a time. Beneath the thalamus is the insignificant-looking *hypothalamus*, which regulates hunger, thirst, sex, sleep, body temperature and basic emotions (fear, anger and so on). It also controls the hormonal secretions of the *pituitary gland* underneath it. The cerebral hemispheres, including the cerebral cortex, basal ganglia, thalamus and hypothalamus are all part of the *forebrain*.

Mid-brain Underneath the cerebral hemispheres is the *brain stem* or *mid-brain*, a much older part of the brain which began its evolution with the first vertebrate worms 500 million years ago. Apart from carrying ascending sensory nerves and descending motor nerves between the brain and the *spinal cord* it contains centres that control automatic functions like respiration and heartbeat. Now, in the central core of the brain stem lies a dense network of neurons called the *reticular activating system;* this controls our sleeping/waking cycle and arouses us to attention-demanding stimuli; it accomplishes these crucial functions because it has connections that fan out to all areas of the cerebral cortex. In other words the level of activation of the cortex depends on this more primitive part of the brain. Consciousness, as we know it, is mediated by the reticular activating system; without it, we would be in a state of impenetrable somnolence.

Hindbrain Behind the brain stem and beneath the occipital lobe is the *hindbrain* or *cerebellum*, the non-stop monitor of all movements commanded by the motor area of the cortex. It is the cerebellum which gives our movements smoothness and precision; well-learned motor skills, like playing tennis, require minimal conscious attention because of the detailed movement information stored in the cerebellum.

Memory

Intrinsic to the brain's primary function of producing adaptive behaviour is the ability to store a greal deal of information about events in the environment and about the sort of responses which 'work'. The huge multiplication of neurons in the human brain during the most recent stages of evolution represents a huge increase in storage capacity. Information storage probably involves some modification of the transmitting properties of nerve junctions or synapses.

What does seem to be clear from our knowledge of the brain is that no psychological process, no mental event, no manifestation of mind, occurs without an underlying physical event in the brain. Conversely, any significant physical modification of the brain – whether by external 'psychological' stimuli, accidental damage, psychosurgery, electric shocks or drugs which act on the nervous system – produces changes in an individual's psychological state. This apparently perfect correlation between mental events and physical events in the brain would appear to be the vital premise from which to start any discussion about the complex relationship between mind and brain.

Mental illness

Brain damage Damage to the brain may be localised or diffuse, affecting all brain regions. Diffuse damage is often the result of disease, general degeneration in the case of neurosyphilis, cortical atrophy in the case of Alzheimer's disease. More circumscribed damage is likely to be the result of physical injury: the brain may be damaged by bruising or by haemorrhaging of the blood vessels inside the skull. Brain tumours, strokes and cerebral ischaemia (reduction in blood supply) can also cause localised damage.

Mental retardation

Destruction of brain tissue is usually accompanied by some impairment of the higher mental functions, particularly language, memory and learning ability. Failure to recognise certain objects, an impairment known as agnosia, may be total or restricted to a particular sense. Patients with prosopagnosia, for example, have difficulty recognising people, even close relatives, until they speak. Someone with tactile agnosia cannot recognise objects by touch but identifies them correctly by sight. Body image disorders are another possible consequence of brain damage: the person may lose awareness of one half of his body, and point to it indignantly demanding why he is in bed with a complete stranger. Other brain injuries can lead to language disturbances (aphasia). Inability to use spoken language may be total or quite specific; one patient lost the word 'no' from his active vocabulary, although on one occasion he got so irritated by lengthy questioning about his problem that he lost his temper and shouted "Can't you understand that I don't know how to say the word 'No'?"

The most common manifestation of diffuse brain damage is dementia, progressive deterioration of all intellectual processes – patchy memory, confused thinking, loss of concentration and marked personality changes involving a lack of inhibition, growing emotional and sexual coarseness, self-neglect and finally incontinence.

Although damaged brain cells cannot regenerate, some recovery of lost function is possible, probably because other parts of the brain take over the functions of the injured area. This flexibility is greater in youth than in older adulthood, but in both cases a caring environment with constant stimulation can often speed recovery.

Brainstorming A technique of group problem-solving, based on the assumption that many heads are quicker and better than one. The 'storm' starts with everyone putting forward their ideas, no matter how crazy or expensive. During this phase, the 'green light' phase, no wet-blanket criticisms are allowed. In the next phase, the 'red light' phase, each idea is evaluated until one emerges as meeting general approval.

Brainwashing Brainwashing, or 'thought-reform' as it is more technically and less luridly known, refers to the use of intensive propaganda techniques applied under conditions of great physical and psychological stress. The term was coined by George Orwell in his novel *1984*. Most of what psychologists know of brainwashing is based on the evidence of political dissidents and prisoners of war.

Conditioning

Prisoners of war in Korea were at one time persuaded by their captors to make statements and broadcasts indicating their conversion to Marxism. Initially they were subjected to serious physical abuse – vicious beatings, exposure to cold, starvation, and so on – but later, more refined techniques of persuasion were adopted, the aim of which was to induce a state of DDD, debility, dependence and dread. The approach used was threefold.

Sensory deprivation

One tactic was *isolation*. Leaders were removed and informers were introduced to create an atmosphere of suspicion and to prevent trust or intimacy developing between prisoners. In some instances prisoners were subjected to complete sensory deprivation. These procedures destroyed morale and *esprit de corps*, and led to increased vulnerability to threats and bribes.

The second tactic used was *thought control*. Prisoners were forced to choose between co-operating on the one hand and starvation, torture, or death on the other. They were confused and worn down by unpredictable treatment, sometimes harsh, sometimes friendly. These manipulations produced anxiety, dread and guilt as well as confusion about how to act.

The third tactic was *political conditioning*. This consisted of daily repetitious instruction in communist doctrine. Ideological co-operation was rewarded and resistance punished. More 'advanced' prisoners were used to persuade their more 'backward' comrades.

In the case of these American servicemen in Korea, conversions were surprisingly rare. Only 15 per cent of those who returned home were judged to have complied unduly. Following initial adjustment problems the majority readapted well. It may not be too callous to suggest that the effects of brainwashing are neither as extensive nor as permanent as is sometimes believed.

Brain waves Minute voltage fluctuations, recorded by EEG, representing the synchronised electrical activity of thousands of neurons in the brain. Under certain conditions regular fluctuations or waves of activity are recorded. These vary in frequency (number of waves per second), and for convenience are divided into four wave bands; in order of descending frequency these are beta (β) waves, alpha (α) waves, theta (θ) waves and delta (Δ) waves.

Sleep

Delta activity is characteristic of deep sleep. Theta activity is rare in normal waking adults but is commonly found in children; there is evidence that adults with abnormal personalities show an 'immature' EEG pattern in the form of increased theta activity. In one study two-thirds of murderers and 85 per cent of aggressive psychopaths showed theta patterns, as compared with 15 per cent of the normal population.

The most striking feature of the normal adult EEG are the alpha waves. These are best seen when one relaxes with eyes closed. When you open your eyes or start to think hard about something, alpha rhythm is 'blocked' and replaced by fast irregular activity. Practised meditators can maintain alpha activity even with their eyes open. Beta activity is characteris-

Meditation

tic of unrelaxed, wakeful states.

Breast envy In psychoanalytic theory, the consequence of suppressing a breast complex (anxiety and frustration associated with withdrawal of the breast after weaning); may lead to the development of overt homosexual traits.

Cannabis (see Marijuana)

Cannon-Bard theory of emotion The theory that the physiological changes and subjective feelings associated with emotion occur simultaneously because the nerve impulses generated by an emotion-arousing stimulus split when they get to the thalamus, some going to the cortex to produce the subjective experience and some to the hypothalamus, which controls physical arousal. A very neat proposition, but unsupported by physiological research. The currently popular *cognitive labelling theory* of emotion is really a refinement of the ideas of Cannon and Bard.

Castration anxiety Fear of injury to or loss of the male genitals. According to Freudian psychoanalysts a common phenomenon in young boys, related to bowel training, weaning experiences or a castration threat made by a parent. Freud saw castration anxiety as destroying the earlier Oedipus complex. Severe castration anxiety may persist as an element of adult fantasy, producing neurotic conflict.

Catalepsy Maintaining an immobile, fixed posture for long periods, as in *catatonic schizophrenia*, certain cases of hysteria, and some forms of brain disorder; can also be induced by hypnosis.

Catecholamines Hormones produced by the adrenal glands, notably adrenaline, noradrenaline and dopamine.

Catharsis In psychoanalytic theory, any discharge of emotion which relieves tension or anxiety, enabling the Ego to regain control over the Id; usually regarded as therapeutic.

Cathexis In psychoanalytic theory, charging an idea or object with intense meaning; a breast-fed infant is said to *cathect* its mother's breast.

Raymond Cattell, b. 1905

Cattell, Raymond B. Cattell's theoretical goal has always been to predict individual behaviour in specific situations by applying the statistical method of factor analysis to measurable aspects of behaviour. To that end his experimental designs have always been 'multivariate', concerned with measuring the behaviour of individuals or groups in many different test situations and correlating those measures.

Like most personality theorists Cattell accepts that there are such things as durable mental structures, or traits, some directly observable, others only inferred from statistical analysis. Traits of the observable sort he labels *surface traits*; underlying and producing these are what he calls *source traits*. Shyness and aggression are both surface traits, produced by a combination of deeper-lying traits. Intelligence on the other hand is a source trait, since it partly determines several surface traits. From this description it follows that Cattell regards source traits as far more important and far less numerous than surface traits. The Cattell 16PF personality inventory, widely used in North America, is the practical application of Cattell's indefatigable research into personality.

Cattell has also postulated that personality traits have various origins. Traits which prompt action of some kind he labels *dynamic traits*; those which have a physiological basis are *constitutional traits*; those attributable to characteristics like energy level, impulsiveness, or sensitivity, are *temperamental traits*; those imposed by external circumstances are *environmental-mould traits*. All these ideas and their experimental roots are set out in his *Handbook of Multivariate Experimental Psychology* (1966) and *Personality and Motivation, Structures and Measurement* (1957).

Cattell was born in Staffordshire, England, in 1905 and studied chemistry and psychology at the University of London, where his chief mentor was Charles Spearman, the 'father' of factor analysis. He moved to the United States in 1937 and taught at Clark University, Massachusetts, and at Harvard. He later became director of the laboratory of Personality and Group Analysis at the University of Illinois and is now at the Institute for Research on Memory and Adjustment at Boulder, Colorado.

Cattell 16PF   One of the major personality inventories used in North America. It investigates 16 fundamental personality traits from which others are derivations.

Central nervous system   That part of the nervous system which comprises the brain and spinal chord.

Central traits   The key elements in one's personality as perceived by others. Our perception of others is rarely based on their total personality but on key aspects of it. The most commonly perceived central traits are 'warmth' and 'coldness'; if you are warm, people also assume you are generous and likely to have a sense of humour.

Cerebellum   One of the oldest structures of the brain, dating back to pre-reptilian evolution (350 million years ago); heavily involved in balance and co-ordinating movement.

Cerebral cortex   (see Brain)

Cerebral dominance   The tendency for one cerebral hemisphere of the brain to be more active than the other during certain tasks and in certain people. The left hemisphere seems to be more active during verbal tasks, the right during spatial tasks. In most right-handed people the left hemisphere dominates in many tasks. With the left-handed people the picture is less clear; most left-handers have normal left-side dominance, others mixed or reversed dominance.

Cerebral hemispheres (see Brain, Split brain)

Learning

Chaining Combining a series of separate learned behaviours into an automatic sequence (switch alarm clock off, get out of bed, put slippers on, put kettle on, let cat in ...). Each behaviour in the sequence is the stimulus for the next.

Character disorder A diagnostic term available to psychoanalysts, though not much used by psychologists. A character disorder affects the whole personality and, psychoanalysts would argue, stems from repressed infantile wishes; the disordered person typically believes his behaviour is appropriate, valuable, responsible and directed by moral and rational considerations. Someone who repeatedly checks whether they have their door key with them is, in their eyes, being properly careful.

Getting the mind's eye down on paper: a case of the right brain not knowing what the left hand is doing? Not necessarily. To some extent all forms of thinking involve both hemispheres.

Chemotherapy Drugs used as therapy or in conjunction with other forms of therapy. Chemotherapy can range from Librium prescribed by the family doctor for mild depression or anxiety, to the mind-altering drugs prescribed by psychiatrists for schizophrenia.

Childbirth Simple learning theory might suggest that the pain and anxiety of childbirth might condition the female of the species against birth and babies. But the reverse is true. In Western cultures today the pain of childbirth is increasingly seen as some sort of investment; mothers who want to get it over with as quickly and as painlessly as possible invest less than mothers who prefer to remain conscious participants in the process of birth. In one study 57 per cent of mothers who were anaesthetised during the birth felt negative about it afterwards and only 3 per cent felt positive. Yet 91 per cent of those who were fully conscious felt positively, and only 3 per cent negatively. Attitudes to the baby were similarly affected: 59 per cent of those who felt positive about the birth breast-fed their babies for at least six months; 51 per cent of those who felt negative did not even attempt to breast-feed. Positive mothers were also eager to keep their babies with them rather than allow them to be taken to the hospital nursery.

Today in the West there is increasing emphasis on active preparation for childbirth and a reaction against general anaesthesia and epidurals (partial anaesthesia). Studies such as that outlined above suggest that the more knowledge and training one has, the more aware, conscious and positive one is about both birth and baby. Preparation can range from reading books and magazines to full PPM (psychoprophylactic methods) training. One of the most widely used methods of 'natural' childbirth (involving medical aid only where there are complications) is the LaMaze method; the mother-to-be practises relaxation of her abdominal muscles so that she can remain in control of the contractions of labour.

So much for the mother, but what of the child? In his famous book *Birth without violence* French obstetrician Frederick Leboyer argues that birth is equally painful for the baby. He advocates dim light and slow, quiet movements in the delivery room so that transition from the womb to the outside world is untraumatic. He also advocates immersing the newborn in warm water.

An oft-quoted cultural comparison between attitudes to childbirth is that between the Curra Indians of Central America and the Siriono Indians of Bolivia. Among the Curra the facts of life are not revealed until the marriage ceremony and birth takes place in a ritualistic fashion with only women in attendance. Among the Siriono sex and procreation are openly discussed and birth is a social event which everyone can attend. By comparison with their Siriono sisters Curra mothers have a hard time of it!

Childhood   *Sheldon White, Barbara Notkin White*

No one, whether parent or psychologist, has open access to the private life and thoughts of a child. How do we estimate what happens to a child's conceptions about himself during the course of his development? We remember our own childhood. We interpret small signs – things a child remarks about himself, attitudes he seems to take, the things he does willingly, the things he refuses to do at all, the stories and myths he creates and responds to. And we use the case studies and the theories of those who do clinical, psychological and psychoanalytic studies of children. The best of them offer the truths of science mixed with the truths of poetry.

Discovery of self As a child's sense of self grows, idiosyncratic items of behaviour appear which cannot be interpreted as easily as the emerging ability to do up a button. Two-year-olds go through a period of frequently saying 'No!' with a half-playful, half-triumphant air. Why? They seem to be announcing a kind of discovery: 'You can do what you want and I can do what I want.'

The four-year-old girl has long discussions with her doll, serves it tea, tells it how to behave, whispers secrets in its ear. Why? Maybe she finds this 'pretend' game a pleasing way to talk to herself, to air ideas and feelings. She has a nice sense of ceremony and theatre but, underneath it all, she knows the doll is really a little bit of herself.

The six-year-old boy endlessly draws pictures of planes, tanks and guns. Why? Maybe in a small way he is living through what he thinks it is like to be big and powerful. The eight-year-old suddenly reveals a talent for lying. He has picked up all those cognitive skills that psychologists regard as eminently desirable – the ability to plan, to take the role of the other – and now suddenly he fashions them into a weapon for use in his social negotiations at home. The twelve-year-old turns positively uncommunicative, meeting reasonable questions with a grunt and a shrug. Why? Maybe the eight-year-old and the twelve-year-old are exploring just how much communication with their parents they are willing to permit. Only so much is constructive for what they need and feel.

Meeting adult demands Children learn to guard themselves, conceivably because the basic processes of socialisation and education repeatedly remind them of the difference between what they are and what they might be or ought to be.

We demand of children that they 'show self-control', 'develop self-discipline', 'make something of themselves' and, occasionally, that they 'have self-confidence' – much ado about the child's self. We seem to be telling children that there is something wrong with them as they are.

When guilt creeps in Children compare themselves with others around them and, out of that comparison, establish definite notions about their comparative strengths and weaknesses. For psychiatrists eight is traditionally the age at which

A back-garden world of make-believe. Self-consciousness comes later.

C

it becomes possible to diagnose neurosis, because this is when something like a sense of guilt emerges, and some children begin to think of themselves as being 'bad'. By the age of eight children have become moral thinkers. They have a sense of the self they would like to be.

Learning: a twofold task When children learn something their task is twofold. They must learn something about the outside world and something about themselves. Self-knowledge is just as important as academic learning: every time we teach a child something, we have to ask not only "What has he learned?" but also "What has he learned about himself?"

Child psychology The study of the intellectual, emotional and behavioural development of human beings from (and before) birth to the end of adolescence.

Psychologists interested in child development tend to define it as a series of orderly stages, leading to the maturity of adulthood. While fine in theory, most parents know to their cost, that progress through childhood is not smooth and orderly, and certainly not always in the direction of maturity. Searching for some kind of order in the development of the normal healthy child is worthwhile, however, for the light it sheds on problems of development.

Unfortunately, there is little agreement between psychologists about what constitutes the most meaningful division of childhood into stages. Some, like Arnold Gesell, simply divide childhood into stages based on age groups. Others, like Piaget and Erikson, emphasise various plateaux of development, in Piaget's case plateaux in thinking and reasoning, in Erikson's plateaux in social interaction. Psychoanalysts on the other hand view development as being almost exclusively related to stages of psychosexual development.

Many child psychologists have turned to alternative approaches which bypass the concept of stages altogether and focus instead on critical and common tasks which children have to master in the growing-up process. Examples of such tasks are weaning, urinating and defecating, sexual expression, aggression, and so on. Many psychologists find this approach useful, because it leads to a more direct understanding of the problems which most frequently present themselves in child-guidance clinics.

Chlordiazepoxide The non-proprietary name for Librium, one of the most frequently prescribed minor tranquillisers for cases of anxiety and neurosis.

Chlorpromazine One of the major tranquillisers and the drug of first choice in the treatment of schizophrenia; also, because of its anti-emetic action, a somewhat drastic remedy for travel sickness!

Piaget
Erikson

Psychosexual development

Choice reaction time The time taken for the brain to identify and respond to one of a number of stimuli. Try sorting a
pack of playing cards first into colours (2 alternatives), then
into suits (4 alternatives) and finally into numbers and pictures (13 alternatives). Do this a number of times to get a
reliable average time for each task, and subtract from each
average an estimate of the non-thinking time it took you to
physically place the cards into the piles. You will be left with a
rough estimate of your brain's choice reaction time!

Genes

Chromosomes Long paired strands of de-oxyribonucleic
acid in the nucleus of every cell in the body; the coded chemical messages they contain (genes) control every single function of the body, including its development, maintenance,
form, size, sex and capacities. Human beings have 23 pairs of
chromosomes, the twenty-third pair being the sex chromosomes (XX in women and XY in men). Abnormal pairing of
paternal and maternal chromosomes at fertilisation can result
in chromosomal abnormalities such as mongolism.

Memory

Chunking A method of making information, especially numerical information, easier to remember by re-coding it into
fewer 'chunks'. Try remembering 22436913410151984 as two-
two-four, three-six-nine, one-three-four, ten-fifteen, nineteen
eighty-four.

Phobias

Claustrophobia The fear of being confined in small spaces,
without means of escape; typically experienced as a feeling of
suffocation in lifts, trains, buses and cars.

Client-centred therapy *Gerald C. Davison*

Client-centred therapy, now a very popular form of psychotherapy, was pioneered by the American psychologist Carl
Rogers
Rogers. The basic assumption of the client-centred approach
is that people are naturally good and capable of healthful
growth ('self-actualisation'), and that problems arise when
Psychotherapy
they deny fulfilment of their true needs and try instead to meet
the demands and expectations of others.

When the client decides The overall task of client-centred
therapists is to help people explore their feelings, and trust
their desires and emotions. And it is of utmost importance
that therapists do not impose standards or goals on their
clients. Establishing such 'conditions of worth', as Rogers
calls them, would only repeat the circumstances which contributed to their problems in the first place. Skilled and sensitive
'Rogerian' therapists have what is called *unconditional positive regard* for their clients, respect for their dignity and their
potential to fulfil themselves by coming to know their basic
needs. Such therapists refrain from judging or directing their
clients. Rogers assumes that as people discover their selves,
they will begin to make their own decisions and change their

C

behaviour in ways which fulfil their true needs. Central to client-centred therapy, and to other humanistic therapies, is the insistence that clients assume full responsibility for their behaviour; this sometimes extends to asking them to decide how often to come for therapy and even when to terminate it.

Client–therapist exchanges A principal technique of client-centred therapy (though Rogerians dislike viewing themselves as using 'techniques', which conjure up the image of the therapist as a manipulator) is *empathy*, knowing and understanding what the client is saying and feeling. By reflecting back to the client the feelings they are expressing, or trying to express, the therapist encourages them to continue exploring their life, perhaps facing up to things they would rather not confront.

But the stereotype picture of the client-centred therapist, merely parroting back to the client what the client has just said, is erroneous. It does little justice to the complexity and difficulty of client-centred therapy, and its potential for promoting healthful change. To appreciate the power of this approach some distinction must be made between 'primary' empathy and 'advanced' empathy.

In the early stages of therapy, the therapist helps the client to feel at ease talking about intimate details of his life; the client must learn to trust this stranger, whose professional credentials are only part of the reassurance he needs before he starts baring his soul. Primary empathy is the therapist's attempt to view things through the client's eyes or frame of reference. For the purpose of empathising, reality must be taken to be what the client perceives it to be. It is the way people construe the world that determines how they react to it, a philosophical position called phenomenology. If you feel guilty about taking a holiday no amount of careful planning and expensive hotels will make you have a good time. In primary empathy, the therapist must communicate to the client that he understands his point of view, that he respects him no matter what.

But if the therapist stays on the primary empathy level, the client may remain stuck within the phenomenological framework he feels they need treatment for. If his way of looking at the world is working for him, why should he hurt so much? Why should he be wanting treatment?

So the therapist must subtly begin offering different viewpoints or interpretations of what the client is saying and feeling; he must tie together the impressions he has formed of the client and, with tentativeness and skill, begin to suggest different ways of looking at the world. This is empathy at an advanced level. The belief is that advanced empathic suggestions help clients to find out what they truly want and need, and to assume the responsibility for deciding how to satisfy those wants and needs.

Clinical psychology That branch of psychology which applies the findings of experimental psychology to a broad range of problems, mental and physical, for which people seek treatment. Clinical psychologists undertake specialised diagnostic work as well as various forms of psychotherapy, and usually draw on a much broader spectrum of study and experience than psychiatrists.

Gestalt
Perception

Closure A concept in Gestalt psychology referring to the release of tension experienced when a problem or task is completed or 'closed', and wholeness is established. A very simple example of closure is the general tendency to remember incomplete figures as complete.

Cocktail party effect The attentional process which enables us to filter out the buzz of many conversations and attend to the conversation which interests us! Our attentional 'filter' is also alerted by the sudden absence of a familiar noise (a clock ceasing to tick) or something of personal relevance (hearing someone say our name).

Tuning in and tuning out

Cognition With its adjective *cognitive*, ubiquitous in psychology. All conscious mental processes - perceiving, remembering, appraising, imagining, reasoning, willing and judging - are cognition and cognitive. Cognitive is the opposite of affective (to do with emotion and feelings) or behavioural, although of course intellectual processes influence both emotion and behaviour.

Cognitive dissonance Holding two conflicting ideas at once, a concept in social psychology developed by Leon Festinger. Typically we reduce the unpleasantness of dissonance by rationalising, by downgrading our attachment to one of the conflicting ideas, or changing both ideas so that they fit together better. Adults paid a lot of money to tell a lie rationalised lying simply by telling themselves that the amount of money justified a single, solitary lapse of honesty. People offered less money managed to convince themselves they weren't really lying at all - the bribe was worthless so the lie didn't matter.

Approach-avoidance

Cognitive labelling theory A modern refinement on the James-Lange theory of emotion; the hypothesis that the same physiological state of arousal underlies all emotions, the subjective difference between them being due to cognitive factors. Feeling aroused and knowing you're late equals panic; feeling aroused and listening to Beethoven's *Pastoral* equals bliss. In other words, it is the label one attaches to arousal that determines the quality of the emotion.

Emotions

Cognitive psychology Broadly speaking, that area of psychology concerned with perception, language, thinking, problem-solving, memory and attention – all the intellectual aspects of behaviour as opposed to the emotional or motivational (there are overlaps of course – cognition influences motivation and motivation perception). Cognitive psychology today makes wide use of models and analogies drawn from computer technology.

Cognitive style Each person's individually consistent way of looking at objective reality and of attaching form and meaning to their experiences. 'Sharpeners' are people who make acute discriminations between objects and events; 'levellers' miss changes and blur distinctions. Some people are 'field dependent', others 'field independent'; the latter are better at taking in and processing visual information. Attempts to associate field independence, discriminatory ability and other cognitive styles with personality traits have been widely criticised as lacking validity.

Cognitive therapy Any technique in psychotherapy which encourages the client to reconceptualise or think differently about problem areas in his or her life. Psychoanalysis is primarily cognitive in that unconscious impulses or tendencies are brought into consciousness and submitted to rational examination. Rational–emotive therapy is also essentially cognitive.

Psychoanalysis

Rational-emotive therapy

Collective unconscious A somewhat mystical but nevertheless intriguing concept developed by Jung, based on his notion that certain mental images or *archetypes* appear to be inborn in all of us. These archetypes represent the accumulated residue of human experience over millennia of evolution (rather than the experience of a single lifetime, the personal unconscious). For ideological ends Jung's concept was perverted to 'racial consciousness' or 'racial memory'.

Jung

Colour blindness There are three sorts of colour receptors in the human eye, one sensitive to red, one to green and one to blue light. The combination of these gives us the experience of colour. Colour blindness occurs when one or more of these colour receptors is deficient or missing. About 10 per cent of people, mostly men, are colour blind in some degree. The condition interests psychologists because it influences certain aspects of perception.

Perception

Comparative psychology Investigating animal behaviour, often using *conditioning* techniques, in order to shed light on human behaviour; investigating animal behaviour for its own sake is the task of the ethologist.

Complex Conflicts and anxieties surrounding a particular area of a person's life and affecting their attitude to many situations and relationships. Freud distrusted the word and used it very rarely. But Jungians speak of father, mother and sister complexes, and complexes connected with almost any traumatic event in life – Jung is famous for his oft-repeated accusation that Freud had a badly resolved father complex!

Compos mentis Legal Latin meaning 'of sound mind'; *non compos mentis* is a plea of insanity, on the evidence of a psychologist or psychiatrist. If accepted, the defendant is not held responsible for his actions. The diagnosis of insanity poses acute problems; IQ and other tests are variable measures of mental competence. Are schizophrenics insane despite their periods of apparent normality? The diagnosis of *non compos mentis* can also be a sentence of indefinite committal to an institution.

Mental illness

Compulsion An action one feels compelled to perform, repeatedly, however irrational, bizarre or against one's better judgement. The psychoanalytic view is that such actions temporarily assuage the guilt or anxiety attached to forbidden impulses. Some compulsions, they point out, such as handwashing or neatness, may reflect the exact opposite, an unconscious desire to be dirty and untidy. Some compulsions are amenable to behavioural therapy, in particular to response-prevention and aversion techniques.

Neurosis

Concept formation The process of formulating ideas from scratch, investigated experimentally because of the light it sheds on our basic powers of reasoning. One major finding of concept formation experiments is that many people test their ideas by trying to verify them; trying to falsify them often gives correct answers just as rapidly. People also find concrete problems easier to solve than abstract ones.

Conceptualisation A recent coinage, meaning the whole web of ideas, values, and feelings one attaches to a certain area of one's life; sometimes synonymous with perceptual set.

Concrete operational stage According to Piaget the gradual development between the ages of seven and eleven of systematic and rational thought about physical objects, the ability to think in a framework of space, time, number and causality, and to realise how other people feel.

Piaget

Conditioning Any natural or experimental process which brings about the relatively permanent changes in behaviour we call learning.
Classical conditioning, à la Pavlov, involves modifying some naturally occurring response (salivation) to a certain stimulus (food) by introducing another stimulus (a buzzer). After a few

Behaviour therapy

Pavlov

repeats the natural response is elicited by the buzzer alone; it has become a *conditioned response*, with the buzzer the *conditioned stimulus*.

Reinforcement

Skinner

Operant conditioning, à la Skinner, is effective because behaviours which are *positively reinforced* (rewarded, or at least not punished) are likely to persist and strengthen, and behaviours which are *negatively reinforced* (punished, or not rewarded) are likely to disappear. This applies equally to automatic and voluntary behaviour. Behaviour which is desired but not automatic (a rat pressing a lever) must be gradually conditioned or *shaped*, first by offering rewards for remote approximations, then for exact fulfilment only.

Remote though they may seem from the complexities of human behaviour, classical and operant conditioning occur quite naturally throughout our youth and childhood.

Social psychology

Conformity One of the most powerful tendencies identified by social psychologists; adapting or altering one's behaviour or opinions for fear of deviating from one's social group. Several well-known experimental studies have demonstrated the importance of this process. In one, the subjects were asked either individually or collectively to report on the movement of a spot of light in a totally dark room; in fact the light was stationary, but the perception of illusory movement under such conditions is very common. Tested alone, subjects diverged considerably in their judgements of the extent and direction of movement, but tested together they came to very similar conclusions. They also maintained this judgement when tested alone afterwards!

Dropping out but fitting in

Conscious Any degree of self-awareness. Because consciousness is so difficult to define, psychologists have concentrated on exploring states of consciousness (trance, meditation, sleep) markedly different from our normal waking state. In Freudian theory, consciousness is identified with the activities of the Superego or part of the Ego. In his later writing (1940) Freud observed that consciousness is a highly elusive state: "What is conscious is conscious only for a moment." William James, on the other hand, asserted that consciousness does not consist of discrete flashes of awareness; it flows like a stream (novelists like James Joyce and Gertrude Stein popularised the 'stream of consciousness' as a literary device).

Conservation The amount of a substance remaining constant even when its shape is altered, a concept younger children find impossible to grasp and therefore a useful distinction between two stages of intellectual development, the pre-operational and concrete operational.

Consolidation theory This proposes that learning involves creating patterns of neuron activity in the brain which would fade and disappear if they were not consolidated and made permanent by chemical changes.

Constancy Making sense out of sensations; the operation of memory and experience on a vast variety of sensory stimuli in order to make them reliable, meaningful and familiar. The Bambuti pygmies of the Congo forest have no experience of wide open spaces and so interpret buffalo grazing in the distance as insects!

Consumer psychology The research which goes into influencing you to buy one product rather than another. Advertisers are often, in Vance Packard's phrase, 'hidden persuaders'.

Suppose you're buying a new car. What factors are going to influence your choice? Price, petrol consumption, horsepower, boot space, racy extras? Certainly all of these, but according to researchers G. H. Smith and R. Engel, other factors may be even more important.

To test their idea, Smith and Engel created a car advertisement which included a provocatively clad model from *Playboy*, and another which depicted the identical car minus Ms Provocative. Then they asked two groups of men to rate the design of the car on a 5-point scale from 'excellent' to 'poor'. One group was shown the ad with the model, but the second group, the control group, saw the ad with the car alone.

Result: the first group rated the car as more appealing, lively, youthful, better designed, faster, more expensive ... than the control group did. Predictable perhaps. But, more significantly, the men who saw the first ad not only denied that the model had influenced them but said they had hardly been aware of her!

IQ

Control group A group of subjects or patients in all possible respects identical to the main group(s) of subjects or patients in an experiment. The only difference in their treatment is that they are not given the drug or therapy whose effect the experimenter is investigating.

Conversion reaction As seen in hysterical pregnancy or hysterical paralysis; a little understood phenomenon which appears to represent a compromise between a forbidden impulse and the wish to express it, or, according to other writers, the conversion of external pressures into physical symptoms as a way of avoiding them (e.g. writer's cramp). When clinically examined, the symptoms of conversion reactions appear to have no physiological basis.

Corpus callosum The bridge of nerve tissue connecting the two hemispheres of the brain. When surgically severed, in the procedure known as the 'split-brain' operation, the two hemispheres operate independently.

Correlation A relationship between two sets of statistics. Degrees of correlation are expressed as *correlation coefficients*, perfect positive correlation being $+1$, perfect negative correlation -1, and no correlation at all 0. There is, for example, a high positive correlation between educational achievement and socio-economic status, but no correlation at all between musicality and breast-feeding.

Counter-conditioning Weakening an existing conditioned response by conditioning an incompatible response; one of the elements of desensitisation treatment, where relaxation is taught in the presence of anxiety-producing stimuli.

Culture-fair tests Tests of intelligence or ability which do not bias against a person unfamiliar with the language and culture of the test inventor. Many critics of psychological testing doubt that current tests meet this criterion.

Daydreaming That state of consciousness in which censorship is relaxed and one's thoughts take an aimless, pleasurable, wish-fulfilling turn; seen by some psychoanalysts as a return to a stage of development when there is no difference between wish and action; a way of obtaining satisfaction denied in the real world.

Death instinct A term coined by Freud in his later theorising. He became convinced that in all of us there is an inborn tendency to retreat back into a peaceful womb-like state of existence. Just as the life instinct, *Eros*, is guided by a libidinal pleasure principle, so the death instinct, *Thanatos*, is guided by a *nirvana* principle (extinction of individuality). We supposedly fight against the regressive pull of the death instinct by turning it outwards on to the world. Freud believed that self-annihilation is actually more basic than aggression; masochism more basic than sadism; and passivity more basic than activity. With the influential exception of contemporary analysts of the Kleinian school, this belief of Freud's was not developed by his followers.

Defence mechanism One of the most accessible terms in Freudian psychology and the means by which the Ego seeks to defend itself against the experience of unwanted or denied emotions, or emotionally loaded character traits. No fewer than 18 different defence mechanisms have been identified, but the most important of them is *repression*, the forgetting or making unconscious of feelings unacceptable or painful at the conscious level. The most frequently repressed emotion is anxiety. Another defence mechanism is *reaction formation*: we sometimes cover up one trait by cultivating its polar opposite; for example, a fascination with dirt and excreta during the anal stage of infancy may be countered by the development of an obsessively clean and tidy personality. Another defence is *projection*, whereby undesirable traits in oneself are projected on to another person, so making the uncomfortable traits easier to live with. Other defence mechanisms are *ambivalence* (simultaneous opposite feelings towards people or objects), *conversion* (transforming anxiety into physical symptoms), *denial* (refusing to recognise the claims of external reality), *displacement* (doing one thing as an unconscious substitute for doing something else), and *fixation* (arrested development).

The fact that so many people accept Freud's ideas on defence mechanisms supports their existence, but denies their being quite so unconsciously organised as he supposed.

Psychoanalysis

Deindividuation Something which happens when a person

is immersed in a crowd and feels he is unseen, ineffectual and worthless as an individual. The experience of soldiers in combat or of students in demonstrations suggest the obvious: that anonymity leads to a lowering of normal restraints and inhibitions and sometimes to barbarous behaviour. A particularly disturbing research finding is that many otherwise normal people seem prone to brutalisation of this kind. The evidence suggests that the situation is overwhelmingly more important than the individual.

Déjà vu That quirky feeling that you've seen it all before. Some parapsychologists claim that *déjà vu* is evidence of clairvoyance, but it seems more probable that immediate cues are partially triggering recognition of similar rather than identical situations. It has also been suggested that an infinitesimal time lag between the functioning of the two cerebral hemispheres, or a confusion between long- and short-term memory receptors, could be responsible. A related phenomenon is *déjà raconté*, the feeling of having heard it all before.

Ambivalence: a case of the right hand not knowing what the left is doing?

Delinquency As many as 80 per cent of crimes are never reported; the majority of people will admit, when asked 'off the record', to having broken the law. That said, juvenile delinquents (age 10 to 17) account for one-third of all known crimes with criminality peaking at around 15, though for no very clear reason. Amongst some groups of youngsters, especially from underprivileged industrial areas with decreasing populations and poor housing, delinquency appears to be the norm. A substantial minority (about 25 per cent) drift into recidivism, a 'life of crime', spending a large proportion of their lives in prison. Many recidivists have psychiatric problems (e.g. depression) which make it difficult for them to adapt to the demands of conventional society.

Another delinquent sub-group are the professional criminals who lead a fairly profitable life of crime and tend to be well adjusted to their unusual lifestyle. Less well known are the 'white collar' delinquents who use their respectability to cheat and defraud society, often with complete impunity; these 'middle class' offenders are difficult to detect and often get the benefit of the doubt in court.

Many social psychologists argue that in view of the potential profitability of crime more attention should be devoted to understanding why most of us do not become criminals.

Delirium A state of mental excitement and incoherence, accompanied by delusions, hallucinations and fever; may be brought on by withdrawal of alcohol or barbiturates; at one time a not uncommon reaction to prolonged use of bromides.

Delta rhythm Synchronised low frequency brain waves (0.5–4 Hertz) recorded by electroencephalograph and typical of deep dreamless sleep.

Sleep

Delusion A false belief. Delusions are very common in psychotic patients, particularly in paranoid schizophrenia where they are usually delusions of *grandeur* and *persecution*. However, the word delusion has wider significance. Many normal people are subject to delusions from time to time. It could be argued that since we all impose our own structures on reality, and often perceive ourselves and others in ways which do not accord with reality, we are all deluded! But *psychotic delusions* are characterised by their all-pervasive influence on the life of the person concerned; delusions of this kind are not dissipated by reason or reality. *Neurotic delusion* is a less profound condition. The neurotic may, for example, transfer feelings about a harsh parent to her employer, and suffer a consequent delusion of persecution which is not entirely supported by reality. Psychologists use techniques derived from personal construct theory to identify minor delusional problems.

Neurosis

Dementia Deterioration of mental powers; in *senile demen-*

tia due to widespread atrophy of cells in the cerebral cortex; *dementia praecox* is the now obsolete term of schizophrenia.

Denial A defence mechanism, but a defence against unpleasant external stimuli rather than internal ones. Denying a traumatic event keeps it out of consciousness.

Dependency A personality trait. People who are high in dependency constantly seek reassurance from their social environment. Some psychologists claim that dependency shows up in the perceptual measurement of *field-dependence*. A field-dependent person finds it relatively difficult to distinguish figure from background (or field) in certain situations, for instance when they are asked to isolate the outline of a complex geometrical design. Someone who leans heavily on drugs is also said to be dependent.

Depersonalisation A term used by psychotherapists to describe the state in which a patient feels he has lost a firm view of his self-hood. Such a patient may go through the motions of acting normally, but somehow feels it's all a sham. For existentially inclined therapists, depersonalisation is a necessary first step on the path to rethinking self-hood.

Depression *A. John Rush*

Virtually all of us experience feelings of sadness and hopelessness at some time in our life. But as these feelings and the experiences associated with them are shared with others, and as we begin to accept the situation as it is, the sadness gradually goes away. The feelings just described are what psychologists call *situational depression*, negative emotions directly attributable to external events.

Signs and symptoms That a person is depressed can be inferred from the following non-verbal behaviours: moving slowly, talking in a low or muffled voice, replying slowly to questions, using few words, rarely speaking unless spoken to, downcast gaze, slumped shoulders, speaking at the end of an expiration and/or outright crying and sobbing. Most people who exhibit such behaviours will readily admit they feel depressed if asked (though there are people with medical or neurological disorders who look sad but don't actually feel sad inside).

Depression is a syndrome, a basketful of symptoms felt by the sufferer and of signs obvious to the trained observer. But a depressive syndrome is unlikely to be diagnosed unless at least four of the following signs and symptoms are present in addition to sadness: a reduction or increase in appetite or weight; a reduction in one's usual rate of thinking or moving, or frenetic movement and thinking (in scientific parlance, psychomotor retardation or agitation); excessive sleep or an inability to sleep; lack of energy/easy fatigability; impaired con-

Big cities can be lonely places. Loneliness is an element of depression that is often overlooked.

centration/decision-making; excessive guilt or self-reproach; recurrent thoughts of death or suicide; a general loss of interest in usually enjoyable activities.

Suicide

While a person who is grieving over the death of a spouse or loved one may experience some of these signs and symptoms, in general grief reactions are self-limited. Only if grieving lasts for longer than six months or so might a physician diagnose a depressive syndrome.

Bereavement

Depression from within *Endogenous depression*, or internally caused depression, has many causes: thyroid, adrenal and other endocrine diseases (diseases of the glands which secrete various vital hormones), diseases of the nervous system such as Parkinson's disease, auto-immune disorders, vitamin deficiencies, etc. There are also depressive syndromes that fall primarily into the category of psychiatric disorders; these are the so-called *manic depressive* illnesses or *bipolar depressions*, characterised by alternating depressed and manic states. A manic state has various ingredients – feelings of euphoria or irritability, racing thoughts, a pressure to speak, distractability, excessive energy, decreased need to sleep, impulsive behaviours which display poor judgement (reckless driving, gambling sprees, sexual indiscretions, etc.).

Mania

The dividing line between situational and endogenous depression is very fuzzy. Most depressions have both situational and endogenous elements. Depressions which are mainly situational are usually self-limited, perhaps accompanied by mild weight loss and sleep difficulties. In mainly endogenous depressions symptoms are usually more severe and set in gradually over a few weeks. Insomnia and weight loss are more marked, and the person feels a heavy burden of guilt and hopelessness.

An interesting cross-cultural sidelight on depression is that whereas we in the West tend to feel guilty and suicidal when we are severely depressed, non-Westerners are more likely to experience severe depression as bodily aches and pains and/or acute suspiciousness of others.

Unfortunately women are twice as likely as men to experience a depressive syndrome other than grief at some time during their life. Researchers have found that some people are genetically more vulnerable than others to developing certain depressions, especially manic-depressive illnesses. There are also data which suggest that some depressions, especially severe or endogenous cases, are due to certain chemical changes in the brain. Other researchers attribute depressive tendencies to specific psychological factors, especially attitudes and ways of thinking. Many forms of depression certainly appear to be associated with rather fixed, stereotyped, negatively-biased ways of looking at oneself and the world.

Treatments Can depression be cured? It most emphatically can, and it yields faster and more surely to professional help than to self-help methods. If psychological factors and attitudes appear to be the culprits, psychotherapy may be the answer – various psychotherapies have been specifically developed to treat depression. If some derangements of brain chemistry are suspected, drugs may be prescribed, notably antidepressants, several of which have appeared on the market since 1957. Antidepressants have much to recommend them – they appear to remove the symptoms of depression and also prevent recurrence in patients vulnerable to repeated episodes of depression. Electroconvulsive therapy is also

Electroconvulsive therapy

used. Despite public repugnance to ECT, it is highly effective and even life-saving in severe endogenous depression. It should be stressed, however, that very careful and thorough medical evaluation of signs and symptoms is needed before the right treatment can be prescribed.

Deprivation A term used by psychologists to describe various states of discomfort. *Maternal deprivation* is a whole field of study in itself, with proponents such as Michael Rutter, Harry Harlow and John Bowlby arguing its definitions and effects. This lack, or loss, of essential 'caring' on the part of the mother has little to do with the phenomenon of *sensory deprivation*, which involves the withdrawal of some or all sensory stimuli, and is one of the techniques of brainwashing and of 'biological clock' experiments.

Depth psychology Psychology based strictly or loosely on the theories of Freud. The word 'depth' refers to the idea that many important desires and conflicts lie deep down beneath our conscious awareness. A range of psychoanalytical techniques can be used to try to uncover these buried parts of the self and identify their effects on behaviour and personality.

Desensitisation A technique used by behavioural therapists to diminish unwanted fears and anxieties; particularly effective with certain kinds of phobia. The patient, in imagination or in reality, is encouraged to confront her fears in a gradual fashion while also being taught to relax. Sometimes the patient's perception of the phobic object can be changed in a positive direction – fear of spiders, for example, has been cured by persuading patients to look after spiders and discover interesting aspects of spider life! Desensitisation, when it works, is probably effective because it functions on many levels at once. It teaches new thought strategies and new control over bodily symptoms of anxiety and it produces a

Behaviour therapy

feeling of achievement (positive reinforcement) when confrontation of the phobic object or situation is successful.

Developmental psychology The study of all psychological processes to see how they develop and change throughout life. The main areas of study in developmental psychology are the unfolding of perceptual and intellectual processes in infancy,

Life cycle

childhood and adolescence; the development of personality at each stage of the lifecycle; physical maturation and decline and their effect on behaviour.

Diagnostic tests These are used, particularly by clinical and educational psychologists, to identify physiological as well as psychological disorders. Some general tests, for example IQ tests, can be used to study specialised patterns of performance which have specific diagnostic implications. Others enable diagnosticians to acquire a summary view of an individual's abilities, aptitudes, interests, temperament, self-concept, values, emotional state, and so on.

Diathesis-stress hypothesis This states that certain disorders result from an interaction between psychological stress and an inherited weakness in a bodily system. For example, stress plus an acidity-prone stomach potentially equals a stomach ulcer.

Dichotic listening A method of studying the processes involved when people attend to conflicting auditory stimuli. Two different messages are played simultaneously, one into each ear, and the subject has to concentrate on one of them by 'shadowing' it, i.e. repeating it back as it is received. Subjects usually report no knowledge of the unattended message, and yet it is possible to show that the meaning of the unattended message has somehow been processed without their conscious knowledge. Some dichotic listening studies have investigated the effects of presenting messages including words associated with pain. Subjects received mild electric shocks in conjunction with these words, and then words of similar meaning were presented as part of the unattended message. Measurable physiological responses were provoked even though the words had not been consciously heard.

Memory

Digit span A measurement procedure used in memory research as part of IQ assessment. A person's digit span is assessed by presenting them with a list of random numbers (digits). The investigator calls out the numbers at one second intervals and asks the person to repeat them back in the correct order. Most people can manage lists of about seven digits. The number of digits remembered is their digit span.

Conditioning

Discrimination learning A term used in operant and classical conditioning to describe the process of training an organism to respond selectively to one of two stimuli. Selective reinforcement of one of the stimuli teaches the organism to discriminate it from the other. One psychologist, T. Verhave, was so successful at teaching pigeons to pick out defective capsules on a production line in a pharmaceuticals factory that hundreds of men nearly lost their jobs!

67

Dispersion A statistical term. When data on a large number of people are collected (IQ scores, for example, or scores of reading ability) they are usually summarised by calculating the average score. Averages, however, can be misleading. Sometimes the scores are clustered around the average value, but just as often there is a wide variability of scores. So average tells us little unless we know the range of the scores and whether they are clumped or scattered around the average. This is called the *dispersion factor*, and is measured by a calculation known as the *standard deviation* of the scores. A large deviation tells us that scores are widely scattered.

Displacement A defence mechanism; substituting an attainable and acceptable goal for an unattainable and unacceptable one; frequently used in the phrase *displacement of aggression*, when hostility is transferred from its rightful target to a substitute target: you kick me, I kick the child, the child kicks the dog, the dog kicks the cat ...

Dissociative reaction Amnesia, sleepwalking and multiple personality are three of the best-known dissociative reactions. All represent a separation of one part of consciousness from the rest. The person finds this a way of dealing with sudden or mounting troubles.

Genes

DNA Short for de-oxyribonucleic acid, the acid of which genes and chromosomes are made; takes the form of long double chains of units called nucleotides (these consist of a sugar molecule, a phosphoric acid molecule and an organic base molecule bonded together in a special way). A sequence of nucleotides constitutes a gene.

Dominance A term most frequently used by students of animal behaviour to describe the phenomenon of hierarchies within animal groups. Every hierarchy has its dominant members, who get first choice of mates or food. The term is also used in psychophysiology when discussing the relative functions of both halves of the brain (cerebral dominance), and in genetics when discussing the way inherited characteristics express themselves; some characteristics are dominant (expressed), other recessive (not expressed). Some personality theorists refer to certain personality traits as being dominant over others.

Neurotransmitters

Dopamine A neurotransmitter substance found in the brain which acts as a chemical bridge for nerve impulses travelling between neurons in certain parts of the brain. A lack of dopamine has been implicated in Parkinson's disease, which occasionally responds to L-dopa, a synthetic drug which mimics dopamine.

D

Double-bind An unpleasant disturbance of direct communication between two people, resulting in a situation where neither can win. It is particularly used to describe parent-child interactions in which the parent gives conflicting cues to the child, particularly in the area of expressing emotion. For example, the child may be led to expect approval for certain action, but instead is met with confusing disapproval. Some psychiatrists believe that a history of double-bind is common in schizophrenic patients, but there is a lack of evidence to show that such a history is more frequent with schizophrenics than with the rest of us.

Double-blind A technique for making certain experiments proof against experimenter bias and self-fulfilling expectations on the part of test subjects. Both the experimenter administering the tests and the participants in the tests are left in ignorance of key features of the experiment, such as whether a drug or a placebo is being given.

The risk of bearing a mongol baby is approximately 1 in 800.

Down's syndrome (Mongolism) A chromosomal abnormality (the 21st pair of chromosomes consisting of three rather than two chromosomes) marked by varying degrees of mental retardation, and by 'mongoloid' features (slanting eyes, flattened skull, thickened tongue, broad hands and feet). Mongols are usually cheerful and co-operative despite their mental handicaps, but their life expectancy is relatively short.

Sleep

Dreaming Needs no definition as such, but psychologists have various theories as to why we dream. Freud was the first to pay close attention to dreams. He postulated that dreams are expressions, often heavily symbolic, of impulses which are unacceptable at a conscious level. Their function is to relieve tension. According to Freud, a nightmare is a dream which has been unsuccessful; the dreamer wakes because his or her thoughts are so threatening that conscious defences must be mobilised to keep them under control. Jung, on the other hand, suggested that dreams are a kind of balancing act between different elements of the personality, enabling the individual to maintain psychological equilibrium. The Gestalt approach to dreams is that they symbolise the dominant and submissive parts of the personality. In short, most theorists recognise that dreaming is somehow necessary to the wholeness and balance of the individual personality. Dream analysts try to find an interpretation of a dream which 'clicks' with the dreamer, and use it to unravel buried conflict.

D

The physiological nature of dreaming, – altered brain wave patterns, rapid eye movements (REM) etc. – has been extensively researched. Humans and cats dream a lot, but birds hardly dream at all. It also seems that if REM sleep is denied over a period of time, compensatory extra amounts of dreaming occur later.

Motivation

Drive In the psychology of motivation, drive is sometimes equated with a general 'push' towards the gratification of a basic biological need, for food, for sexual activity and so on. It is also used to refer to specific drives such as hunger or thirst. But modern psychologists find the term too imprecise to be useful. What, they ask, is added to the concept of hunger by referring to it as a 'hunger-drive'?

Drug dependence *Jerome Jaffe, Robert Petersen, Ray Hodgson*

Definition and classification Faced with endless confusion about the meaning of the terms 'addiction' and 'habituation' the World Health Organization abandoned both terms in 1965 and adopted the more neutral term 'drug dependence', which it defined as: "A state, psychic and sometimes also physical, resulting from the interaction between a living organism and a drug, characterised by behavioural and other responses that always include a compulsion to take the drug on a continuous or periodic basis in order to experience its psychic effects, and sometimes to avoid the discomfort of its absence. Tolerance may or may not be present. A person may be dependent on more than one drug."

The WHO then attempted to categorise patterns of drug dependence, suggesting nine classes of dependence-producing substances: the alcohol-barbiturate group; amphetamine-like substances; cannabis (marijuana, hashish); cocaine; hallucinogens (LSD and related drugs); *khat* (a stimulant used in Yemen and Ethiopia); opiates (including drugs made directly or indirectly from opium or synthetic substances which have similar effects); volatile solvents; and tobacco. Although such categories are valuable, drug users seldom fit neatly into them. 'Polydrug abuse', the use of several drugs, is common.

Alcoholism
Amphetamines
Marijuana
Cocaine
Hallucinogens
Opiates.

Where the habit leads Most drug experts would probably agree that it is psychological dependence which looms largest in the public mind when the word 'addiction' is mentioned.

At one time it was believed that only drugs which cause 'physical dependence' (produce biological changes so that withdrawal symptoms appear when use is discontinued) produce a severe dependence syndrome. Drugs which did not produce biological changes merely caused 'habituation' or 'psychological dependence'. This distinction, although beguilingly simple, is misleading. Giving up tobacco or amphetamines does not produce withdrawal symptoms as visible or as predictable as giving up heroin, yet both are associated with

71

Halfway to heaven or to hell

Anxiety

behaviour patterns that are exceedingly difficult to modify. Millions of smokers can attest to the difficulties of giving up cigarettes, and even heroin addicts frequently comment that giving up cigarettes is more difficult than giving up heroin. Heavy amphetamine users often find the compulsion to continue use overwhelming, despite the havoc it creates in their lives. In fact, withdrawal syndromes do follow the discontinuation of tobacco or amphetamine, but the relationship between a withdrawal syndrome and drug dependence is extremely complex.

There are a number of drugs which, if given repeatedly over a long period, produce physical dependence and therefore a withdrawal syndrome when discontinued. But the syndrome is not necessarily accompanied by severe discomfort, anxiety or a marked desire to get more of the drug. So physical dependence need not necessarily equal 'addiction' or 'psychological dependence'.

We now recognise that there are distinct stages in the natural history of drug use and dependence and that different factors can have their impact at different stages. Researchers now ask which factors (psychological, sociological, biological, pharmacological) determine whether there will be *initial use* (experimentation), whether an initial user will repeat the experience and become a *casual* or *recreational* user, whether such a user will go on to *intensive use*, or to dependence.

Drugs and mental disorder

Nearly 50 per cent of visits to family doctors are for treatment of primary and secondary emotional disorders. In fact more psychoactive drugs are prescribed by general practitioners than by psychiatrists. Since the 1960s there has been an enormous proliferation in the number of antipsychotic and antidepressant drugs available. There is however a growing realisation that drugs are not sufficient treatment in themselves and that counselling and therapy are often more important. Properly speaking, psychotherapy excludes the use of drugs, although they may be prescribed in conjunction with specific therapies. Psychiatrists' attitudes are changing from an exclusive focus on drugs towards combined pharmacological/psychotherapeutic treatments. Outlined below are the major classes of drug used to alleviate anxiety, depression and schizophrenia.

Anti-anxiety During the 1920s the drugs most commonly used to relieve anxiety were the bromides and barbiturates. By the 1930s it became apparent, however, that bromides were cumulative and created more problems than they solved (i.e. toxic delirium). For a time the field was left to the barbiturates but by the 1950s it had become apparent that they produced physical dependence and withdrawal reactions similar to those produced by alcohol. The late 1950s marked the advent of a whole family of new drugs, the tranquillisers, first meprobamate and chlordiazepoxide (Librium), and then other benzodiazepines (like Valium). These are now among the most heavily prescribed drugs both in psychiatry and general practice.

The physiological manifestations of anxiety (rapid pulse, increased sweating, increased muscle tension, etc.) affect virtually all the organ systems in the body. The main brain centres involved are the reticular activating system (the part of the brain which controls sensory input and arousal), the limbic system (the part concerned with the experience of emotion), and the hypothalamus (which controls the peripheral autonomic nervous system and the pituitary endocrine system) and it is on these that the benzodiazepines are thought to act. Their effect is that of a muscle-relaxant, anticonvulsant and sedative combined. There are no major side effects and drug dependence only develops with high doses.

In the past decade various injectable tranquillisers (fluphenazine, flupenthixol decanoate and fluspirilene) have been introduced. Their major advantage is that patients do not need to be persuaded to 'keep taking the tablets'.

Depression

Anti-depressant drugs The first drugs used to treat depression were the amphetamines, introduced in the 1930s. The two main groups of anti-depressants now in current use, the tricyclics and monoamine oxidase inhibitors, were developed in the 1950s. These are used primarily in the treatment of endogenous depression, in the well-founded belief that depression is related to a deficiency of two neurotransmitter substances, noradrenaline and serotonin. Concentrations of these are increased by tricyclics and MAO inhibitors.

Before antipsychotic drugs were invented, manic depression was usually treated by electroconvulsive therapy (it still is in many cases). Occasionally various types of sedative, such as the barbiturates and bromides, were prescribed, but it was the antipsychotic drugs (see below) which provided more permanent control of the marked hyperactivity and elevation of mood characteristic of mania.

By the 1960s a new drug, lithium, came on the scene. Lithium is undoubtedly effective in cases of manic depression - it is an element, as sodium and potassium are elements, and has many biochemical actions, although the most significant ones have not been identified yet - but like the tricyclics and MAO inhibitors it produces side effects with prolonged use.

Today is cancelled

Antipsychotic drugs Alcohol and opium are two of the most widely used natural antipsychotic substances; these affect the brain centres implicated in the dopamine system. The main synthetic drugs in the antipsychotic category are the phenothiazines, the thioxanthenes and the butyrophenones. Phenothiazine was synthesised in 1883 and was originally used as a treatment for worms and urinary infections. Its derivatives, notably chlorpromazine (Largactil), were found to have tranquillising effects without sedation; they are there-

D

Sedation

fore used to alleviate delusions, hallucinations and disturbed behaviour, especially among schizophrenics. However it now seems that they are not the wonder drugs they were once thought to be; it is now questionable whether they can cure schizophrenia or even substantially alter its natural history. Their value seems to be that in suppressing target symptoms they facilitate other forms of therapy. Unfortunately, they also have unwanted side effects with prolonged use.

The search is now on for drugs which do not have debilitating side effects. One that shows particular promise is propranolol, a beta-blocker (blocks the beta brain wave frequencies which accompany states of high arousal); in high doses propranolol has been found to relieve psychotic symptoms.

Dynamic psychology What all psychologists would like their psychology to be! Less flippantly, that school of psychology which investigates motivation, the drives, needs and impulses which make us 'tick'.

Dyslexia Difficulties in learning to read and write are very common in children, and can be caused by a wide range of factors including low intelligence, lack of stimulation and encouragement, poor teaching, high anxiety levels and undiagnosed physical handicaps. But some children make poor progress in reading and writing for a completely different reason – dyslexia, or 'word blindness'. This is characterised by a lack of ability to recognise or remember written words, and confusions between individual letters and words. Word and letter reversals and transpositions are especially common among dyslexics. *Dysgraphia* is the name given to similar and often related difficulties with writing.

Dyslexia has traditionally been associated with minor forms of brain damage, but the precise causes and nature of the disorder remain uncertain. The disability is certainly commoner in countries where there are a lot of inconsistencies between the written and the spoken word, as in English.

Autism

Echolalia Repeating sounds which seem to 'echo' the patterns of normal speech. Echolalic babbling is the name given to an early stage in the language development of infants, where it appears that children imitate the sounds of adult speech and practise variations in tone and rhythm. Autistic children, however, seem to revert to echolalia as a condition rather than a stage, with no appearance of progression.

Educational psychology The application of psychological theory and practice to educational methods is a complex and contentious field. One of the major areas of disagreement concerns methods of instruction for children, and whether, for example, direct instruction is preferable to 'discovery' (in the latter method children are encouraged to discover underlying processes through experiment and activity).

Direct instruction has been criticised because it tends to encourage passivity in children, robbing them of the opportunity to attach meaning through their own efforts. The discovery method, on the other hand, has been held responsible for a decline in the attainment of basic skills.

Personality

Experiments have shown that there is a significant interaction between the personality of children and the educational methods used. Extraverts learn better with discovery methods than introverts, while introverts learn better with direct teaching methods. Learning experiments suggest that discovery learning work would be improved if children were grouped in pairs of similar ability level but dissimilar anxiety level.

Perhaps, then, it can be said that no educational method is intrinsically good or bad, merely that its usefulness depends on the personality of the children to whom it is applied. Gone are the days when learners had to adapt to the constraints of the system; we now encourage educationists to adapt learning situations to the needs of the learners.

Ear   *John Boddy*

The sounds we hear arise from travelling pressure waves in the air generated by the vibration of objects in the environment. The sounds of speech, for example, are generated by the vibration of our vocal cords. The pitch of the sounds we hear depends on their frequency, their rate of vibration. Humans are able to hear sound waves with frequencies ranging from 15 cycles (waves) per second to 20,000 per second, but with a lot of variation between individuals. We are most sensitive to sounds between 1000 and 2000 cycles. Bats and porpoises can hear high-pitched sounds up to 100,000 cycles per second – the ability to do so is part of their navigation system. They locate obstacles by emitting very high frequency sounds whose echo informs them how far away objects are by the time it takes to bounce off them and return. Blind people are also able to learn to avoid objects by 'echolocation', but not as effectively as bats or porpoises because they cannot generate or hear such fast-travelling high-frequency sounds.

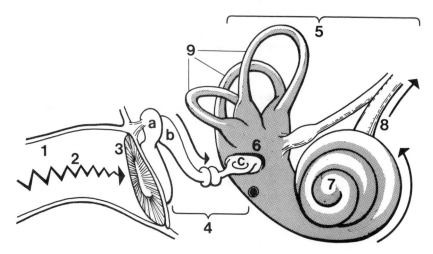

Inside the ear
1 Ear canal
2 Sound waves
3 Eardrum
4 Middle ear with ossicles a, b, c
5 Inner ear
6 Oval Window
7 Cochlea
8 Cochlear nerve to brain
9 Semicircular canals
responsible for balance

Brain

The ear is a very remarkable piece of engineering. Sound waves strike the eardrum (tympanic membrane) at the inner end of the external ear canal, and cause it to vibrate at their frequency. The eardrum is so sensitive that a movement only one-tenth of the diameter of a hydrogen atom is sufficient to produce an auditory sensation. Any greater sensitivity would result in our hearing the molecules in the air 'rattling' in Brownian movement. The bony levers of the middle ear (the ossicles) amplify the movement of the eardrum and apply it to the oval window, the membrane which seals the tightly coiled, fluid-filled tube of the cochlea, the real organ of hearing. The vibration of the oval window sends waves of fluid up the cochlea, bulging the long basilar membrane inside it at locations corresponding to the frequency of the sound. Where the basilar membrane bulges, receptors called hair cells are squashed and in protest generate electrical impulses. These are transmitted to nerve cells whose long axons feed into the auditory nerve, and from there it takes only a few thousandths of a second for them to reach the brain. We 'hear' only after impulses from the auditory nerve reach the brain.

There are about 28,000 nerve fibres in the auditory nerve and yet we can discriminate between 340,000 different sounds on the basis of pitch and loudness. Our brain also detects the minute time lapse between sounds reaching either ear, and uses this information to tell us the direction of the sound.

Central nervous system

Efferent Meaning 'away from'; efferent neurons carry nerve impulses from the central nervous system to 'effectors', usually muscles or glands; in this context 'motor' and 'efferent' are interchangeable.

Ego Latin for 'I', and used by psychoanalysts to describe the most accessible structure of the human mind. The Ego represents that aspect of the self which deals with conscious experiences. It also has access to what Freud called the 'preconscious', which contains material not immediately available, but accessible if the Ego so chooses (the pre-conscious contrasts with the unconscious, to which access is both difficult and highly restricted).

The Ego functions in several ways: it determines the way in which we deal with the world; it acts as a public 'front' for the instinctual demands made by the *Id* and the moral demands made by the *Superego*; sometimes, when the demands of the Id contradict those of the Superego, it becomes the arena for their conflict and resolution.

Eidetic Used to describe the peculiarly vivid images of persons with so-called photographic memory. *Eidetikers* experience these images as if 'seeing' them with extraordinary clarity and detail 'projected' on a wall or screen in front of them; they can examine and describe them in meticulous detail. While some psychologists claim that as many as 50 to 60 per cent of children under the age of 12 have some form of eidetic imagery, the number drops off in late adolescence to about 17 per cent of the adult population. It has been suggested that eidetic imagery is a primitive form of visual memory which gets replaced by a more conceptual or linguistic form of memory as children become older.

Electra complex The female equivalent of that cornerstone of Freudian psychoanalysis, the Oedipus complex. Freud suggests that around the age of four girls become powerfully attracted to their fathers and fearful of jealousy and punishment from their mothers. Unresolved this conflict can lead to problematic adult relationships with other men, none of whom can 'take the place' of the loved father. Girls who successfully surmount their attraction to their father come to identify positively with their mother. In Greek mythology Electra revenges her father's murder by her mother.

Electrical stimulation of the brain (ESB) In 1870 German scientists Fritsch and Hitzig discovered that stimulating certain areas of the brain with electric wires (electrodes) caused involuntary leg and arm movements. Today there are back-injured patients walking around with tiny radio transmitter-receivers (stimoceivers) implanted in their chests which stimulate the brain by remote control, enabling them to lead a pain-free existence. Though ESB has other analgesic uses, and has also been used as a cerebral pacemaker to prevent epileptic fits, it is primarily a research tool, and until quite recently a fairly crude, hit-and-miss one. ESB experimental subjects are usually chimpanzees, because their brains most closely resemble ours; electrodes are inserted in pre-planned locations in the brain through a small hole drilled in the skull; when the electrodes are activated the animals sneeze, yawn and flex their limbs to order. In one dramatic experiment, brain researcher José Delgado halted a charging bull by means of electrode implants in its brain! However, the idea of controlling unacceptable or antisocial behaviour by ESB is one which many psychologists and social scientists find repugnant.

Electrocardiogram (ECG or EKG) A pen-tracer record of heart-rate activity. Used by psychologists to measure autonomic or emotional arousal.

Electroconvulsive therapy (ECT) The application of brief electrical currents to the brain. The patient is first injected with a muscle relaxant, to reduce the severity of the seizure and to prevent physical injury during convulsion. Between 70 and 150 volts are applied through electrodes attached to both temples, or to the back and front of one side of the skull. Typically each electric shock lasts for less than 1 second, causing a convulsion for about a minute. The convulsions produced by ECT resemble epileptic fits.

Brain damage

ECT or EST (electroshock therapy) is the centre of considerable controversy. It appears to relieve symptoms of depression and mania in many patients, some of whom show immediate and marked improvement, but its long-term effects are less clear. No one really knows what electrical shocks do to the brain, and there is no conclusive evidence that they 'work'. Supporters of ECT take the line that possible brain damage (manifested as memory loss) is preferable to suicidal tendencies or psychotic symptoms.

Electroencephalogram (EEG) An ink-on-paper record of
Brain
electrical activity in the brain. Electrodes are attached to the scalp and the rhythmic electrical fluctuations in the brain are amplified (up to two million times) and translated into pen-
Brain waves
tracer 'waves' on graph paper. Brain activity varies according to one's state of consciousness and the area of the scalp which has the electrodes.

The most useful application of the EEG is in the diagnosis of epilepsy, and in detecting localised damage to the cortex, seen as slow wave activity over the affected area. However, EEG records are not easy to interpret; what they show are many superimposed patterns of activity and it takes a skilled analyst to pick out which frequencies predominate.

Electromyogram (EMG) A pen-tracer record of the tension in muscles. EMG recordings from the tongue and larynx while people were asked to solve mental problems led some psychologists to suggest that thought might be the product of sub-vocal speech.

Emotions Cross-cultural studies have identified various quite distinct and universally felt emotions (joy, anger, fear and so on) and we all intuitively understand what the word 'emotion' means, but there is no generally accepted theory of emotion among psychologists, though there are areas of agreement. Most psychologists agree for example that emotion has a *physiological component* and a *cognitive component*: symptoms such as a pounding heart, flushed face and sweating palms indicate physiological *arousal*; our mental reaction to this stirred-up state and the label we attach to it is the cognitive component. By no means all psychologists are convinced that the physiological component precedes the cognitive; a minority subscribe to the *Cannon-Bard theory* which suggests that both occur simultaneously, the argument in favour of this view being that we have to perceive something to get churned up about. *Feelings*, by the way, are what one experiences as the result of having emotions.

Physiological arousal

The fact that our physiology appears not to differentiate between seemingly opposite experiences – fear and joy appear to produce closely similar states of physiological arousal, although the thoughts and feelings they involve are vastly different – has led a few psychologists to suggest that emotions form a kind of continuum, with emotion quality corresponding to arousal quantity. Others, the majority, theorise that we have just one emotional state or emotional mode which we label according to context. This is known as the *cognitive labelling theory* of emotion.

Part of the difficulty psychologists face in studying emotion lies precisely in this labelling process, which is different for different people and therefore resistant to empirical analysis. Physiological arousal can be monitored, measured and compared by polygraph, GSR, EEG, ECG and so on, but individual interpretation, which incidentally affects arousal, is less co-operative. Until clear correlations are established between arousal and interpretation the more subtle emotions – irritation, curiosity, amusement – will remain unstudied. Most research to date has concentrated on intense emotional states like fear and anger.

Political anger or personal vendetta? Different labels for the same body symptoms

Most hypotheses about emotion are tested in fake social situations, where the subject unwittingly displays the required emotion in response to a person or persons acting in league with the experimenter, or by showing arousing films to subjects and asking them to give a running commentary or answer questions afterwards.

Empathy The ability to share and accept another person's feelings, while respecting their dignity and refraining from value judgements; a quality more valued by clients and therapists today than in the past. Freud's recommendation that a therapist should be "impenetrable to the patient and, like a mirror, reflect nothing but what is shown to him" has been much diluted, even by psychoanalytic therapists. The quality of 'humanness' is essential to most client-therapist relationships, particularly in client-centred therapy and various forms of group therapy.

Client-centred therapy

Encounter groups Groups of 8 to 20 people who meet informally once or twice a week, sometimes for extended periods, to improve their interpersonal skills and the quality of their daily lives. Each group has a leader (sometimes, though not necessarily, a trained therapist) and decides on its own goals and how to work towards them. The leader's job is to create an atmosphere of trust, acceptance and sympathy in which group members can express themselves freely and shed inhibitions; she/he also keeps the group on track and calls attention to the subtleties of personal interaction and the dynamic functioning of the group as a whole.

Group psychotherapy

The encounter movement is strongest in the United States. As American psychologist Carl Rogers has pointed out, it seems to strike a special chord in American consciousness, satisfying "a hunger for something the person does not find in his work environment, in his church, certainly not in his school or college, and sadly enough not even in modern family life. It is a hunger for relationships which are close and real, in which feelings and emotions can be spontaneously expressed ... where deep experiences can be shared ... where new ways of behaving can be risked and tried out." Some groups focus on personal growth, others on the enrichment of married life, family life or work relationships. There are even groups for criminals, drug addicts and delinquents. Some groups concentrate on improving sensory awareness, others on social sensitivity, or creativity, or problem-solving, or the spontaneous expression of emotion and affection, hence the proliferation of aliases such as T-groups, sensitivity training groups, marathon groups, body awareness groups.

Rogers

Psychotherapy

Endocrine glands The ductless glands of the body which secrete their hormones directly into the blood stream.

Endogenous Literally 'generated from within'. Used mainly of signs and symptoms which have no identifiable external cause, as in endogenous depression, depression which cannot be related to any particular situation or event.

Enuresis Involuntary urination (see Bedwetting).

E

Encounter groups: a reaction
away from the 'cool'
pushbutton ethos of today?

Environmental psychology In the widest sense the study of all psychological processes which are in some way influenced by the external environment, particularly by inorganic aspects of it (the houses we live in, the offices we work in, the streets we walk along, environmental nuisances like noise and traffic fumes). The environmental psychologist has an important contribution to make to architecture, town planning and interior design. Behaviour, thoughts and feelings are strongly environment-influenced. Are you really the same person in a warm candle-lit restaurant as you are on a crowded bus in the rush hour?

Epilepsy A condition in which the nerve cells of the brain spontaneously go into spasm. A severe fit causes loss of consciousness and violent muscular spasms (grand mal) while milder fits result in only momentary loss of consciousness (petit mal). Epileptics are not qualitatively different from non-epileptics: anyone can have an epileptic fit if wired up to an electrical shock generator; some people go into an epileptic fit under stroboscopic lighting. Brain surgery on severely epileptic patients, involving the severing of the corpus callosum in the brain, led to experimental interest in split-brain responses.

Epinephrine (see Adrenaline)

81

Erik Erikson, 1902–1979

Erikson, Erik Erik Homburger Erikson was Danish by birth but was brought up in Germany. His early love was art, until he began teaching art at a small school run by Anna Freud, Sigmund Freud's younger daughter. In 1933, after graduating from the Vienna Psychoanalytic Society, he went to the United States, and became Boston's first child psychotherapist. His later travels in the academic world took him to Harvard, Yale, Berkeley and back to Harvard. He retired in 1970, and died in 1979.

Erikson won great acclaim for his writing and for his clinical work, winning the American National Book Award and a Pulitzer Prize. The concepts for which he is most famous are: *epigenesis, life cycle* and *man's search for identity*. Epigenesis means growth or development, and according to Erikson human epigenesis is a sequence of eight developmental stages in which certain aspects of the personality come to the fore. The more crucial stages are those between birth and adolescence: (1) *mutuality of recognition stage*, the first stage between baby and mother, and the basis of all later feelings; (2) *trust stage* without which the individual would be emotionally handicapped in the later stages of the life cycle; Erikson saw the trust stage of infancy as very important for the emergence of a well-rounded personality; (3) having learnt to trust his/her environment the child proceeds to the *autonomy stage*, and then to the *initiative stage*, learning to cope independently with the external world; (4) during the *industrious stage*, the child learns what is expected of him or her, and acquires a sense of achievement in fulfilling those expectations; (5) with adolescence comes the *identity stage*, and the search for personal values.

Erikson's concept of *identity crisis* is now part of everyday language. At each new stage of the life cycle there are potential hazards and crises to be negotiated. But the most serious turning point is adolescence, when individual identity emerges. Erikson recognised, nevertheless, that identity crises can occur in adult life as well.

Adolescence

Erogenous Giving rise to sexual feelings. Erogenous zones are parts of the body where touch, pressure or other stimulation produce sexual excitement. Freud, in his concept of *libido*, pointed out that the drive for erotic pleasure can make any part of the body an erogenous zone. The most common areas are the oral, anal and genital ones, but practically every part of the human anatomy has been reported as sexually responsive to stimulation - even teeth! It has been said that the most important erogenous zone in humans is the mind - fantasy and imagination can produce intense states of sexual arousal, up to and including orgasm.

Eroticism

Eros The creative life-loving instinct which expresses itself as *libido*, sexual energy. Freud contrasted Eros with Thanatos, the death instinct, expressed as *destrudo* or destructive aggression.

Eroticism Feelings associated with sexual excitement. The objects of erotic stimulation are potentially unlimited, but in most individuals they consist primarily of the *erogenous zones*. Disorders of eroticism can take the form of either excessive interest in the pursuit of sexual excitement (erotomania) or the misdirection of sexual interest (fetishism, sadism, etc.). Decreased capacity for sexual activity (impotence, frigidity) is usually regarded as a separate category of disorder and labelled *sexual dysfunction*.

The commoner and the rarer forms of adult eroticism have been sung in all the great literatures of the world, but one area of eroticism was unsuspected until Freud: *infantile eroticism*. In his attempt to account for disorders of adult sexuality, Freud found it necessary to postulate the existence of infantile eroticism. He proposed that newborn infants suck not just because they are hungry but because they seek erotic gratification – most infants suck their thumbs or a corner of the pillow between feeds. At about 18 months the focus of erotic concern shifts from the mouth to the anus. At around three or four the organ which provides most erotic gratification is the clitoris in girls and the penis in boys. A little later interest in the sexual apparatus of the opposite sex is aroused, at which juncture the child's sexual feelings change from autoerotic (self-directed) to alloerotic (other-person-directed).

Freud's views are based on anecdotal evidence only. Objective studies of infant sexuality are rare and it is not easy to determine what infants experience when they play with their genitals. The only study to probe the norms of infant sexuality has been that of Kinsey, the famous American sexologist. He provides evidence of adult-like orgasms in young children, reportedly elicited by a wide range of stimuli, including friction of clothes, fast bicycle rides and most emotionally arousing objects and situations. Anthropological studies also indicate that overt sexual behaviour is common in young children in societies with liberal sexual attitudes.

Ethics and psychological research The moral dilemma which faces research psychologists arises from two conflicting needs, the scientific need to acquire new knowledge and the human need to respect individual freedom and dignity. In extreme cases the ethical implications of a particular piece of research are unequivocal: the medically meaningless and sadistic experiments carried out by Nazi doctors on concentration camp inmates are universally condemned. Unfortunately most ethical questions are by no means as clear cut.

Studies conducted in the early 1960s in the United States into the psychological determinants of obedience required subjects were at first asked and subsequently ordered to

Sexual dysfunction

The lineaments of desire

Experimental psychology

administer painful electric shocks to a stranger sitting on the other side of a partition. Despite the obvious pain experienced by the stranger a high proportion of subjects were prepared, if pushed hard enough by a forceful experimenter, to administer higher and higher levels of shock. In actual fact the stranger was an actor who received no shocks at all. This research was justified as giving insight into, amongst other things, the behaviour of concentration camp guards who committed atrocities because they were 'following orders'. Many psychologists have argued that there is no justification for subjecting individuals to such extreme levels of distress.

When new forms of psychotherapy are being subjected to clinical tests it is usually necessary to compare the progress of a group of patients receiving the treatment with that of an identical group of patients not receiving the treatment or receiving a bogus treatment. Is it right to withhold a possibly effective treatment from a patient whose need for it may be great? With illnesses that are poorly understood new research is constantly necessary. This too can pose moral problems. Should schizophrenic patients be asked to forego their medication, and re-experience their psychotic symptoms, to test some new theory of schizophrenia?

Nowadays such ethical decisions are only partly left to the conscience of the individual researcher. In Europe and America each major professional psychological organisation has its ethics committee (e.g. the American Psychological Association Ethics Committee) which establishes comprehensive guidelines concerning the use of human and animal subjects in research.

Ethnocentrism The tendency to think all other groups or races inferior to one's own; one of the components of authoritarianism and of most ideologies.

Ethology The comparative study of animal behaviour, usually in the interests of animal husbandry, habitat preservation or species conservation.

Euphoria A lift of mood, a feeling of expansive warmth, well-being and optimism; a quite natural reaction to good food, good news and good fortune, but in manic depression and other psychoses quite unfounded. Euphoria can also be drug-induced (alcohol, barbiturates).

Evoked potentials EEG records of the activity which occurs in the brain in response to selected stimuli. A bright light flashed in the eyes, for example, or loud clicks heard through earphones will result in a series of waves rather different from the rhythmic ones which occur all the time. Evoked potentials can be analysed in various ways: one can look at their amplitude (strength), or their latency (speed with which they follow the stimulus), or their complexity. Brain damage can be identified by careful interpretation of evoked potential patterns. More recently evoked potentials have been claimed to be a measure of intelligence.

Exhibitionism In childhood a very natural and normal instinct for self-display; shame and diffidence only come with social awareness. What is considered indecent in one society is proper and acceptable in another. In the West far more men are arrested for indecent exposure ('flashing') than women; exposure of the genitals usually achieves all the gratification the flasher wants – the act is an end in itself and not an invitation to intercourse, and the more shocked the onlooker is, the greater the pleasure. Stripping is also exhibitionistic but it is seldom for self-gratification only; it is almost always intended to give pleasure to others.

Existential therapy An approach to psychotherapy, based on existential philosophy, which stresses the importance of being fully aware of one's feelings and experiences in the here and now, and taking full responsibility for one's choices and actions whether they involve pain or pleasure. The existential therapist tries to heighten his client's sense of being a free agent, of being 'in charge' of his existence. The relationship between therapist and client in existential therapy is one of authentic give-and-take; in contrast to the psychoanalyst or client-centred therapist, who generally reflects back his client's thoughts in modified form, the existential therapist actually expresses his own feelings and opinions.

Experimental psychology The oldest specialised form of psychology, and the dominating influence in psychology today. Most psychologists agree that experimental psychology was born in 1879, when Wilhelm Wundt opened the first psychological laboratory at the University of Leipzig in Germany. In these early days, experimentation was largely concerned with attempts to study the processes of thinking and feeling. John Watson's shift to the study of learned behaviour, and to related experiments, marked the beginnings of the modern experimental approach.

Experimental psychology is largely carried out in laboratories, and often based on work with animals such as rats, pigeons, dogs and cats. The aim of controlled experimentation in psychology – as in any science – is to investigate the effects of one factor while holding all the others constant. Rats are an especially popular choice for experimental work because their genetic make-up can be standardised over a short time-span, they are relatively cheap to rear, and they respond well to laboratory conditions. Humans share certain similarities of the nervous system with such animals, and these can be exploited and studied in detail. The ethics of

Just covering the proprieties

using animals for research are complex; most psychologists would say that the discomforts endured by experimental animals are justified in the service of humankind.

Today, experimental psychology includes a number of subdisciplines, such as perception, learning, memory, psychophysiology and psycholinguistics.

Experimenter bias Experimenters can unwittingly come up with a distorted picture of reality by seeing what they want to see. In one well known study a number of experimenters were asked to count the movements made by two groups of flatworms; one group, they were told, could be expected to be more active than the other. In fact all the worms were identical, but two to three times as many movements were reported in the 'active' group – a case of the researcher researched! Nor is chivalry dead; male experimenters tend to be more pleasant and friendly with female subjects.

Experimenter effect Psychologists have learned that subjects in experiments are easily influenced by the experimenter. There is a tendency for them to do what they think the experimenter wants, and however careful the experimenter may be subtle or indirect cues can be conveyed. There are a number of ways in which these unwanted and distorting effects can be avoided. The most common technique is to ensure that the experimenter remains unaware of parts of the experiment. This form of working in the dark is called *double blind*.

Extinction Abolishing a natural or a conditional response by not reinforcing it or by conditioning another.

Extrasensory perception Knowledge of thoughts, events and objects gained by other than ordinary sensory means; clairvoyance or precognition concern events and objects, and telepathy thoughts. ESP is a growing field of research, but the psychological community appears just as divided over the existence of parapsychological phenomena as the general public. Some psychologists see the rejection of such phenomena by their fellow psychologists as an admission of insecurity.

Extravert A person whose basic orientation is towards the external world. Extraversion (and introversion, its dimensional 'opposite') can be investigated by a whole range of personality tests. Extraverts are out-going, sociable, rather impulsive, and require constant stimulation from the environment. Their academic performance tends to be lower than that of introverts, especially at higher levels of education because concentration is not one of their strong points; they also appear to be more sensitive to extra-sensory phenomena like telepathy, presumably because they have lower anxiety levels.

It was Jung who first developed the concepts of extraversion

Personality

and introversion, although they have since been altered and developed by others, notably by Hans Eysenck. Jung believed that no one is entirely characterised by one or the other orientation, rather that everyone has qualities pertaining to both. He believed that personality disorders are the result of an incorrect balance between such opposing forces.

Extrinsic motivation Doing something not for the sheer enjoyment of it but for some external reason, like money, status, favours or the good opinion of others; fear of punishment also counts as extrinsic motivation.

Eye *John Boddy*

The eye is the brain's camera. The light reflected from objects passes through the cornea and lens of the eye to form an upside-down image on the eye's 'film', the dense, light-sensitive mosaic of 125 million rods and 6 million cones which make up the retina. The lens of the eye bulges or stretches to bring objects into sharp focus on the retina; when the ciliary muscles get tired and cannot stretch the lens far enough to focus distant objects we start wearing spectacles to compensate for short-sightedness. The eye's aperture device is the iris, which controls the size of the pupil, closing it in strong light, dilating it in dim light.

Inside the eye
1 Cornea
2 Lens
3 Pupil
4 Iris
5 Ciliary muscles
6 Retina containing cones and rods
7 Choroid layer containing lots of blood vessels
8 Optic nerve
9 One of six pairs of muscles which rotate eyeball in socket
10 Blind spot

Find your blind spot. Close your right eye, look at the white rabbit and move the page slowly away from your nose until the black rabbit disappears

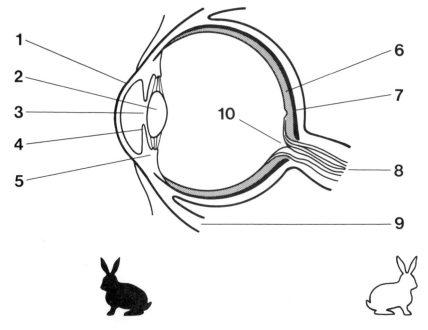

In daylight the 6 million cones in the retina give us a detailed technicolour picture of the world. As it gets dark both colour and detail are lost (the cones being insensitive to low light intensities) and vision is transferred to the more numerous rods away from the centre of the retina. When light strikes the rods or cones electrical signals are generated in them. The optic nerve, which has just one million nerve fibres, has to accommodate the signals coming from all 131 million rods and cones, so the messages it carries to the visual cortex of the brain are already in coded form. We cannot 'see' until those messages reach the brain – only the brain can give rise to conscious experience.

Colour blindness

The muscles of the eye socket, which move our eyes and enable us to follow a racing car as it roars down the straight, took on an added significance a few years ago when it was discovered that they give the eyeball a continuous tremor. Far from blurring our vision, as one might expect, this tremor provides the non-stop stimulation necessary for the rods and cones to keep sending signals. Without it our vision would quickly fade. Having two eyes (binocular vision) and therefore two slightly different sets of information going to the brain, we have a three-dimensional impression of the world, an appreciation of distance.

Perception

Eysenck personality inventory (EPI)   Developed by H. J. and Sybil B. G. Eysenck in 1963 and widely used in Britain and Europe; contains 57 questions which give a reasonably reliable and statistically independent measure of extraversion and neuroticism; incorporates a brief 'lie scale' which validates the reliability of the other responses given.

Nervous system

Facilitation The amount of neurotransmitter substance at a nerve junction (synapse) may be insufficient to enable a nerve impulse to cross it but it will 'facilitate' the crossing of a second impulse. The opposite phenomenon is called inhibition: the arrival of an impulse makes the synapse less, not more, likely to fire the neuron on the other side of it. Social psychologists also refer to a person's behaviour being facilitated by that of others: a reluctance to indulge in a calorie-packed dessert may dissolve when everyone else orders one!

Factor analysis An important statistical technique for reducing vast amounts of data to bare essentials; used extensively in the field of personality and intelligence assessment. If certain items in an IQ test, say, correlate very highly, they can be regarded as measuring the same 'factor' - verbal reasoning, for example, or numerical ability. One then finds that there are high correlations between such factors, indicating that they are all measuring an additional, higher-order factor. In an IQ context this higher-order factor would be general intelligence, sometimes referred to as the g-factor. With questionnaire-type tests, which have literally hundreds of items, the significant factors can be quickly picked out by computer.

Family *Rhona Rapoport, Robert Rapoport*

The earlier phases of the life cycle are, in a sense, a rehearsal for the 'main act' of our lives, which comes with 'the establishment phase'. Typically, in advanced societies nine out of ten adults get married, and during the establishment phase most couples have two or three children. But 'getting married and living happily ever after' includes many possible life styles.

Changing options Women can now plan their pattern of fertility in a way that was previously impossible, and childbirth is less risky now than at any time in history. Young people marry earlier and can plan to have fewer children in a shorter space of time, freeing women to return to the job market and perhaps to another 20 years of profitable employment or career development.

Men's attitudes to family life are changing. Increasingly they are taking more part in domestic duties, from giving the occasional helping hand to willingly taking their full share of running the house and looking after the children. Some men resent the meaninglessness of their factory or office life and their reaction has been to try to enrich their private lives. Many men place their own ceiling on career advancement if it means frequent absence from home, or overtime.

Changing preocupations We divide the establishment

period not into decades, or into age categories, but into sub-phases which are marked by different preoccupations.

Naturally, few family life cycles fit perfectly into this pattern, but the table below offers a rough guide to the major preoccupations and the likely problems of most parents while they have children at home.

Sub-phase	Preoccupation	Potential problems
Early establishment (pre-school children)	Concern with *productivity*: choices and plans	Conflicts in the allocation of one's energies
Mid-establishment (children at school)	Concern with *performance*: effectiveness; competence at what is chosen	Conflicts of loyalties and obligations; dissatisfaction
Late establishment (children out of school)	Concern with *evaluation*: the meaningfulness of commitments (psychological 'payoffs')	Depression, boredom; feelings of being trapped, isolation; whether to change (what? how?)

Queen Victoria was a working monarch from her accession in 1837 to her death in 1901. She had eight children and was a devoted, not to say meddling, grandmama.

Family therapy Psychotherapy involving parents and children together (and sometimes relatives), the assumption being there is an intimate link between neurotic parents and disturbed children. The therapist's task is to form a clear picture of the actions, reactions and interactions going on within the family, as mirrored in verbal and non-verbal exchanges during therapy sessions. This is why the whole family is seen together. Parents and children are encouraged to communicate freely during therapy in order to understand themselves and each other better. The therapist provokes discussion by putting forward the idea that the family is a dynamic institution; that it reflects the efforts of two people to survive, grow, and deepen their intimacy; that it is a setting into which children come sometimes as welcomed additions, sometimes as intruders; that children in their turn act, interact, and react, and provoke change.

The main task of the family therapist is to make it as clear as possible what the problems are, how they come about and how they can be solved. However, therapy *en famille* has many sceptics: for one thing, the children are usually outnumbered by the adults present, nor are they as verbally articulate; parents, for their part, are usually reluctant to talk about sexual matters in front of their children.

The monsters are coming

Fantasy At the conscious level fantasy can take the form of pleasant day dreams or highly charged imaginings; both represent wish-fulfilment. Fantasy plays a part in a healthy sex life, during love-making and masturbation, though reaching orgasm solely through fantasising is pretty rare! Psychoanalysts also talk of unconscious fantasy: you find yourself humming a tune which turns out to have lyrics related to something you are daydreaming about.

Fear The subjective experience which goes with physical arousal (pounding heart, legs gone to jelly, sweaty palms) when you are faced with something threatening. Like all the emotions fear seems to operate on three levels: cognitive (I feel afraid), physiological (I'm in a sweat, my heart is thumping) and behavioural (let's get the hell out of here!). However the three do not always perfectly correlate. Some people feel terribly afraid even in the absence of physiological arousal. Other people register massive physiological activity, but claim to be unafraid, perhaps because they have learnt to label danger as exciting or challenging.

Femininity   *Judith M. Bardwick*

'Femininity' and 'masculinity' are very difficult terms to define. Although most ordinary people intuitively believe they know what femininity and masculinity are, both concepts are abstract and as such can only be measured in derivative form.

Historically the great bulk of the relevant social science literature has concerned itself with the differences between the sexes. As professional interest in the psychology of women grew - one of the great achievements of Feminism - and as the role responsibilities of the sexes began converging, it became a scientific and political mandate to establish the existence of similarities between the sexes. We now tend to emphasise the similarity of the sexes by demonstrating how they share in the distribution of any characteristic, by focusing on individualism, and by stressing how sex roles are learned.

Androgyny

Magnifying the differences Early studies of psychological sex differences were strongly influenced by evolutionary theory. Because Darwin and his successors gave great prominence to biological and especially reproductive differences, and emphasised the genetic innateness of characteristics, early students of psychology were predisposed to dwell on gender differences and turn a blind eye to gender similarities. The stereotyped feminine woman was described as passive, fragile, dependent, non-competitive, non-aggressive, intuitive, receptive, afraid to take risks, emotionally labile, supportive, maternal, empathic, having low pain tolerance, unambitious, sensitive to inner feelings and to responses from other people. The comparable stereotype of masculine men described the exact opposite.

Stereotyping

The scientific approach demands that one tries to measure what one sees. Accordingly investigators have measured verbal sex role identity (one's perception of oneself as masculine or feminine and one's judgement of how others evaluate one), sex role preferences (the activities or character style one prefers) and sex role adoption (the activities or character style one actually adopts). What society and psychologists have considered to be healthy femininity, and by implication masculinity, is fairly evident from such major tests as the masculinity-femininity scale of the Minnesota Multiphasic Personality Inventory, which measures the extent of culturally feminine occupations and denial of interests in culturally masculine occupations.

Until recently, then, psychologists measured femininity and masculinity by how much one is like (or says one is like) the stereotype of one's sex and by how much one is different from the stereotype of the opposite sex. But within the stereotypical expectations of what is feminine, we do not know how generalised the significant personality characteristics are. The adjective most often used to describe the caring, supportive, providing, maternal aspects of female behaviour is 'nurturant'. Now, are women who are very nurturant, nurturant all, most, or some of the time? Are they equally nurturant with everyone, or are they more nurturant with the young, aged and ill? Are they appropriately or inappropriately nurturant? Are women high on nurturance necessarily low on assertiveness? Do women who have many feminine interests have few that are masculine?

Will this little girl reach a satisfying compromise between her gender and her aptitudes?

Towards a blend of interests As Feminism generated the awareness that psychologically healthy people are unlikely to be one-dimensionally feminine or masculine, new tests were created. These are based, first, on the assumption that femininity and masculinity are *not* opposite ends of the same dimension but two independent dimensions. Anyone can score high or low on either. The second new assumption is that people are complex rather than simple, complex in the sense that anyone can be simultaneously masculine and feminine, and that participation in non-traditional roles speeds up the development of a complex personality. The third assumption is that people who score high on both the feminine and masculine scales have the highest levels of self-esteem.

Cultural and biological consistencies The truth is that we do not really know how physical gender - the physiological fact of being male or female - enhances or limits what each sex can do. The nature of the human species is to learn. Any genetic or physiological tendency that we have will be, from birth, intertwined with learning. If women are forbidden to act aggressively or are kept away from situations in which aggressive responses are appropriate, then, in a self-fulfilling prophecy, everyone will conclude that women do not have the capacity to act aggressively and scientific studies will confirm what everyone knows!

Neither sex has a monopoly on getting their hands dirty.

Although it is hard to perceive basic consistencies underneath the specific differences in style and emphasis of different cultures, some sex differences seem to be universally or almost universally recognised. Eleanor Maccoby and Carol Nagy-Jacklin report that in every culture that has been studied, and these cultures differed very widely, the most consistent sex difference is the greater aggressiveness or assertiveness of males. Even so, Ronald Rohner found that there are greater differences in aggression levels *between cultures* than between young boys and girls of the same culture (unfortunately the data for adults is less conclusive).

Hormones

The idea that sex hormones increase tendencies towards particular behaviour has some experimental support. The sex hormones, it appears, are influential long before puberty. Some studies even suggest that male and female characteristics result partially from the effects of sex hormones on the central nervous system before birth. Girls exposed to abnormally high levels of androgen prior to birth are characterised by more dominating behaviour than is generally characteristic of girls. But an equally plausible hypothesis, supported by studies done with animals, is that acting in a particular way increases levels of the relevant hormone.

What such data imply are tendencies, perhaps relative differences, in the frequencies of particular emotions that lead to dominating or nurturing behaviour. These tendencies appear to be associated with one sex far more than the other and the great majority of cultures expect, want and socialise for them. As a result any sex differences that exist in early childhood are greatly enlarged. While identical experience may lessen differences linked to gender physiology, it is unlikely that such differences will disappear.

Feminism and psychology *Sarah E. Hampson*

The Feminist Movement is more than a campaign for equality within contemporary society. It is a philosophical, political and moral system of thought and, as such, has had a significant impact on psychology.

Feminism has influenced psychology in two ways. First, it

has had an effect on the sort of research psychologists choose to do. Whatever differences there are between the female and male personality and intellect, they have been more thoroughly studied and disputed in the last 20 years than at any time in history and have proved to be far less pronounced and more difficult to demonstrate than is commonly believed. Some psychologists have focused their attention specifically on the study of women and girls. They have investigated women's 'under-achievement' in school and at work and proposed that women's attempts at realising their full potential are sabotaged by a 'fear of success' motive. Female criminality has also received considerable attention recently – previously it was dismissed as a rarity unworthy of investigation.

Achievement

The fact that most people still believe in wide-ranging intellectual and emotional differences between the sexes, despite evidence to the contrary, has also intrigued psychologists. The nature of these widespread beliefs has been very thoroughly studied. Research on sex roles has demonstrated the prevalence of the stereotypic belief that women are passive, dependent, talkative, emotional and vain, whereas men are aggressive, self-confident, ambitious and objective. Psychologists themselves are not immune to these stereotypes: clinical practitioners have been shown to hold a stereotype of the healthy mature adult which more closely matches the male stereotype than the female.

Femininity

Stereotyping

The second way in which Feminism has influenced psychology is one step removed from research. It is at the theoretical level that Feminism, as a system of thought, is beginning and has the potential to make its most profound impact. Take the one adult sex difference about which we can be reasonably confident, that women are superior to men in verbal ability whereas men are superior to women in visual-spatial skills (ask a woman for the meaning of a word and ask a man to map read). In the absence of a feminist input, psychologists developed a theory which explained this difference in biological terms. They suggested that it reflects an underlying biological distinction between the sexes that must have come about as the result of evolution, and that therefore the behaviours associated with it must be adaptive – perhaps verbal skills were adaptive for successful child rearing and spatial skills for successful hunting.

Graced with a biological explanation a sex difference acquires an air of respectability: if nature made us that way, who are we to argue? But the feminist perspective shows us that this type of theorising contains a fatal flaw. Hitherto, observed sex differences were taken as starting points of explanations, not as phenomena to be explained. The feminist perspective makes us ask *why* there are sex differences. It then becomes apparent that the form the dichotomy between the sexes takes is the product of the society in which we live. An adult sex difference is the result of the continuous interplay

94

between heredity and environment and it is impossible to separate the two influences.

In highlighting the inadequacies of the old nature–nurture debate, Feminism opens up the possibility of breaking down the barriers surrounding disciplines such as psychology and sociology and integrating the pure and applied aspects within these fields. By advancing the intellectual quality of enquiry, the Feminist Movement has begun to raise the consciousness of psychology and psychologists.

Fetishism Sexual attraction to a particular part of the body, to a type of clothing, or to something bizarre and normally unconnected with erotic stimulation. Mild forms of fetishism are quite normal (one speaks of buttock-men, breast-men or leg-men). Nor is there anything particularly abnormal about mild clothes fetishism (liking one's partner to dress in leather, PVC, rubber or any other of the sexy 'super-skin' materials which form the common fetishes).

Fixation

Problems begin when private fetishistic games turn into an obsessional and single-minded interest in the fetish object without the partner! If a man occasionally makes love to his wife while she is wearing a rubber mackintosh ... well, variety is the spice of life. But if he starts making love to any old mackintosh in a cinema queue, he needs treatment. Fetishism is probably the result of conditioning, but not in any simple way; fetishes seem to be selective (not accidental) pairings of object/sexual arousal. Fantasy and a heightened capacity for fixation of sexual interest are also likely components.

Field Mainly used in the terms *field dependent* and *field independent*, which are measures of cognitive style; in this context the 'field' is a line pattern from which one has to pick out a certain shape (Hidden Figures Test, Embedded Figures Test). *Field theory* is a concept in personality theory developed by Kurt Lewin: the individual is considered to exist in a force field (the analogy here is with electromagnetic theory), in which the dynamically interacting forces are both psychological and physical. A change anywhere in the field will affect its equilibrium and require compensating change elsewhere. *Field studies* are studies conducted in the real, everyday world, not in the laboratory.

Fixation In psychoanalysis, the attachment of sensual pleasure to objects associated with a certain stage of psychosexual development. A person 'fixated' at the oral stage may smoke or eat compulsively, or be woundingly sarcastic; an anal fixation may lead to stinginess, stubbornness or compulsive neatness. Fixations are allegedly the result of excessive frustration or excessive gratification of sexual feelings in infancy and childhood.

Flight   Used in such psychoanalytic terms as *flight into illness* and *flight into fantasy*, denoting the conscious or unconscious wish to escape from unpleasant external reality. *Fugue* is an extreme form of flight from self.

Flooding   An intensely unpleasant experience; the overwhelming flood of sensations, images and thoughts reported by some schizophrenics, or the unbearable surge of emotion experienced when a habitual anxiety-reducing response is prevented. In the latter case, repeated exposure to an anxiety-provoking stimulus gradually reduces both the urge to avoid it and the discomfort experienced at being prevented from avoiding it. Response-prevention treatment works well with phobics and obsessive-compulsive neurotics.

Obsessive-compulsive neuroses

Phobias

Folie à deux   Literally 'madness in twos' or 'folly for two'; bizarre or psychopathic behaviour arising out of a delusion or a delusional world shared by two people (commonly twins, brother/sister, husband/wife). The 'Moors Murderers', Brady and Hindley, were diagnosed as suffering from *folie à deux*.

Forepleasure   The pleasure of anticipation, particularly the sexual tension which mounts in anticipation of the *full pleasure* of coitus and orgasm. Male impotence is often exacerbated by a neurotic desire to achieve orgasm at all costs and as quickly as possible, at the expense of a longer and helpful period of forepleasure.

Forgetting   Never to forget anything would reduce us to a state of total confusion. In a sense, forgetting is essential to survival. Several factors are involved in forgetting, but the list is less straightforward than one might imagine. There is no scientific evidence, contrary to popular belief, that time itself causes forgetting. Learned skills like cycling, or swimming return very rapidly even after long periods of neglect. All of us can recall events from our childhood. People in solitary confinement make their deprivation more bearable by reliving their memories, dredging up past experiences...

Memory

But time is *indirectly* implicated in forgetting. During quite short periods of time, events can occur which interfere with the laying down of information in the memory stores. Copy out the twelve 'nonsense' syllables shown in List 1 and get a friend to do the same. Both of you should spend five minutes learning the syllables. Now ask your friend to relax for five minutes while you try to memorise List 2. Finally, on separate sheets of paper, both try to write out the syllables from List 1.

You will almost certainly find that your friend does much better than you do. By learning List 2, you have interfered with the establishment of List 1 in your memory. Your friend did not have this problem. List 2 acts backwards, as it were, and hampers your recall of List 1. This process is known as 'retroactive inhibition'.

But interference, or inhibition, can work forwards as well, 'proactive inhibition'. Learn List 3, then, as in the first experiment, get a friend to join you in learning List 4. Now, as before, both of you attempt to recreate List 4 on separate pieces of paper. Again you lose. Learning List 3 has interfered with learning the last list - proactive inhibition is at work.

List 1
| FOF, | DUT, | LEB, | PID, | HAF, | ROP, |
| SUW, | BOC, | RIS, | BAF, | GIR, | HAB, |

List 2
| CIR, | DAC, | GIZ, | WAB, | POG, | RUZ, |
| HES, | JUQ, | KIW, | QON, | MIB, | LUW |

List 3
| POR, | GAR, | NOL, | GAC, | LUN, | BEC, |
| KEB, | BIV, | TUL, | FID, | KAC, | PES. |

List 4
| LUB, | MOJ, | RIJ, | KIB, | HUJ, | JUP, |
| PAG, | QUD, | WUF, | GAJ, | CEV, | DOB. |

Formal operations stage The intellectual passport to adulthood! In Piaget's system of cognitive development, the stage at which we begin to reason hypothetically, work out the consequences of imaginary courses of action, distinguish the form of an argument from its content, deduce principles from abstract data (if As and Bs make up a common class C, and all Cs are D, then As and Bs are also Ds).

Psychoanalysis

Free association In psychoanalysis, the standard method of cajoling unconscious material into consciousness. However the ability to free associate revealingly requires practice as well as trust. The client is encouraged to relax normal censorship over his/her utterances. What the analyst wants is an uncensored documentary of what is going on inside the client's head, however nonsensical, embarrassing or bizarre.

Memory

Free recall Recalling lists of words or objects in any order whatever; a classic technique in memory experiments. Free recall usually reveals that words at the beginning and end of lists are remembered better than words in the middle.

Frequency curve If one plots the frequency of an observation or a score along the vertical axis of a graph, and the variable being measured along the horizontal axis, one usually finds that the plots lie along a curve, a frequency curve. The more scores one plots the smoother the curve and the easier it is to see how the frequencies are distributed. Plotting the frequency of variables like height or intelligence gives a symmetrical or 'normal' distribution. Other variables might give skewed frequency curves.

Frequency effect A tenet of behaviour theory; the more frequently a particular response is connected with a particular stimulus, the stronger the connection becomes. J. B. Watson maintained that recency has much the same effect as frequency.

Sigmund Freud, 1856–1939

Neurosis

Hysteria
Psychoanalysis

Hypnosis

Freud, Sigmund Freud was the founder of psychoanalysis, revolutionised the treatment of mental illness, and raised controversies to which we are still trying to find answers. Although his theories are complex, several of his books, including *The Interpretation of Dreams* and *Three Essays on the Theory of Sexuality*, continue to reach a wide audience.

Sigmund Freud was born in 1856 in what is now Czechoslovakia. At the age of 17 he enrolled as a medical student at the University of Vienna. After qualifying he worked for a short while at the Vienna General Hospital, and then, in what was to be the most influential move in his life, went to Paris to study at the Salpetrière, a famous hospital for nervous diseases. It was here that he began to see that neuroses (the old name for nervous diseases) might be more psychological than physiological in origin.

On returning to Vienna in 1886 Freud set up a clinic for the treatment of in nervous diseases. Increasingly, however, he became involved with the treatment of what he called psychoneuroses, psychological disorders having no obvious physical cause. It was Josef Breuer, a friend and medical colleague, who introduced him to the idea that hysteria might be the result of a forgotten physical trauma. Breuer succeeded in getting his patients to recall their traumas, and the emotions which accompanied them, under hypnosis, and the method seemed to relieve their hysterical symptoms. Freud also tried hypnosis, with promising results, and so began the whole edifice of ideas we now know as *psychoanalysis* - the term was coined by Freud himself.

Slowly Freud gained patients as well as pupils and disciples. By the 1930s he was a figure of world standing in medical circles, and a member of that most august of institutions, the Royal Society. When Hitler invaded Austria in 1938, Freud was permitted to leave Vienna, unscathed. He settled in London, increasingly afflicted by the cancer which killed him a year later.

Freud was a determinist in mental as well as physical matters, believing that universal laws govern the function of the human organism. His primary aim was to discover the key which would reveal those laws. *Hypnosis* had made it clear to him that there are active parts of the mind which are not transparent to inspection either by analyst or patient. Freud called these parts of the mind the *unconscious*. Hypnotic suggestion seemed to be only a partial instrument; there seemed to be mental forces which actively interfered with this method of analysis. He called this phenomenon *resistance*. To overcome it he developed the technique of *free association*; he asked his patients to offer him whatever thoughts came into their heads.

Unconscious

At this stage in his work Freud conceived of the unconscious mind as consisting of desires and wishes, usually sexual or destructive, which derive their energy from primary physical instincts. The conscious mind, which he saw as concerned with adapting to external reality, was often in conflict with the unconscious. Freud suggested that it is this conflict which leads to anxiety; if the anxiety cannot be coped with the conflict is repressed, or relegated to the unconscious. *Repression* is one of the most important *defence mechanisms* we use to exclude unacceptable impulses from our consciousness.

Defence mechanism

In Freud's view it is the unresolved conflict between unconscious childhood desires and the checks and obstructions which parents and society place on them which lay the foundation of adult neuroses. The course of sexuality in infancy and childhood influences and colours all adult relationships. Freud's theories about infant sexuality, which postulate an *oral*, *anal* and *genital* stage of *psychosexual development* and of course the well known *Oedipus complex*, shocked Viennese society and many of his intellectual contemporaries. That young children should have erotic urges and sensations, and relate sexually to their parents, was unthinkable.

Dreaming

Dreams, for Freud, were a far more important source of information about the unconscious than either hypnosis or free association. He saw dreams as the product of conflict and compromise between primary unconscious impulses and secondary, often repressive, conscious ones. Dream analysis made it possible to guess at the hidden unconscious desires of neurotic patients.

Dreams also enabled Freud to classify the important differences between events in the conscious and unconscious. He found, for example, that the unconscious was not subject to any sort of organisation; each impulse seeks satisfaction independently. Later in his life Freud proposed finer distinctions between the conscious and unconscious. The uncoordinated and wholly unconscious instincts he called the *id*; the organised and realistic function, part conscious and part unconscious, he called the *ego*; and the conscious critical, moral and socially-determined function the *Superego*. This is the general structure still accepted by most psychoanalysts.

Freud's daughter Anna, born in 1895, became a psychoanalyst in her own right. Children were her particular interest and the Anna Freud Institute in London continues work in this field today. Anna Freud was especially concerned with the relationship between the child patient and the adult analyst. Children, she pointed out, do not seek their own treatment, as adults frequently do, but are 'brought along' against their will, often unaware of their 'problems', and sometimes not even suffering from them! Her book *Psychoanalytical Treatment of Children* (1946) remains a key text in child psychology.

Freudian slip A slip of the tongue or the pen which betrays unconscious feelings. Even the British Psychological Bulletin is not immune; in a recent issue it referred to 'The Fraud Memorial Professorship'.

Frigidity Supposedly lack of interest in sex or inability to feel arousal or pleasure; exclusively used of women, and usually by insensitive or misinformed sexual partners.

Orgasm

Until the pioneering work of Masters and Johnson and others it was standard psychiatric practice to label a woman who was not orgasmic (unable to experience orgasm) as 'frigid'. But as William Masters (of Masters and Johnson) put it, frigidity "means a woman who doesn't have orgasm and it means a woman who has orgasm once a week and her husband thinks she ought to have it twice". In psychiatry and psychology the term has largely been abandoned as pejorative and vague, and been replaced by 'orgasmic difficulties' or 'orgasmic dysfunction'.

Sexual dysfunction

Dysfunction may be primary (anorgasmia, lack of orgasm under all circumstances) or situational (orgasm is experienced only in certain situations, e.g. during masturbation). Occasional orgasmic difficulty is often due to emotional dissatisfaction with the sexual partner, or to the man not maintaining erection for long enough. Also many women still suffer from society's double standard, which sanctions male sexuality but denies or ignores women's. Drugs, alcohol and fatigue decrease sexual responsiveness in women, though not to the point of making coitus impossible. Other forms of female dysfunction, such as vaginismus (spasm in the outer third of the vagina) and dyspareunia (pain during intercourse), usually have psychological causes, though the latter may be the result of vaginal infection.

Sex therapy

Therapy for psychologically caused dysfunction usually tries to abolish performance-oriented sex, and emphasises non-demanding, mutual pleasuring and better verbal and non-verbal communication. 'Sensate focus' exercises encourage women to show their partners which kind of stimulation they find arousing. Most women who have primary orgasmic difficulty can become orgasmic through 'directed masturbation' therapy.

Erich Fromm, 1900–1979

Fromm, Erich Erich Fromm was German by birth but emigrated to the United States in 1933 with the rise of Nazism. In his later years - he died in 1979, aged 79 - he divided his time between private practice, a professorship at New York University and a fellowship of the William Alanson White Institute, also in New York.

A prolific and fluent writer, Fromm made his mark on psychology by stressing the importance of social influences on the individual personality. He was heavily influenced by the writings of Karl Marx, to the extent that less than generous fellow psychologists sometimes referred to him as 'Marxian personality theorist'.

Alienation is a basic theme in Fromm's writings. Man has cut himself off from other human beings and from the world of nature. Society and social institutions are the expression of various uniquely human needs, namely: *relatedness* (having divorced ourselves from nature we need to relate to others, the most fulfilling relationship being love for another human being); *transcendence* (the need to raise ourselves above our animal nature by being creative); *rootedness* (the need to have roots, to belong, satisfied in infancy and childhood by parental care and acceptance and in later life by friends and spouses); *identity* (the need for self-esteem and the esteem of others); and *frame of orientation* (the need to have a consistent and reliable way of seeing the world).

Frontal lobes The frontal regions of both cerebral hemispheres; considered to be the seat of personality because they have extensive links with the limbic system, suggesting that they are important in the integration of motivational and emotional experience. The frontal lobe of the dominant hemisphere also mediates certain aspects of speech.

Brain

Frustration In 'psycho-jargon' frustration is the omission of an expected positive reinforcer! More colloquially, frustration is not getting what you want when you want it. Recent work strongly suggests that frustration has much the same effect as punishment - most people look on it as a signal to begin new response patterns. Learning to tolerate low levels of frustration is part of learning to be a tolerable social being. According to the *frustration-aggression hypothesis*, frustration can produce a number of responses, one of which is aggression; most forms of aggression, so the theory goes, can be traced back to some form of frustration.

Aggression

Fugue state Nothing to do with J. S. Bach, but a rare neurotic dissociative state in which loss of memory (amnesia) is coupled with physical escape; the person may turn up in some distant town, assume a new identity, create a new lifestyle. It is not known how many 'missing persons' remain missing because no one penetrates their re-constituted identity.

Amnesia

Functional autonomy The urge to continue doing something long after the original motive has gone, like continuing to amass money when the motive for amassing it (security, power, leaving it to the children) ceases to matter. In other words, functional autonomy = habit.

Functional disorders Disorders caused by psychological stress rather than organic or physical damage; neuroses and psychoses are functional disorders.

Functional fixedness A mental 'set' or staleness which limits the way one thinks about objects and the relationships between them. Children are often better at looking at things in novel ways because their ideas are less fixed.

Anxiety

Lying

Transactional analysis

Social interaction

Pain

Galvanic skin response (GSR) When you are anxious or otherwise emotionally aroused, various physiological changes take place. One such change is a decrease in the electrical resistance of the skin as it becomes more moist. In the USA, the GSR has been used as one component of a lie-detector device called a polygraph. However, it takes a very skilled operator to interpret GSR data, because the conductivity of the skin fluctuates spontaneously whether or not one is in the grip of a powerful emotion.

Games A term used in transactional analysis to describe basically dishonest ways of behaving towards other people, which are superficially plausible, have an ulterior motive, and are commonly used by the individual in question. The word 'game' is not used to imply enjoyment, but to refer to the often ritualised patterns of behaviour which are described. The founder of transactional analysis, Eric Berne, outlined a number of such games in his book *Games People Play* (1964), giving them appropriate names. The most common game played between couples is called 'If it weren't for you', in which one partner typically blames the other for cramping his or her style, or in some way hampering or restricting his or her activities. The underlying truths of the relationship may be very different though. Game analysis is often used by marriage guidance therapists in the counselling of couples.

The word 'game' is also used by social psychologists; the analogy between games (which have goals and rules) and various types of social interaction has proved useful in analysing and teaching social skills.

Gate control theory of pain A theory developed in 1965 by psychologists Robert Melzack and Patrick Ward, elegant because it integrates physiological and psychological knowledge and accounts for the well-known fact that emotions and cognitive processes (attention, memory, expectations) influence our perception of pain. Pain messages fed into the spinal chord (central nervous system) can be blocked from or admitted into consciousness by a 'gate' mechanism; when pain occurs selective brain processes instruct the nerve cells in the spinal chord to increase or decrease their sensitivity to pain messages. Acupuncture is thought to work because stimulation of certain large fibres in the sensory nerves prevents the gate from opening by short-circuiting normal transmission pathways.

Generalisation An important aspect of conditioning. When an organism learns a response to a particular stimulus, it is found that stimuli similar to the original 'training' stimulus will also elicit the response to some extent. The strength of such responses can be related to the similarity of the stimuli, to produce what are known as *stimulus generalisation gradients*. In many phobias fear of a specific object is generalised to other related objects.

Phobias
Alcoholism

Genes The biological units of inheritance which determine one's species and one's characteristics as an individual. In addition to largely determining obvious characteristics like physiognomy, stature and eye colour, genes may also influence the development of such complex attributes as intelligence and personality. The ratio of gene influence to environment influence is a matter of fierce controversy. Undoubtedly our genes contain the seeds of everything we are, but the plants we grow into depend on the sun, rain and hail of personal experience.

Behavioural genetics

The notion that there are such things as units of inheritance was purely hypothetical until the brilliant work of biologists Watson and Crick in the 1950s. Now we know that genes are discrete parts of long chains of *DNA* (de-oxyribonucleic acid) molecules in cell nuclei; these DNA chains, or *chromosomes*, are arranged in pairs, twisted together in a spiral fashion. Every cell in the human body – except the red blood cells and the sex cells – contains 23 pairs of chromosomes. In the sex cells there are only 23 single chromosomes. When sex cells – sperm and ovum – fuse at fertilisation the single chromosome sets come together to give the new individual the full number of pairs. Now, the way in which the maternal and paternal sets of chromosomes pair up ensures two things: first, that the new individual is unique, within species limits; and second, that some genes are blocked and others activated. The latter are known as *dominant genes*; those which never get a chance to express themselves are called *recessive*. So, if your eyes are brown like your mother's, but your father's are blue, it is the gene for brown eyes which is dominant and the blue which is recessive. If you are intelligent, and both your parents are intelligent, your chromosomes probably contain up to 100 different mainly dominant genes, all interacting in your favour. Studying the action of large sets of genes is the province of the behavioural geneticist. Exactly how many genes we have is not really known, but certainly they run into thousands if not hundreds of thousands.

Genetic factors Theories of conditioning have led to the belief that most behaviour patterns are formed by the ever-shaping and controlling environment. But genetic inheritance is also known to play a significant role. So how important are genetic factors?

The inheritance v. environment or nature v. nurture debate is unlikely to be resolved in our lifetime. But there is a growing body of experimental work involving the study of identical and fraternal twins. Twins provide two routes of investigation: one can compare identical twins reared in different environments, where any similarities in behaviour must be due to genetic factors; and one can compare identical twins and fraternal twins, where the expectation is that the former will have more traits in common than the latter, if heredity is indeed paramount.

Identical twins reared apart typically show significant similarities in personality traits, as great as those shown by identical twins brought up together, thus demonstrating the relative unimportance of environmental factors. Identical twins are very much more similar in personality than fraternal ones, supporting the same conclusion. Although such evidence supports the claim that heredity (and thus genetic factors) plays a very important role in producing personality differences, it is less easy to define the role in precise terms.

The phenomenon of *regression to the mean* is also used as an argument in support of the pre-eminence of genetic factors, for environmental factors alone would surely produce increasingly greater deviations from the norm. The children of tall or outstandingly clever patients, for example, also tend to be tall or clever, but less so than their parents; at the other end of the scale there is also balance-restoring movement, this time upwards towards the mean.

Genital stage The last of Freud's psychosexual development stages in which the libido (sexual energy) becomes largely invested in what Freud described as 'mature genital relations'. Not all libido can be thus invested, however; spare sexual energy can be sublimated (re-channelled) into non-sexual areas.

Genotype All the genes contained in one's chromosomes, whether expressed or not; not to be confused with phenotype, the genes which actually get expressed. One's phenotype may be blond, but one's chromosomes may contain the genotype for both blond and auburn hair.

Gestalt A movement in psychology which began in Germany in the 1920s and has a growing number of adherents today, possibly because the essentially humanistic beliefs underlying Gestalt chime very exactly with today's emphasis on 'doing your own thing'. To quote the Gestalt 'prayer': "I do my thing and you do your thing. I am not in this world to live up to your expectations. You are not in this world to live up to mine. I am I and you are you. If by chance we find each other, that's beautiful. If not it can't be helped".

The German word *Gestalt* has no direct translation; its nearest English equivalent is 'configuration'; a configuration can be any perceptual 'whole'. The concept of wholeness is central to Gestalt psychology; you, the whole person, are far more than the sum of your parts.

The three founders of Gestalt psychology – Wolfgang Kohler, Max Wertheimer and Kurt Koffka – were among the first

Psychotherapy

psychologists to concentrate on the organisational aspects of visual perception, the way in which our brains naturally organise things into 'wholes', even though there may be elements missing. We tend for example to complete an incomplete drawing of a familiar object when asked to recall it. The phenomenon of insight in learning, involving as it does a sudden total response to a problem rather than piecemeal, random investigation of it, is an essential tenet of Gestalt.

In *Gestalt therapy* the individual is encouraged to rethink himself or herself as a whole in relation to the environment; this involves restructuring self-perception, confronting attitudes and behaviours one normally prefers to ignore. According to Fritz Perls, the originator of this form of therapy, we tend, at our peril, to block out awareness of aspects of ourselves and concentrate on only part of our identity. The Gestalt therapist's job is to restore us to wholeness. Whole, self-actualised individuals are aware of all aspects of their personality and experience and accept them.

Gestalt therapy frequently takes place in groups, although its emphasis is on the individual. As well as discussing ignored aspects of identity with clients, or perhaps pointing out aspects of their behaviour they may not be aware of, the therapist also encourages clients to act out dialogues (playing both themselves and the other person) which express the conflicts and tensions they are experiencing.

James Gibson, b. 1904

Perception

Gibson, James J. James Jerome Gibson, born in 1904 and currently professor of psychology at Cornell University, USA, made his mark on psychology by challenging the classical 'naive realism' view of human perception.

Perception, he argued, is not simply a matter of sensations which the brain organises into perception. Our sensations are too changing and variable to account for perceptual constancy. A white plate seen from the side in semi-darkness stimulates the retina in an entirely different manner from a green plate well lit and seen from above. Both plates cause a different sensation. But we still see them as plates. Gibson therefore proposed that our senses detect certain invariant properties in objects, actively selecting information from stimuli and actively imposing patterns on it. The label he attaches to this theory is *psychophysical correspondence*. In his best known book on the subject of perception, *The Perception of the Visual World* (1950), he explores the processes which take place in our sense organs in relation to the properties of external stimuli and the way in which our senses co-operate to obtain information. If one of our sense organs is inoperative, for example, our other senses compensate.

Graphology The analysis of handwriting to determine personality is viewed with great suspicion by many psychologists. However, Hans Eysenck has pointed out that there is some experimental evidence to support graphologists' claims that they can read character from handwriting. In one study involving 50 subjects handwriting analysis correlated with the results of personality inventories with a higher than chance success rate.

Group psychotherapy To begin by stating the obvious, any group psychotherapeutic process involves treating several people simultaneously and encouraging each person to participate equally. A basic assumption of group psychotherapy is that to a minor extent every person in the group is a lay therapist for the others, under the overall guidance of a trained therapist. Since the pioneering work of Jacob Moreno in the early 1940s, group psychotherapy has travelled the world, and found applications for all sorts of social and emotional problems. Something like 60 different methods of group psychotherapy are practiced today.

Encounter groups

T-groups

The aims of group treatment are essentially those of individual treatment, to alleviate psychological and social problems, but the group context elicits interactions and provides feedback of the kind not produced by individual therapy. Group psychotherapists require special training. They must learn how to confront groups and encourage interactions within them, how to absorb aggressive outbursts from several members at once, yet react positively and with equanimity. They must also learn how to handle tenderness and affection.

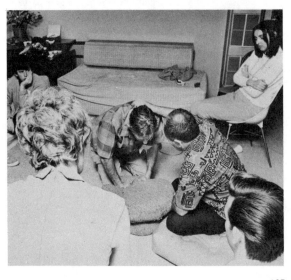

Personal crisis in a group setting

A gifted group therapist eventually acquires an almost intuitive grasp of the events and feelings taking place between people, but always guards against being over-analytical or getting too involved with particular individuals.

Groupthink The process which underlies the blunders made by highly cohesive groups throughout history, the overriding concern being group morale. Psychologist Irving Janis has identified eight major components of groupthink: excessive optimism and risk-taking in the belief that the group is invulnerable; collective rationalisation which conveniently quashes doubt or remorse; a belief in the unimpeachable morality of the group and its decisions; a low opinion of opponents and outsiders; strong internal pressure to conform; individual self-censorship of thoughts incompatible with the consensus; an illusion of unity and unanimity; the emergence of self-appointed 'mind guards' who monitor deviation from the consensus and suppress facts hostile to it.

Ideology

Guilt The concept of guilt is familiar to us all, but psychologists are interested in the role which exaggerated guilt feelings play in mental disturbance. Many depressive and neurotic people suffer consciously or unconsciously from a deep sense of guilt, related to real or imagined actions in their past. The guilt may be acknowledged and specifically described, or it may form part of a diffuse set of negative self-assessments which lead to self-hatred. In either case, guilt feelings can colour future actions, and inhibit feeling and choice. Many psychoanalysts see freeing their patients from obsessional guilt-feelings as a major part of their work.

H

Hallucination A perceptual experience which has all the vividness of real perception without the external stimuli which usually go with it. Unlike eidetic images, hallucinations seem to be 'inside the head' rather than 'out there'. They are private and idiosyncratic. Though often associated in the popular mind with severe psychiatric disorders like schizophrenia, or with hair-raising 'trips' on hallucinogenic drugs, hallucinations are fairly common occurrences; they are, for example, quite frequent in hypnagogic and hypnopompic states (just before sleep and waking) and can also be induced by hypnosis, sensory deprivation, malnutrition, sleep deprivation and emotional stress.

Altered state of consciousness

Hallucinogens Psychedelic ('mind expanding') drugs like LSD (lysergic acid), mescalin (the active ingredient of peyote, a cactus which grows in Mexico and Central America), psilocybin (the active ingredient of a mushroom, *Psilocybe mexicana*, also a native of Mexico and Central America) and phencyclidine or PCP (a synthetic drug originally used as an anaesthetic). Hallucinogens appear to act by blocking or decreasing serotinin, a brain chemical which plays a key role in the transmission of central nervous system impulses.

Drug dependence

Halo effect A real problem in psychological testing and diagnosis, no matter how standardised test instructions and test materials are; because the tester likes the person being tested, he or she gives biased ratings on certain items, resulting in a score which does not meet the criterion of reliability – another tester might obtain quite different results.

Test construction

Harlow, Harry Harry Harlow and his associates hit the headlines during the 1940s and 1950s with their novel investigations into the development of affection in infant monkeys. Using surrogate (substitute) mothers made of wire or padded terry cloth, they demonstrated that *maternal deprivation* seriously handicaps emotional and social development, certainly in monkeys, and most probably in human beings too.

It was Harlow's caution about drive-reduction theories (which state that behaviour fulfils the function of satisfying or reducing drives) which led him to devise experiments which demonstrated that young animals develop affection independently of the drive associated with hunger. Their response to their mother is determined by a web of factors, including the need for tactile comfort, warmth and movement (in the absence of real mothers Harlow's infant monkeys consistently preferred substitutes which were soft and warm, and which

Harry Harlow, b. 1905

109

rocked, to substitutes which stayed still and provided no contact comfort).

Harlow also devised a number of experiments to test the way in which monkeys learn. His monkey subjects proved they could solve complicated puzzles without being offered extrinsic rewards; in fact, rewards made learning less efficient. This seems to suggest that puzzle-solving is in itself a rewarding experience.

Harry Harlow was born in Iowa, USA, in 1905. Most of his research life has been spent at the Regional Primate Research Center at the University of Wisconsin.

Hebb, Donald Donald Olding Hebb is best known for his theories about the nature of thinking. His major work, *The Organisation of Behaviour: A Neurological Theory*, was published in 1949. In it he suggests a neurological basis for abstract thought, indeed for all behaviour involving memory and the formation of ideas.

Starting from the observation that thought processes are relatively independent of input from the sense organs, Hebb reasoned that the brain must to some extent operate independently of incoming sensory information. It operates, he suggested, by means of *cell assemblies*, networks of brain cells which are the physiological equivalents of associated ideas and memories.

A cell assembly becomes established when two or more neurons are repeatedly activated simultaneously. In time regular pathways for nerve impulses become established, so that activity in one neuron automatically triggers off activity in the others. The formation of new assemblies and larger assemblies represents learning. Also, activity within one assembly can induce activity in other assemblies. Sustained thinking about a particular subject involves a whole series of cell assemblies firing off in a co-ordinated fashion, or in *phase sequence* as Hebb put it.

Like so many of his contemporaries – he was born in 1904 – Hebb did not begin his working life as a psychologist. His first love was writing, and it was while struggling to become a novelist that he became interested in Freud. The two men who most influenced him were Pavlov and Karl Lashley – he worked with Lashley at Chicago and Harvard. Since 1948 Hebb has worked at McGill University, Montreal.

Hebephrenia (see Schizophrenia)

Hedonism The doctrine that pleasure is right and proper because it leads to the greatest happiness for the greatest number, was first advanced by the early nineteenth-century philosopher Jeremy Bentham, though of course the idea that the mainspring of human motivation is the gaining of pleasure and the avoidance of pain goes back to Ancient Greece and

Maternal instinct

Donald Hebb, b. 1904

Brain

Nervous system

Pleasure principle

no doubt earlier. The hedonistic viewpoint was the fulcrum of early psychological theories of learning: one learns because learning is rewarded (pleasurable) and because failure to learn is punished (painful). Freud and his followers drew on hedonistic theory, proposing that pleasure is the final aim of the human organism and that all behaviour is a means to that end. When discussing motivation psychologists usually distinguish between hedonistic elements, the so-called *hedonistic theory of motivation*, and instinctual (physiological) or cognitive (rational) elements.

Heroin One of the opiate drugs (derived from opium), introduced in 1898 as a cough suppressant and still used therapeutically. Used recreationally, heroin produces euphoria and a general indifference to threatening situations, although both sensations become increasingly fleeting with increasing use. Withdrawal produces anxiety, sleeplessness, fever, stomach cramps and diarrhoea. Drugs known as opioid-inhibitors, which block the effect of opiates and opioids, have been used to wean addicts from the heroin habit but their long-term efficacy is uncertain.

Drug dependence

Heterosexuality Sexual interest in members of the opposite sex; the 'socially acceptable' mode of sexual activity in almost every society in the world. Most social and legal conventions are based on the idea that heterosexuality is 'natural', 'healthy' and ordained for the purpose of procreation and the maintenance of family life.

Homeostasis The principle of 'negative feedback' at work in all living organisms, from amoeba to man; when any body process goes too fast or too slow, or creates a surplus or a deficiency, mechanisms are set in motion which restore the ideal balance. Though primarily a biological concept, the principle of continuous balance-seeking is fundamental to the thinking of many psychologists.

Homosexuality Alfred C. Kinsey, working in America in the late 1940s and early 1950s, concluded that perhaps 4 to 6 per cent of men and possibly 2 per cent of women are exclusively homosexual most of their lives. More recent research confirms Kinsey's estimate. Kinsey et al. view sexual orientation as a continuum, with 100 per cent heterosexual behaviour at one end and 100 per cent homosexual behaviour at the other, and all possible gradations in between. Indeed some 50 per cent of men and 28 per cent of women say that at some time in their lives they have responded physically and emotionally to someone of their own sex.

The differences between the behaviours of male and female homosexuals reflect those between male and female heterosexuals. Homosexual women have sexual relations less regularly and with fewer partners than male homosexuals, and like heterosexual women lesbians tend to look on sexual aggressiveness and promiscuity as offensive and unfeminine. Like heterosexual men, homosexual men tend to assert their masculinity through sex and dominance.

Homosexuality: constitutional or environmental? Or more pertinently, how well adjusted are the people concerned?

There are basically two views about the origin of homosexuality. One is that hormones active in the embryo bias the nervous system in its reaction to environmental influences (it has not been shown, however, that there is a relationship between sex hormone levels and homosexuality). The other view is that environmental factors predispose some people to difficulties in psychosexual and psychosocial development. A frequent pattern in the family background of male homosexuals is an over-protective mother and an emotionally distant or hostile father, with a reversal of these parental roles in the case of female homosexuals.

Just as many homosexuals seek psychotherapy as heterosexuals – for anxiety, work problems, depression and a range of problems unrelated to sexual orientation. Help with changing homosexual orientation is only given if asked for.

Sadly there are still mental health professionals who condemn homosexuality. In many countries homosexual acts, even between consenting adults, are illegal. Surely the decriminalisation of homosexuality is only a matter of time. In the United States the 'gay liberation' movement now appears to have the backing of the American Psychiatric Association.

Hormones The hormone system is to the nervous system what surface mail is to air mail, reliable but slower! Whereas a nerve impulse can travel from head to toe in perhaps one-fiftieth of a second (250 miles per hour), a hormone message can only travel at the speed of the blood (about 15 inches per second in the arteries, and much more slowly in the capillaries and veins). Hormones are complex carbon compounds secreted by the endocrine (ductless) glands of the body, and they get emptied directly into the bloodstream on instructions from the hypothalamus. There are dozens of hormones in the human body, some concerned with metabolic rate, growth and repair, others with homeostasis, others with sexual identity and the regulation of emotion.

Emotions

As the 'master-switch' of the endocrine system, the hypothalamus responds to messages from other parts of the central nervous system, and therefore occasionally to messages from higher mental processes (reasoning, memory and feelings), and instructs the pituitary gland to release hormones into the bloodstream; these then travel to 'target' glands in the body, which respond by manufacturing other hormones to carry out specific jobs. Hormone concentrations in the bloodstream are infinitesimal (measured in picograms, or millions of millionths of a gram). The hypothalamus and pituitary are sensitive to hormone levels in the bloodstream, and can therefore act to increase or decrease production in the glands which they control.

Hypothalamus

Pituitary

The gland geographically nearest the pituitary is the thyroid; this secretes three hormones, including thyroxine, which stimulates body metabolism generally, and growth. Embedded in the thyroid are the four parathyroid glands, producing parathormone for controlling the body's calcium levels. The pancreas, sited between the kidneys, controls sugar levels in the body. The two adrenal glands, one above each kidney, are functionally subdivided: in the medullary part a group of hormones known as catecholamines are produced; these include noradrenaline (norepinephrine, USA), the neurotransmitter substance of the sympathetic nervous system, and adrenaline (epinephrine, USA), the 'stress' hormone. The cortex of the adrenal glands produces small quantities of sex hormones in both sexes, and also corticoids, responsible among other things for regulating blood volume and reducing inflammation and allergic responses.

Sex hormone production is, however, largely the job of the gonads, ovaries in the female and testes in the male, with the pituitary playing much the same role as an air traffic controller. At puberty testosterone secretion begins in the male and oestrogen secretion in the female; whereas a man continues to produce testosterone for the rest of his life, a woman ceases oestrogen production with the menopause. However, our sexual activities and proclivities are not totally at the mercy of our hormones.

Oestrogens

Most endocrinologists estimate that well over 90 per cent of impotence problems are psychological rather than hormonal (due to lack of the male hormone testosterone). Attempts to detect hormonal differences between homosexual and heterosexual men, and whether transsexuals are hormonally abnor-

Testosterone

mal, have arrived at no very clear conclusion. Nor do low hormone levels necessarily correlate with low libido, though in some cases abnormally high levels correlate with unconventional sexual interests. One's gender depends on hormones, but one's sexuality is the product of a wide range of cultural and psychological factors.

Clark Hull, 1884–1952

Hull, Clark Few other psychologists have been so keenly devoted to the knotty problems of scientific methodology as Clark Hull. He specifically set out to make psychology as susceptible to mathematical interpretation as other sciences. Many of Hull's critics believe that he developed his deductive-mathematical approach too soon, that he was, perhaps, a victim of his own enthusiasm for mathematical analysis.

Hull is best remembered for his work at the Institute of Human Relations at Yale University during the 1930s and 1940s. He died in 1952 at the age of 68.

Hull's theory of behaviour stresses the relationship between an organism and its environment, with the environment providing the stimulus and the organism giving the response. The most significant variable in this interaction is what Hull called the *reaction potential* of the organism, the strength of which is determined by the probability of a response but also by four variables: drive, stimulus intensity, incentive and habit strength. To give a very simple example, if a rat has been conditioned to jump over a barrier when it receives an electric shock, the probability of its doing so on future occasions is very high, so its reaction potential to the shock stimulus is also high. It is not difficult to see that if the shock was weak, or the rat sleepy, or the jumping habit only half-formed, the reaction potential would be lower.

A lifetime of unsatisfied hunger

Hunger One of the primary drives in man as in all other species, primary because absolutely essential to individual and species survival. Dieticians are fond of telling us 'You are what you eat', but it makes more sense to put the cliché the other way round: you eat according to what you are. Hunger is overwhelmingly psychological and only partly a response to the demands of the 'inner man' or 'inner woman'. Our attitudes to food, our thoughts about food, the norms of slenderness and beauty propagated by films, magazines and advertising – these are all powerful influences.

Hyperactivity A subject of major concern to educational and child psychologists because of its effects on academic achievement; hyperactivity is a syndrome, a combination of symptoms including physical recklessness, impulsivity, lack of concentration or application, and difficulty with fine motor control (entailing problems with writing, drawing, etc.). Aggression is not in our definition; hyperactive children are not necessarily unduly aggressive. The condition has been attributed to MDB (minimal brain dysfunction), thyroid dysfunction, high sugar diet and lack of parental discipline. Treatment may involve behaviour therapy and, where appropriate, reduction of sugar in the diet. Drug treatments have also been used (e.g. methylphenidate and dextroamphetamine), especially in the United States, but their use remains controversial.

Hyperphagia Compulsive, uncontrolled eating, demonstrated experimentally to be due to impaired functioning of the hypothalamus.

Hypertension High blood pressure. Estimates of the prevalence of hypertension in Western societies varies from 10 to 30 per cent of the adult population. In more than 90 per cent of such cases the cause of the condition is not known, but stress and anxiety are strongly implicated. The condition involves added risk of heart failure, heart attack and kidney problems. Normally tranquillisers are prescribed, but more recent treatments include biofeedback and rational-emotive therapy.

Biofeedback

Hypnagogic state That state of consciousness half way between relaxed wakefulness and the first stage of sleep; the half-awareness that one is 'nodding off'.

Hypnosis and self-hypnosis *Martin T. Orne and Kevin M. McConkey*

The discovery of modern hypnosis is generally attributed to Franz Anton Mesmer (1734-1815), who considered that its effects were due to animal magnetism, a magnetic fluid which flowed from the magnetiser to the patient, bringing about a cure. A more accurate description of modern hypnosis was first given by Le Comte Maxime de Chastenet de Puységur (1751-1825), who recognised that the hypnotic effect was actually due to suggestions given to patients. The term hypnosis was introduced by James Braid (1795-1860), who emphasised that to produce what he considered to be artificial sleep, patients must be induced to focus their attention.

Hypnosis played a major part in the early treatment of hysteria by Sigmund Freud as well as an important role in the development of psychoanalysis. Modern hypnotherapy owes much to the work of Milton Erickson (1902-1980), who considered hypnosis to be a way of bringing out individuals' inherent capabilities. The first serious investigation of hypnosis was probably that carried out in 1784 by the French Royal Commission, a group of leading scientists of the day headed by Benjamin Franklin (1706-1790). Modern scientific research into hypnosis, however, began around the turn of this century, a major milestone being the application of systematic quantitative techniques of analysis by Clark Hull.

Hypnotic aptitude Despite a general belief that the hypnotist has some sort of power over the hypnotised individual, there is very little evidence for this view. In fact hypnosis and self-hypnosis involve a high level of self-control and self-direction by individuals, even when they are deeply hypnotised. Although hypnotised individuals generally show a high degree of relaxation and ignore distracting events, relaxation is not essential. Well-motivated people can experience hypnosis while standing up or taking physical exercise. What is essential, however, is that the individual focuses his attention and narrows his awareness of peripheral events. If he doesn't he will not successfully experience hypnosis.

During hypnosis people respond to suggestions in a way that allows events to be experienced as if they were actually occurring. For example, a responsive individual told to focus on his or her hand becoming light and floating upwards will experience it rising as if by itself; but not all individuals are capable of having such an experience. Although almost everyone participating in research or therapy sessions will raise their hand if specifically asked to do so, only some will do so during hypnosis, indicating that hypnosis is not simply a matter of obeying instructions. Rather, what makes hypnosis interesting is that the behavioural response of the hand rising slowly reflects the *subjective* experience of the hand floating upwards as if by itself.

An individual's responsiveness to hypnosis depends much more on his or her aptitude than on the skill of the hypnotist. Given the correct motivation, a tape recording can be just as effective as an experienced hypnotist. The ability to be hypnotised is not related to intelligence, education or gullibility, but to whether one engaged in imaginative play as a child and whether one is capable of becoming absorbed in a book or play. Hypnotic aptitude is greatest during the early teens, becomes relatively stable during adulthood, and declines during old age.

Hypnotic experiences A wide range of phenomena may be experienced during hypnosis. Ideomotor suggestions involve vividly imagining movement of a particular part of the body (e.g. a hand floating), with the result that the movement seems to occur as of itself. Challenge suggestions involve telling an individual that he or she cannot carry out a particular movement and then asking them to attempt it (e.g. an arm being too stiff to bend); this leads to the temporary illusion of being unable to perform the movement. Distortions of perception and memory are a particularly compelling facet of hypnosis. Such distortions include hallucination (seeing things not present), amnesia (failing to remember events), and age regression (apparently reliving earlier events). Highly responsive individuals will also carry out suggestions after hypnosis in response to a pre-arranged cue (post-hypnotic suggestions) provided the suggested behaviour is not unacceptable. All of these phenomena can be experienced during self-hypnosis as well, but most individuals focus on the relaxation and inner exploration afforded by self-hypnosis rather than on responding to specific suggestions; but in some instances suggestions designed to assist the individual in practical day-to-day living may be employed.

Despite active research into and widespread clinical use of hypnosis, there is no single accepted theory of hypnosis. Some theorists consider hypnosis to be an altered state of consciousness in which suggestions are passively and uncritically accepted, but others emphasise that hypnotic behaviour involves actively thinking along with and imagining suggestions so that events are vividly experienced. Be that as it may, there is general agreement that responsive individuals are capable of experiencing a wide range of suggested events as if they were real. The controversy lies in the mechanisms involved in bringing about such experiences. Support exists for both the major theoretical positions outlined and most investigators adopt concepts from both in order to interpret their observations.

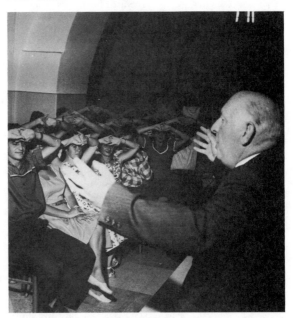

Hypnosis in a group psychotherapy context

Uses of hypnosis Many medical, psychological, and dental professionals throughout the world use hypnosis clinically, and also train their patients in self-hypnosis. Hypnosis is frequently used to induce relaxation prior to surgery and is particularly helpful during childbirth. It is also a useful method of controlling pain, both acute (e.g. dental) and chronic (e.g. terminal cancer). Suggestion is rarely appropriate to suppress pain that serves a psychological function, however, and should be used with great caution in such circumstances.

Hypnosis is also useful in treating chronic anxiety, insomnia, and some forms of headache. It has helped individuals master some of the disorders of self-control such as smoking and obesity. It is used in psychotherapy in the treatment of specific symptoms (e.g. phobias) and more generally to help patients understand their behaviour and their emotions. Specific techniques such as age regression may be used to assist patients to recall traumatic events and thereby promote resolution of their problems. However, hypnosis should never be seen as the sole treatment but rather as a part of an overall therapy plan. It is not an independent science or art and should be employed only by medical, dental or psychological practitioners who are capable of using a variety of therapeutic techniques and of choosing the technique most appropriate for the appropriate patient and disorder.

The use of hypnosis in sport generally involves attempts to improve an athlete's performance. Since psychological factors often play an inhibiting role, hypnosis is often helpful in relieving anxiety, building confidence and achieving optimal motivation. The common fear that hypnosis can be used to make people do antisocial, self-destructive things is not well founded. Instances where hypnosis is claimed to have caused antisocial behaviour can generally be better understood by looking at the non-hypnotic context in which the offending behaviour occurred.

Increasingly hypnosis is being used to question witnesses and victims of crimes in order to refresh their recall. While people are capable of purposely lying even during deep hypnosis, and also of successfully feigning hypnosis, problems also exist with honest, co-operative individuals. Why? Because during hypnosis our memories of events can be easily distorted in ways that are not obvious either to us or to the person hypnotising us. So although hypnosis can be useful in the investigation of crimes, extreme caution and corroboration of any hypnotically obtained information is essential if it is ever to be used in court.

Hypnosis continues to be a fascinating phenomenon. We now know that the ability to experience hypnosis depends on the aptitude and skill and motivation of the individual rather than on any unusual power on the part of the hypnotist. Hypnosis is a co-operative effort that allows the individual to have experiences that would not otherwise be accessible. Further, with only a little practice, the individual is often able to gain control over imaginative skills in a way that makes it possible to experience the world in novel fashion and to develop more of the broad human potentialities inherent in every one of us.

Hypochondria A far from funny preoccupation with one's bodily processes and state of health. Textbook hypochondriacs have a morbid, all-absorbing interest in every pimple, graze and snuffle, believing them to be the first signs of serious diseases. Some clinical psychologists believe that hypochondriacs develop 'poor health' as a means of gaining 'secondary affection' (sympathy, help with chores). By savouring the fatal implications of their symptoms hypochondriacs convince themselves that they really are physically ill; being mentally ill is unacceptable, even to hypochondriacs.

Hormones

Hypothalamus Literally 'below the thalamus', an accurate description of the location of this physiologically distinct part of the forebrain. The hypothalamus is believed to be the most important automatic control point in the brain; it monitors eating, drinking, sleeping, sexual activity and temperature; it is also directly implicated in emotional experiences and aggressive behaviour.

Neurosis

Conversion reaction

Hysteria A neurosis characterised by intense negative emotions (anxiety, fear, the wish to escape at all costs) which in extreme instances cause disabilities for which there is no medical explanation. Hysterical symptoms such as paralysis, anaesthesia, amnesia, vomiting, loss of speech, sight or hearing, come under the general heading of conversion reactions, and under the particular heading of *conversion hysteria*. Such symptoms may be sustained as long as the underlying threat or conflict continues. Take the case of a young couple expecting their first baby: while the husband is on his way to the hospital to see his baby for the first time he crashes his car; he is uninjured but stumbles away totally blind; eye specialists can find no organic reason for his blindness. Four months later the mystery is solved with the help of a psychologist. It turned out that the husband hadn't wanted a child in the first year of marriage and felt bitter about being 'tricked' into it by his wife. Did he, the psychologist suggested, purposely crash the car, not wanting to get to the hospital? Did he go blind in order not to see his child, the target of his resentment? When offered this explanation, the man's sight was restored.

Id In psychoanalytic theory the unconscious, deepest level of the psyche, the main source of mental energy; the instinctual drives and wishes of the Id are controlled and distorted by the Ego and Superego. The idea that we have a reservoir of instinctual energy pressing for release is outmoded and the term Id is now rarely used outside Freudian theory.

Social psychology

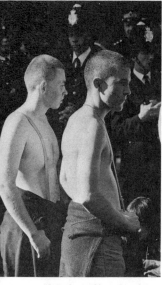

Interchangeable or deep-down different?

Self-concept

Authoritarian personality

Identification Part of the process of finding out who one is and what one's values are; a special case of observational learning, consciously or unconsciously motivated by wanting to be similar to someone loved, admired or respected. Identification begins at birth with the strong bond between child and mother; this is *developmental identification*. Learning prescribed sex roles is thought to occur largely through identification with and imitation of the same sex parent. But identification is not confined to childhood and adolescence. Many adults would be surprised to learn how much of their behaviour is based on subtle forms of hero worship. Advertisers play on this tendency by asking TV and sports personalities to declare that they wear seat belts, brush their teeth with brand X or go on holiday with tour operator Y. Hoping to gain the power and status of a person through identification is called *defensive identification* (you are defending yourself against your own lack of power and status).

Identity A firm sense of identity is part of maturity and essential to any enduring, meaningful relationship or endeavour. Certainly it is something which constantly develops and changes from the womb to the grave, and it corresponds to a person's self-concept.

A housewife shares her husband's friends and interests and rarely goes out without him: what 'identity' has she lost? Think of someone you know well: has their identity changed since you first met? How do you define your own identity? Would others define it in the same way?

One's position within a culture, a socio-economic group or a family, imposes certain roles which are essential to self-concept. *Identity crises* occur when prescribed roles are confused or withdrawn, as in adolescents, the widowed, divorced, retired or imprisoned. Transsexualism is a particularly fascinating problem in identity, especially as the identity the transsexual aspires to is one he or she has never experienced.

Ideology A system of thought combining at least three of the following: (1) a more or less comprehensive explanatory theory about human experience and the external world; (2) a programme, generally stated in abstract terms, of social and

I

political organisation; (3) the belief that some kind of struggle is necessary to carry out such a programme; (4) reliance not merely on persuasion but on active recruiting to ensure loyalty and 'commitment'; and (5) a belief that it serves the needs of a wide public, though it may confer a special leadership role on intellectuals. Communism, several other types of socialism, fascism, nazism and certain kinds of nationalism, are all typical of modern ideologies. In earlier days religious movements such as Christianity could have been classed as ideologies. Today Islam is once more assuming a strong ideological flavour.

Peace and goodwill to all men – a far cry from the militant ideology of the Crusaders.

Implosion therapy A behavioural procedure developed by T. G. Stampfl; the therapist helps the client to imagine feared objects or situations in their worst exaggerated form – imagine youself locked in the reptile house at the zoo for a night! This naturally floods the client with intense anxiety, but if the scene is 'held' in the imagination the anxiety subsides. Sessions are repeated until the feared situation can be faced more calmly in real life. In flooding the feared situation is real, not imaginary. Implosion supposedly brings to the surface repressed material related to the feared situation.

Impotence Rather ponderously defined by W. H. Masters and V. E. Johnson as "the inability to maintain an erection of sufficient quality to accomplish successful coital connection". A whole range of male sexual problems comes under the heading of impotence, which like frigidity has become a highly derogatory term. It is more common now to talk of 'erectile difficulties' which may or may not include ejaculation problems or loss of interest in sex. Masters and Johnson arbitrarily divide erection problems into *primary* (men who have never had intercourse successfully) and *secondary* (men who have). Both groups include men who have erections under some circumstances (on waking, during masturbation) and men who don't have erections at all. The secondary group includes men who can have intercourse on some occasions or with some women – it is not uncommon for men to be impotent only with women they feel strongly about. Causes may be physical (severe diabetes, alcohol, certain drugs, fatigue) or psychological (guilt, fear, lack of knowledge, anxiety) or a combination of both. Although all men have erection difficulties on occasions, for some a single unsuccessful experience is enough to establish a pattern of 'performance anxiety', which of course creates and exacerbates the problem. Modern therapies (as practised by Masters and Johnson, J. LoPiccolo and H. S. Kaplan) all emphasise re-education, with gradual increases in intimacy under conditions designed to reduce anxiety about performance. A recent development in therapy is to teach men to develop erections by showing them erotic slides and giving them feedback on their level of arousal.

Incest Sexual relationships between members of the same family, frowned on by almost every society in the world. Why? Research is hampered by secrecy and the lack of clear definitions. 'Sexual relationships' can range from fondling to intercourse, might happen once or regularly, have the consent of both parties or involve force; 'family' can include uncles, aunts, step-parents and grandparents. In the main researchers have had to glean their evidence from psychiatric patients, a sample which gives a very distorted view of the phenomenon. Incest is not mainly between father and daughter or limited to the lower class, as was once thought. An anonymous national survey in America in 1974 showed that incest was actually commoner in higher social groups and between brother and sister. Cases are rarely reported, partly because the relationship is by mutual consent. Brother-sister incest is more likely when the two share a bedroom or have very permissive parents. Fathers who have sex with their daughters have often lost sexual partners by death, divorce, illness or rejection. As

Sexual dysfunction

Sex therapy

Taboos

we learn more about the factors related to incest (sharing rooms, seductive behaviour on the part of children, even encouragement from the mother) emphasis is shifting from 'treating' the 'offender' to looking at the family dynamics which lead to, and maintain, incest.

Incidence   The frequency of a behaviour, experience or illness, in a population within a specified period of time; a statistic expressed as so many cases *per year* or *per month* is a statistic of incidence. Prevalence, on the other hand, is expressed as so many cases *per thousand of population.*

Individual psychology   A theory of personality and psychopathology developed by Adler, based on the belief that individuals are the outcome of their own creative and organisational powers. Although now mainly of historical interest, Adler's theory contained insights ahead of its time, for example the idea that neurotic symptoms are not the result of repressed conflicts but devices used to gain certain ends.

Industrial psychology   The application of psychological principles to the study of work and work environments; personnel selection, job evaluation, motivation and job satisfaction, training, productivity, equipment design, consumer behaviour, employee-management relationships, human error and industrial accidents all come within the scope of the industrial psychologist.

Stress

Occupational stress is of special interest to industrial psychologists, since stress affects performance, and all work environments have built-in stresses. High levels of responsibility, heavy workload, constant interruptions, distance from shops, loud noise – these are all stressful. The task of the industrial psychologist is to minimise stress and so maximise performance. Though each individual experiences stress differently, one very general effect of stress is increased vulnerability to illness, and illness is a major cause of absenteeism.

Motivation

The factors which influence work motivation, work satisfaction and productivity have received much study. Gone is the old belief that people inherently dislike work and are only goaded into it by monetary reward. Work means a great deal more to most people than a pay packet.

In a now famous experiment psychologist Elton Mayo studied the effects of changing work conditions in a factory assembling electrical relays, working a 48-hour week, each employee producing 2400 relays a week. When piece-work was introduced output went up, as expected. Then two five-minute rest periods were introduced, and output went up again. Then the rest periods were lengthened to ten minutes, and output went up again. Then the company introduced a free hot meal – another rise in output. Then the employees were let out at 4.30 instead of 5.00 pm – output rose again.

Absenteeism dropped by 80 per cent during the experiment. To end the experiment the employees went back to their original hard conditions, and no one was more surprised than Mayo when production broke all records at over 3000 relays per person per week! This phenomenon became known as the 'Hawthorne Effect' after the factory where the experiment was conducted. Mayo explained it as the workers' positive response to having interest shown in them, though the experiment has been criticised on the grounds that a number of other changes also took place. Indeed the whole question of interest is extremely important in motivation analysis. We work best when the work is interesting, not necessarily when it is pleasurable.

Infancy *Martin Richards*
The term 'infancy' comes from the Latin, *infantia*, which means an inability to speak. So, strictly speaking, infancy refers to the period of development from birth to the time when a baby begins to talk, usually early during the second year of life.

Neonate (a newly born infant) The neonate has not seen before but adapts quickly, closing eyes against strong light, and turning towards diffuse light sources. Has a limited focal length of approx. 12 inches. Will 'corner' eyes towards sound sources in a reflex manner – vision should thus be tested with a silent object.

1 month Will turn towards light sources and follow gently moving objects held in line of vision at 6–10 inches away. Will watch mother's face during feeding with increasing alertness.

3 months Shows great interest in human face and will also scan surroundings when held upright. Will follow slowly moving objects held 6–12 inches from face through half-circle. Watches movements of own hands engaging in finger play but cannot co-ordinate hand and eyes.

6 months Has great interest in all surroundings and watches adult activities across room. Will watch objects falling in field of vision. If they roll out of visual field they are 'forgotten' at once. Hand and eye are co-ordinated in grasping close objects. Any squint is now abnormal.

9 months Very attentive to all visual happenings in immediate surroundings. Will observe and manipulate small objects with much interest. Has good ability at eye and hand coordination and observes activities of other people within 10–12 feet for a few moments at a time.

12 months Has wide range of co-ordinated vision in all directions. Drops and throws toys forwards, watching them fall to ground, and also in correct direction for those rolling out of sight. Recognises familiar people within range of 20 feet or more and shows great interest in all situations outdoors where movement stimulates interest. Begins to be interested when shown pictures. Has close range vision up to

Language

The suckling reflex, well developed from birth. Even in the womb a baby sucks its thumb.

Self-concept

Memory

about 10 feet, and will point with index finger at interesting objects or events.

First words As the end of the first year approaches the infant produces his first recognisable word. 'Cat' may mean any animal with fur and four legs or 'mama' any adult who seems likely to offer assistance. Quite frequently the meaning of a word goes through a three-stage evolution: first it is used very specifically, then it is generalised very widely, and finally the meaning is narrowed down to the accepted adult meaning.

It may well be a mistake to always try to place a precise meaning on what the child says at this stage. As with earlier non-verbal communication the point may be more to enter into a conversation and to keep adults talking than to convey a precise wish! Speech at this age has a definite experimental quality; the infant is trying out the effects of saying things.

Watching a child at the one-word stage you cannot but be impressed by his command and understanding of the social world! In a familiar environment with familiar people he seems to understand quite subtle changes in mood of those around him and plays complicated games. His means of expression, however, are still limited. Perhaps his imaginative powers are much more sophisticated than we customarily believe. Watching children play gives some hints that already at this age they have the power to turn bricks into cars and shoes into boats.

Inferiority Low self-esteem and negative feelings about oneself, often an important part of depression (theorists like A. T. Beck give them a central causative role), shyness and social anxiety. When such feelings pervade nearly all aspects of a person's life, they become an *inferiority complex*. That such feelings are often unfounded was proved by a recent American study; researchers reported very few behavioural differences between male students who dated often or seldom, but the 'low daters' had a very negative view of themselves. Feelings of inferiority can arise from real experiences of failure or rejection, but this does not explain why some people get more discouraged than others, persistently compare themselves upwards and distort even successful experiences to fit their low opinion of themselves ("she's only going out with me because she feels sorry for me").

Information processing The processes which intervene between reception, perception and recall of sense data. We modify, categorise, label or even ignore incoming information on the basis of information we already hold. Such processes are usually outside our awareness, but without them we could not maintain a stable world. The jargon used in attentional and perceptual research is often borrowed from computing and communication technology. The 'coding' of information during 'input' can reduce 'load' on 'channel capacity' but unattended 'channels' are to some extent also unconsciously 'processed', as in dichotic listening. The design of programmes which enable computers to perform complex human tasks (translating, playing chess) has provided valuable insights into how we process information.

Inhibition Curtailment, suppression or restraint of behaviour. In classical conditioning, responses which temporarily disappear or take longer to appear than usual are said to be 'inhibited'. More generally, we are inhibited whenever we 'hold back', even though holding back is an essential part of socialisation (controlling bowel movements, controlling sexual behaviour until the setting is right). Problems arise when such behaviour is inappropriate or extreme. Common reasons for inhibition are guilt and the fear of looking foolish or being rejected, usually as a result of punishment in the past. Because it so often results in avoiding pleasurable activities, inhibition is one of the ingredients of shyness, social anxiety and depression. Desensitisation and assertion training can loosen inhibitions and lead to more spontaneous behaviour. Under-inhibited behaviour (overeating, outbursts of anger, promiscuity) can be changed by self-control training and learning new ways of expressing oneself verbally.

Sleep

Insomnia A range of sleeping problems including difficulty falling asleep, waking in the night and staying awake for long periods, and waking too early. Accurate information about sleeping habits is hard to get outside sleep laboratories. People often overestimate the time they take to fall asleep and a 'bad' night might actually provide a full eight hours' sleep despite periods of wakefulness. Most insomniacs seem to sleep less deeply than normal sleepers, and therefore wake more easily; worry and anxiety certainly increase wakefulness. Drugs are not a long-term solution, and sometimes create more problems than they solve. In severe cases desensitisation and relaxation training may be more helpful.

Instinct A fixed but complex behaviour pattern which does not have to be taught or practised (e.g. in birds nest-building, courtship, rearing young). It has never seriously been suggested that any human behaviour comes into this category; used in this sense 'instinct' is strictly for the birds, bees and fishes. However the word is also used to describe any inborn, biological urge which predisposes an animal to respond in a particular way to food, sex, danger and other environmental stimuli. Used in this sense instinct becomes a theory of motivation. Some writers, notably Freud and McDougall, have tried to account for human behaviour in terms of instinctual urges seeking gratification, but they disagree over what the important human instincts are. Freud stressed sex and later aggression, while McDougall proposed a number of social instincts as well. The problem with instinct theories is that they really don't explain anything, certainly not the complexity of human social, sexual and aggressive behaviour or their absence: is aggression inevitable and absence of maternal feelings pathological? The concept of instinct is now rarely used in psychology.

Intelligence *Hans Eysenck*

Intelligence is commonly understood to mean general mental ability rather than high performance in a specific area of knowledge. To psychologists the word has a very similar meaning. Even to the Roman writer Cicero 2000 years ago it denoted overall rather than specific mental agility.

Mental age, chronological age and IQ First of all, how is an elusive quality like intelligence measured? Modern attempts to measure intelligence began in the early years of this century when the French psychologist Alfred Binet put together a number of mental problems of varying difficulty and constructed an 'age scale' for measuring children's intelligence. Scales like this are based on the fact that as children get older they can solve problems of increasing difficulty; by looking at the age at which the average child first solves a problem we get some insight into the difficulty level of that problem. A particular child can then be given a mental age, MA, consistent with his or her performance on a whole battery of problems. A child whose chronological age, CA, is 8 may actually be able to solve problems typically solved by 12-year-olds; his or her MA would then be 12.

Mental age

Intelligence quotient, abbreviated to IQ, is a term of measurement familiar to most people, and it is related to Binet's concept of mental age; IQ is in fact the ratio between mental age and chronological age expressed as a percentage, or $MA/CA \times 100$. So a child of 8 just able to solve problems solved by the average 6-year-old would have an IQ of $6/8 \times 100 = 75$, or below average (100). The actual distribution (slightly idealised) of IQs in the population is shown below. Twenty-five per cent of people have IQs between 100 and 110, but only 2 per cent fall into the 130-140 category.

IQ

Properly designed IQ tests follow objective statistical rules - they are not constructed at the whim of the psychologist. An IQ test is not a test of acquired knowledge but of ability to manipulate the elements of a problem in such a way as to find a solution which has not been part of any formal training.

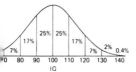

Different abilities General mental ability of the kind discussed above is only one kind of intelligence. Many people possess specialised abilities - verbal, numerical, perceptual, spatial, etc. - which can also be measured by special tests. Elevated to the status of skills these abilities are vital in specialised walks of life, such as interpreting, accountancy, art and design, and in the professional and academic fields.

Although there are no differences in overall intelligence

127

between the sexes, there are differences on some of the specialised abilities. Women are superior to men in respect of verbal and memory skills, but men have the edge when it comes to perceptual and spatial skills. Here is not the place to go into the origins of such differences, but there is a lot of overlap; the fact that differences exist should not be overinterpreted.

There has been much discussion about the origins of individual differences in mental ability, and the evidence is now very strong that genetic factors are about twice as important as environmental ones, at least in our type of society. Some of the evidence for this is outlined in *Behavioural genetics* (page 32) with most of the data coming from studies of identical twins brought up apart, comparisons of identical and non-identical twins, and studies of adopted children, and family and social environments.

Behavioural genetics

IQ tests: do they pass the test?   Do intelligence tests actually measure intelligence? To answer that one has to consider two distinct sets of criteria. The first concerns 'internal' or statistical relationships between different tests. If one's definition of intelligence is that it is general mental ability, then all such tests should intercorrelate positively; in other words a child who does well on one test ought to do well on a whole range of tests. This has always been found to be true. The statistical relationships between IQ tests are strong proof that one is measuring a real quality, namely intelligence.

The second set of criteria is 'external'; if children and adults with high IQs generally do better at school and university, and enter more prestigious and higher-paid professions, than people with low IQs, which in general they do, then intelligence tests are again validated; they do indeed predict success quite accurately. Such predictions, of course, are never perfectly fulfilled; intelligence is a necessary but not a sufficient condition for worldly success. Other qualities are also important, such as ambition, persistence, hard work, and good old-fashioned luck.

Quite recently there have been efforts to discover the biological factors underlying IQ. If these factors were isolated it might be possible to establish non-cultural indices of intelligence. Theory and experiment both suggest that brain wave measurements known as 'evoked potentials' are closely related to our conception of intelligence. People with high IQs show larger, quicker and more complex evoked potentials than low IQ subjects.

Evoked potentials

Attempts to find new types of tests or validate new theoretical concepts have not, on the whole, altered our conception of intelligence. Jean Piaget, for example, formulated a number of interesting theories about mental development in children, but the tests he designed behave in every way like orthodox IQ tests. Other investigators have been concerned with devising tests for 'originality' and 'creativity', but these too correlate well with ordinary IQ tests. On the whole, therefore, IQ tests and the traditional concept of intelligence have stood the test of time and a great deal of criticism. New theories and new methods of measurement have, if anything, reinforced their validity.

Interpretation In psychoanalysis, the analyst's translation of the surface content of a client's dream into its latent or symbolic meaning. Since Freud the term has been widened to include anything the analyst may say which helps make the unconscious conscious. How do we know if an interpretation is correct? Most psychoanalysts would say there are no right or wrong interpretations, only interpretations which speed or retard the analytic process. Many non-analytic therapists regard interpretation with scepticism.

Intrinsic motivation Being motivated 'from within'. Activities which we carry out purely for our own pleasure (playing, solving puzzles, making music) are intrinsically motivated, independent of external rewards. Being given material rewards for doing the things we enjoy generally tends to lessen our interest, application and level of achievement. Praise, on the other hand, increases our interest and enjoyment (musicians get more enjoyment from an appreciative audience).

The new self-propelled REF 24 – fooling around for the fun of it.

Introspection Direct observation of one's own mental processes in the hope of gaining insight into the workings of the mind; an early method of psychological research developed by Wilhelm Wundt and E. B. Titchener, but an approach fraught with problems. How, for example, are conflicting reports to be reconciled? How does one define 'mental processes' or know when a report of a mental process is accurate? Can one distinguish mental processes from the results? - memory is a mental process and also the result of one. Research has shown that we are unaware of many of the stimuli which prompt our behaviour. Introspection can actually disrupt mental and behaviour processes: try analysing how you drive a car while you are driving! Introspection as an approach to psychology was superseded by behaviourism.

Behavioural psychology

Introvert A personality type described by Jung as "hesitant, reflective, withdrawn ... reserved". H. J. Eysenck regards introversion-extraversion as one of the two major dimensions of personality, along with neuroticism. There is evidence that a person's degree of introversion can change after therapy, usually to greater extraversion, casting some doubt on Eysenck's view that introversion is a stable, partly inherited personality type.

Personality

IQ (intelligence quotient) In early tests of children's intelligence (Stanford-Binet) IQ was calculated by dividing mental age by chronological age and multiplying by 100. An average child, one whose mental and chronological ages are equal, has an IQ of 100. Used for adults this formula would incorrectly imply that as one's chronological age increases one's intelligence declines! Tests of adult intelligence (WAIS, for example) calculate IQ not as a quotient in the strict mathematical sense (though the term is kept because people are used to it) but as a 'deviation IQ'. This is a measure of how much a person deviates in statistical terms from the average performance of his or her age group. People who do better or worse than most people of their age score higher or lower than 100. According to psychologist Catherine Cox, who has studied the lives of many famous people, George Washington had an IQ of 140, Mozart 165 and Isaac Newton 190.

Intelligence

James, William William James' reputation as America's greatest psychologist rests almost solely on his two-volume work *Principles of Psychology*, published in 1890 and for many years a leading introductory textbook to psychology. His brother Henry James became America's greatest novelist.

James' formal education was irregular but stimulating (he attended schools in New York, Paris, Boulogne, Rhode Island, Geneva and Bonn) and left its mark on his mind and personality. He was seduced by many interests as a grown man - painting, chemistry, biology, medicine, physiology, psychology and later parapsychology and philosophy. He was, from 1872 until his death in 1910, a Harvard man.

James' main contribution to psychology was his *functionalist* approach, a recognition of the interdependence of mental and physiological existence. He asserted that consciousness is something continuously flowing, not a series of disconnected mental perceptions. This 'stream of consciousness' is the medium for all thoughts and feelings, the vehicle and the essence of the non-material and non-social self. Habitual ways of thinking and feeling, he suggested, become habitual because they prove useful in dealing with the external world.

James' name most often pops up in psychology today in discussions about the origin of emotions. He theorised that emotions are not caused by perception of some significant event but by our bodily reaction to it. In his own words, "we are happy because we laugh and sad because we weep". Because the Danish physiologist Karl Lange arrived quite independently at the same theory, it was dubbed the *James-Lange theory of the emotions*.

William James, 1842–1910

James-Lange theory A theory of the emotions developed independently by two psychologists, William James and Karl Lange, in the 1880s. Both men regarded emotion as the *result* of physiological arousal: the sight of a charging bull produces a 'churned up' internal state *followed by* fear. Though challenged by Cannon and Bard, the theory has a direct descendant in the cognitive labelling theory of emotion.

Jung, Carl To a non-psychologist the difference between psychoanalysis and analytical psychology may seem like hairsplitting, but the difference is really that between Freudian and Jungian psychology. Jung severed his very close connection with Freud and the psychoanalytic movement in 1914, and founded his own school of psychology. The Mecca of analytical psychology today is the C. G. Jung Institute in Zurich.

Carl Gustav Jung was a man of terrific intellectual energy, which he combined with a great sense of fun. His collected

Karl Jung, 1875–1961

works discourse on a wide range of subjects – psychology and psychotherapy, religion, mythology, art, literature, alchemy, astrology, telepathy, clairvoyance, spiritualism, yoga and fortune telling. Jung received his psychiatric training at Basel University and spent most of his life in his native Switzerland, mainly in Zurich, lecturing, researching and running a private practice. He died in 1961 at the age of 85.

In Jungian psychology the whole personality is referred to as the *psyche*; the *ego* is the conscious mind, and co-existing with it is the *personal unconscious*, composed of experiences which have been suppressed, ignored or forgotten; material in the unconscious tends to organise itself into *complexes* centred on significant persons, objects or experiences which attract related material as a magnet attracts iron filings. The *collective unconscious* consists of non-personal experiences, of *archetypes* or mental images common to everyone. Also operating within the psyche are a number of separate systems such as the *self*, really the core of the psyche which impels the individual to seek completeness; the *shadow*, the animal side of our nature, complete with the basic instincts of lower life forms; the *anima* and *animus*, respectively the feminine side of man's nature and the masculine side of a woman's; and the *persona*, the mask we use to conceal our thoughts and feelings from others. In his autobiography *Memories, Dreams, Reflections* (1961), Jung wrote that his whole life was "the story of the self-realisation of the unconscious".

Notwithstanding the variety of evidence presented by Jung for the existence of ubiquitous forms of collective experience, to anyone steeped in behaviourism Jung's concepts appear speculative in the extreme. He gave pride of place to the functions which make us most truly and elusively human, to *intuition* for example (experiences 'out of the blue') and to *transcendency* (the desire for spirituality, meaning and wholeness, expressed in dreams, myths and symbols). It was also Jung who first classified people into 'psychological types' suggesting the two major personality classifications *extraversion* and *introversion*.

Collective unconscious

Persona

Symbolism

Personality

Klein, Melanie   Melanie Klein's contribution to psychoanalysis is the more remarkable in that she never attended a university or received a degree. She was born in Vienna in 1892 and her early experience of psychoanalysis was mainly at the receiving end, first with Sandor Ferenczi in Budapest and then with Karl Abraham. In 1921 she moved to Berlin and began to practice as a child analyst - her first patient was barely three years old. In 1926 she settled in London, and became a naturalised British subject. She died in 1960.

Melanie Klein, 1892–1960

Klein's work created enormous controversy. While Anna Freud, the dominant figure in child psychoanalysis in the 1930s and 1940s, believed that psychoanalytical theory needed some adaptation before it could be applied to children, Klein applied unmodified Freudian techniques to her young patients. Her critics claimed, and still claim, that the processes she attributed to children's minds were too complicated and sophisticated. Klein riposted with clinical evidence of the extent to which feelings of rage, satisfaction, fear, grief and loss are present almost from birth, and form the basis of later patterns of behaviour.

The technique which Klein developed to draw out her young patients was *play therapy.* She equipped a small playroom with simple non-mechanical toys such as small men and women dolls, animals, cars, houses and trees. She also supplied drawing materials, running water, bowls and sand. Klein found that her children were able to express their feelings through play with these materials; often they used them as props to act out parent and teacher roles. In *The Psychoanalysis of Children* and *The Psychoanalytical Play Technique* Klein describes the beneficial results of play therapy.

Klinefelter's syndrome   A chromosomal abnormality in males (instead of two sex chromosomes, X and Y, there are three, XXY) resulting in abnormally long legs, small testes and lack of secondary male characteristics (beard, deep voice, muscular development).

Kohler, Wolfgang   During the last quarter of the nineteenth century, when psychology emerged as an accepted science in Germany, its main goal was conceived to be the analysis of the mind into its simplest elements. Wolfgang Kohler, however, together with two other German psychologists of his generation, Max Wertheimer and Kurt Koffka, rejected this approach, choosing instead to analyse whole experiences and see the natural patterns in them. A new form of psychology, *Gestalt,* evolved around Kohler and his colleagues.

Wolfgang Kohler, 1887–1967

Kohler was born in 1887 and gained his PhD at the Univer-

133

sity of Berlin in 1909. His famous problem-solving experiments with chimpanzees, which led him to develop his theory of *insight* learning, were carried out during his time as director of an anthropoid research station on the island of Tenerife.

In one of his experiments, chimps were required to get fruit which had been placed out of reach in a basket suspended from the roof of their cage. If they pulled a string, the basket swung to and fro, but nearby scaffolding could be used to reach the basket at some point in its swing. The chimps appeared to solve the problem of getting the fruit out of the basket suddenly rather than in any random or hit-and-miss fashion. Once the solution had occurred to them - jumping onto the scaffolding and catching the basket as it swung towards them - they used it successfully over and over again. Unlike Thorndike, Kohler maintained that problem-solving is primarily a matter of insight and perceptual reorganisation rather than of trial and error.

Kohler emigrated to the United States in 1935 and was professor of psychology at Swarthmore College until his retirement in 1963. He died in 1967.

An insight problem for human primates. Given a glass of water, three bottles and four knives, find a way of supporting the glass so that it stands on the knives but does not touch the bottles. The knives must not touch the table top and the bottles must stand upright. Solution on page 141.

Korsakoff's syndrome Severe impairment of recent memory and inability to learn new information, usually associated with brain damage in an area of the sub-cortex known as the hippocampus following many years of chronic alcoholism, although the direct cause may be a deficiency of thiamine (one of the B vitamins); typically Korsakoff's patients confabulate (make up information) to fill in memory gaps.

Psycholinguistics

Thinking

Language A system of symbols for communicating feelings, thoughts and specific instructions. Even in our thinking we use language, though in a 'shorthand' form which short-circuits logical steps for the sake of speed. Having quite literally 'leapt' to our conclusions we then use conventional language to convey them to other people. Behaviourists like Maurice Bowra and B. F. Skinner argue that language is a behaviour, learned like any other behaviour: infants acquire language skills by imitating the speech of adults and by being rewarded, or not rewarded, for their imitations. Other theorists stress the importance of biology in language development; according to them the ability to use language is inborn. Eric Lenneberg, a prominent spokesman for the biolinguistic camp, claims that children cannot be taught to talk until they are biologically ready to do so, at which point language comes rather easily to them.

Karl Lashley, 1890–1958

Lashley, Karl It is no exaggeration to say that Karl Spencer Lashley revolutionised our thinking about how the brain works. His association with Harvard University, where he did most of his research, lasted from 1935 until his death in 1958 at the age of 68.

Lashley was a superb technician, insisting on doing himself what many researchers today leave to their assistants - constructing apparatus, carrying out the necessary surgical procedures, preparing microscope slides, analysing results. Almost all of his experiments involved brain-injured rats. What Lashley was trying to discover was whether selective damage to the brain could impair ability to learn new tasks. The rats he used were taught such tasks as maze-running both before and after damage to specific areas of their cerebral cortex.

As a result of this meticulous work, Lashley put forward two important theories about how the brain functions: *mass action* and *equipotentiality*. The theory of mass action states that the whole, rather than just specialised areas, of the cerebral cortex is involved in the process of learning. The more complex the task, the greater the area involved. The term equipotentiality describes the ability of different parts of the cortex to take over from parts which have been injured. This is particularly true of the area of the cortex involved in vision: when one part of it is damaged, another can do its work. In short, Lashley challenged the previously accepted notion that localised structures in the brain were responsible for learning and other functions.

Brain

Psychosexual development

Latency period That phase of emotional development between resolution of the Oedipal phase (age 5) and puberty

135

(age 11); sexual and aggressive impulses temporarily subside, enabling the Ego and Superego to consolidate and strengthen.

Latent content The underlying, hidden meaning of a dream inferred from its 'manifest' or obvious content; the manifest content symbolises the latent content. Freud viewed dreams as tension-reducing; that latent or hidden tensions should be so heavily disguised in symbols even while in the altered state of consciousness we call dreaming implies that they are very threatening indeed.

Law of effect A key concept in learning theory formulated by E. L. Thorndike in 1898 (before Pavlov or Watson) and the basis of operant conditioning; if the effect of a behaviour is pleasant the behaviour will be repeated, and the connection between the behaviour and the stimulus causing it will be strengthened.

Learned helplessness The belief that whatever one does is useless and ineffectual and that therefore passivity is the appropriate (in)action! According to psychologist Martin Seligman such beliefs and behaviours are the hallmarks of depression. If positive attitudes and behaviours meet with enough opposition, the individual switches to negative attitudes and behaviours. Depressives can be helped by showing them that their actions *do* make a difference.

Learning Humans differ from other animals in their relatively vast capacity for storing knowledge and experience. This is reflected in the largeness of the human cortex and forebrain relative to the older midbrain and hindbrain. We humans have to absorb vast amounts of information before we are competent to look after ourselves and we have created complex systems (languages, both spoken and written) for handing that information down from generation to generation. Each successive generation literally stands on the shoulders of all preceding generations.

Just about everything we do - dialling a telephone number, going to a party, expressing emotions, evolving a personality - involves some form of learning, and every form of learning, at least in human beings, involves information processing, storage and retrieval (see Memory).

Psychologists consider learning to be not only the acquisition of factual knowledge but any relatively permanent change in behaviour which comes about through experience or conditioning. The mechanisms of conditioning have been most thoroughly studied in animals, notably by Pavlov, Skinner, Thorndike and Watson. Animals appear to have inborn instincts which tell them to behave as they do. But it seems unlikely that any human behaviour is instinctive; certainly our lives are to some extent shaped by the physical, glandular

"Wait a minute while I get the hang of it."

Conditioning

Instinct

Language

and nervous constitution we come into the world with, but to survive and fulfil our genetic potential we have to adapt, and to adapt is to learn.

For humans, as for animals, there may be optimum times, 'critical periods', for acquiring certain skills; language is certainly one of them as anyone will know who has tried to learn a foreign language in later life. Sexual expression may also be something we learn in our teens and twenties or not at all.

Lesbianism (see Homosexuality)

Lesioning Destroying selected areas of brain tissue by cauterising or freezing; a technique commonly used in animal research to find out which part of the brain does what.

Kurt Lewin, 1890–1947

Lewin, Kurt Kurt Lewin's major contribution to psychology was *field theory*, a model of the inter-relationship of the individual and society. He saw social groups as fields of dynamically interrelated conditions and forces which affect and determine individual behaviour and used sociograms as a technique of representing relationships within groups.

Lewin was born in Posen, Germany, in 1890, gained his psychology doctorate in Berlin in 1914, and was an infantryman during World War I. He emigrated to the United States in the late 1920s, eventually becoming director of the Research Center for Group Dynamics at the Massachusetts Institute of Technology. He died in 1947.

Lewin envisaged the individual as existing within a *life space*, a psychological shell containing all the factors which determine behaviour. In turn the life space exists within a 'foreign hull', comprising all the non-psychological factors which can penetrate and affect the life space. Lewin believed that, with age, individuals as well as their psychological shells become less flexible, with the result that ideas and feelings gradually become enclosed in separate regions. This enclosing, barrier-making process inhibits change in attitude.

Libido The psychic energy associated with the sexual-creative instinct. Freud's ideas about the libido evolved over more than 40 years, as did those of his psychoanalytic colleagues. In common parlance libido is equated with the itch for sexual activity, but in psychoanalysis libido fulfils not only sexual instinct but 'ego instincts' (non-sexual, self-preserving and creative instincts) as well.

Life cycle   *Rhona and Robert Rapoport*
Psychologists approach the study of growth throughout life by viewing ordinary lives as sequences or stages, each associated with characteristic inner preoccupations. Growth occurs when there is adaptive transition from one stage to the next.

All ways of dividing up our lives are more or less arbitrary.

Shakespeare did it one way, with his seven ages of man. Biologists have their own ground plan - infancy, puberty, prime of life, senility. Psychologist Erik Erikson identified, in all, eight stages of social development. Freud and Piaget, concentrating on childhood and adolescence, proposed four psychosexual and four intellectual stages of development respectively.

The categories we propose are also arbitrary but they fit modern life, and use a combination of psychological and sociological criteria. They are five in number: childhood, adolescence, young adulthood, the establishment phase, and the later years.

Childhood embraces several substages, from earliest infancy to school entry and primary education.

Adolescence is taken to be roughly between the ages of 13 and 19. The main preoccupation in this phase is with the search for 'identity', finding out who one is as an individual.

Young adulthood starts at the time of leaving school, when one is catapulted into a more adult role or goes to university or college. Here people are preoccupied with learning to commit themselves to intimate relationships and social institutions such as marriage and work. This stage lasts until they have 'settled down', probably with the first child (though not all of us want children or marriage).

The establishment phase occurs, very approximately, between the ages of 25 and 55. The main preoccupations here are with making the kind of commitments - work, family, friends and leisure activities - that will constitute satisfying life investments. Commitments may also be to abstract notions such as politics or religion. By this stage, more than 90 per cent of adults are married and most have children. By the end of it the children will have embarked on their own journey through life.

Later years are marked by a preoccupation with attaining a sense of social and personal integration, and the acceptance of mortality as inevitable.

We decline in our physical powers as we grow older, but there is no reason to think that we decline similarly in our capacity to develop or express interests. Growth is possible at every stage of the life cycle if we look on changes as opportunities to be exploited.

Limbic system Literally a 'border' system within the brain, important in regulating emotional behaviour. The system consists of several richly interconnected areas of the brain, including part of the cortex (cingulate gyrus), several areas in the subcortex (septal area, amygdala, hippocampus - all embedded deep inside the cerebral hemispheres) and the hypothalamus. The limbic system is a borderline system in that it integrates evolutionarily 'old' and 'new' parts of the brain.

Brain

Psychosurgery

Lobotomy A questionable form of brain surgery developed by neurologist Antonio Egas Moniz in 1935 and widely used until the mid 1950s to modify the mental lives of obsessive or depressive patients; the procedure involved cutting certain fibres connecting the frontal lobes with the rest of the brain; this was done with a special knife, a leucotome, inserted through a small hole drilled in the skull. Apathy, irresponsibility, impaired judgement, diminished intellectual powers, reduced creativity and even coma and eventual death were some of the 'side-effects' of prefrontal lobotomy. The real scandal of lobotomy was that the 'successful' experiments on chimpanzees on which the technique was based turned out to have been surgically incompetent and inconclusive.

Social psychology

Lost letter technique An ingenious and unobtrusive method of measuring attitudes to political parties, current issues, etc., developed by psychologist Stanley Milgram. The technique relies not on polls, questionnaires or interviews but on people's general willingness to drop 'lost' or 'mislaid' letters into the nearest mailbox. The experimenter simply leaves lots of 'lost' letters, addressed to the same address but to different organisations or individuals, around various postal districts and waits for them to be delivered to the address on the envelope. Fewer letters addressed to disapproved-of organisations (Nazi Party, League for Blood Sports) will turn up than letters addressed to popular ones. As a control the experimenter puts a neutral-sounding addressee (Mr John Taylor) on a proportion of the envelopes.

Love *Leonore Tiefer*

In contemporary Western civilisation romantic love and sexual expression are closely intertwined. Many people feel that sexual feelings are a natural outgrowth of feelings of love and that sexuality provides the greatest pleasure in a relationship of love. The capacity to feel love is highly valued and individuals who seem uninterested or incapable are pitied. Though sexual performance is possible with someone other than a beloved, passion and fulfilment come only in the context of mutual care and devotion.

But this is not a viewpoint shared by members of many other cultures. Romantic passion may be a good foundation for short-lived sexual relationships, but by its very nature romance is brief and passion founded on it quickly wanes. Founding a marriage on such fleeting attraction would be asking for trouble.

Some cultures devalue love because they feel it is based on an idealised rather than a realistic knowledge of the beloved's qualities. Sexual expression of such artificially founded feelings would lead to an unwise choice of marriage partner. At one time in Korea marriage based on love was illegal because it indicated profound disrespect for the wishes of practical-

How many misconceptions do they have about each other?

minded parents. Possibly the absence of publicly shown affection among Orientals is a result of attempts to suppress the temptations of deceptive romance.

A further variation is supplied by cultures where romantic love is unknown yet sexual passion flourishes. When natives of certain South Pacific islands are told about romantic yearning, devotion and the insatiable craving for a greater feeling of union with the beloved, they display amusement or disbelief. For them sexual pleasure is a result of adept technical performance engaged in by individuals who experience transitory attraction for one another.

So what kinds of cultures recognise romantic love? Cultures where individuals of both sexes interact every day, but where expression of sexual feelings for a number of different partners is discouraged or prohibited, seem to breed powerful feelings of wanting to 'belong' to a particular beloved. In these same cultures there is a strong tradition that sex and romantic love go together; so when adolescents experience certain arousing feelings they label them as 'love/sex' feelings. They are also cultures where feelings of individual worth are not readily provided by the entire community and need to be sought out in individual relationships.

Drug dependence

LSD (lysergic acid diethylamide) In the 1960s one of the most widely abused synthetic hallucinogenic or 'psychedelic' drugs; tolerance develops rapidly, and regular use is fairly rare – in this sense there are no LSD 'addicts'. The physical effects of LSD are undramatic: dilated pupils, a slight increase in blood pressure, heart rate and temperature, and occasionally nausea, chills, flushing and shakiness. Psychological effects include exceptionally intense and colourful visual experiences; greatly sharpened sense of hearing, taste, smell and touch; synaesthesia or a 'crossing over' of sense perceptions (seeing or smelling sounds, hearing colours); a slowed sense of time; and a sense of ecstatic detachment. Users frequently see enormous symbolic significance in ordinary objects and events. A 'bad trip' can be truly terrifying.

Lying Psychologists are interested in lying from several different perspectives. Many forms of questionnaire, the Eysenck Personality Inventory for example, include sets of questions designed to tell researchers whether the information given can be relied upon.

Intent to deceive is an important part of any definition of lying. Most normal adults tell lies intentionally, with some ulterior motive and with some awareness of the sanctions against lying. It is our 'conscience' which makes us anxious about being found out. This is why lie detectors were invented. There are small physiological changes associated with anxiety, and these can be measured; signs of anxiety, therefore, can be a good indication of whether a person is lying or

Anxiety

Polygraph

Solution to the insight
problem on page 134

not. Lie detectors are widely used in modern police work, especially in the United States. Psychopaths who are liars have no moral inhibitions about lying, hence no anxiety.

For many clinical psychologists working with children the distinction between lies and fantasy is a fairly subtle one. The lies children tell reveal a lot about their moral and social development. The invention of a non-existent 'friend', for example, who must be fed, clothed and given every consideration by the family, is a common phenomenon among preschool toddlers. Older children, on the other hand, often prevaricate about what happens to them at school. Though the latter behaviour approximates more closely to lying than to make-believe it serves the same purpose as the invisible 'friend': it helps the child to elaborate personal goals and values. Lying, when it is not part of psychopathic behaviour, is often a creative approach to inadequacy. Old people sometimes tell untruths or 'confabulate' to fill in the gaps in a failing memory or enliven a dismal routine; their purpose is not intentionally to mislead but to cope with inadequacy.

Maladaptive A response which is entirely inappropriate to deal with a stressful or changing situation. Evolution is a process of adaptive change; any genetic mutation or behaviour which is maladaptive rapidly dies out - this is what 'survival of the fittest' is all about.

Maladjustment Failure to adapt to the changes which come with successive stages of the life cycle; the teenager has to adapt to the demands of adulthood, the middle-aged couple to children leaving home. Maladjustment often expresses itself as frustration, tension, anxiety and depression.

Mania The popular idea of a maniac (someone in the grip of mania) is not so far removed from the clinical reality: mania is a mental disorder characterised by intensely excited behaviour, terrific alertness of sensory perception and speeded-up thought processes; as mania deepens, thinking and behaviour become increasingly incoherent and disoriented and the person may be extremely aggressive if restrained or criticised. In *homicidal mania* excitement takes the form of a desire to kill.

Marijuana: a strong lobby for legalisation

Manic-depressive reactions Psychotic disorders in which periods of severe depression and extreme elation (mania) alternate, hence the more recent term 'bipolar disorder'. Heredity may be one of the culprits: Franz Kallmann, for instance, found that one in four members of the families of manic depressives was also manic-depressive. Individuals most vulnerable appear to be highly sociable extraverts ('life and soul of the party' types) who have a history of mood swings; in their case extraversion usually marks deep feelings of inadequacy. Typically a first manic-depressive episode strikes around the age of 25-35; attacks can last for several weeks, or up to a year if untreated.

Marijuana (Cannabis) Drug derived from the Indian hemp plant, *Cannabis sativa*, also known as grass, pot, hashish, dagga, ganja, etc. The most controversial of all the psychoactive 'recreational' drugs, alleged by many to be less deleterious to health than either alcohol or tobacco, marijuana induces relaxation, vivid sense perceptions and a slowed sense of time, but these sensations vary with one's mood and emotional state.

Abraham Maslow, 1908–1970

Maslow, Abraham It was American psychologist Abraham Maslow who coined the term 'third force', to distinguish the humanistic approach to psychology from the behavioural

M

and psychoanalytical. The humanistic approach assumes that human nature is essentially good, creative and capable of healthy growth. Unlike many other personality theorists Maslow dwelt on the healthy rather than the disordered personality. The most important of his concepts are *metaneeds*, *self-actualisation* and *peak experiences*.

Need

Maslow asserted that man's metaneeds – as distinct from basic needs like food, air, sex or security – include beauty, goodness, justice and wholeness. He defined metaneeds as being necessary for personal growth and fulfilment. A person who strives to satisfy those needs is engaged in the process of self-actualisation. What are the characteristics of self-actualising people? They are realistic, independent, spontaneous, creative, democratic, problem-centred rather than self-centred, need privacy and detachment, have a fresh rather than a stereotyped approach to others, resist conformity, and are likely to have many peak experiences. Intense happiness is a peak experience, an experience which makes one feel more whole, more alive, more in tune with the world. Peak experiences are, in a sense, landmarks on the road to self-actualisation.

Maslow's academic career was spent mainly at Brooklyn College (now New York University) and Brandeis University. He died of a heart attack in 1970, aged 62.

Masochism Deriving sexual pleasure from humiliation, pain or even injury to a sexual partner or oneself; rarely separate from the desire to inflict pain on a sexual partner (sadism); the practice of both masochism and sadism is known as sadomasochism ('S and M'). The man who gave masochism its name was L. von Sacher-Masoch, an Austrian novelist who described it in a book he wrote in 1885.

Masturbation Deriving sexual gratification from stimulating one's own genitals, usually with the hand, but also in other ways; *mutual masturbation* is the manual stimulation of the genitals of one's partner while he or she stimulates you. Solitary sex behaviours (autoeroticism) can relieve sexual and non-sexual tensions, especially when no partner is available, and almost all men and, according to Shere Hite, the majority of women masturbate. Few areas of eroticism are so clothed in shame and anxiety. The Jewish, Christian and Muslim faiths have traditionally condemned masturbation. Physicians from Hippocrates to the nineteenth-century French doctor Lallemand warned against 'softening of the brain' and premature death as the price of masturbation; indeed in the nineteenth century a whole industry was created to manufacture grotesque devices to prevent male masturbation (women were not thought to masturbate). It is not surprising that a residue of guilt and fear still exists. However, most health professionals today regard masturbation as harmless and

Sex therapy

143

maybe beneficial. Sex therapists use 'directed masturbation' programmes to remedy erectile and orgasmic difficulties, and encourage mutual masturbation to prolong forepleasure or substitute for intercourse when this is not possible.

Mother-child relationship

Maternal deprivation The notion that lack or inadequacy of maternal care and affection seriously and lastingly influence the intellect and personality of a child, a notion developed by child psychologist John Bowlby in the 1960s which led to widespread changes in institutional care for children.

Harlow

Maternal instinct The tender, spontaneous affection of a mother for her child is widely taken to be evidence of an innate and unlearned 'maternal instinct'. Why else should mothers give so many years of selfless devotion to their children? Nevertheless psychologist Harry Harlow, investigating mothering behaviour in female monkeys brought up in isolation, concluded that maternal feelings are far from inbuilt and automatic. When isolated female monkeys gave birth to their first baby they typically ignored it, or, in a few cases stood on it, bit off toes and fingers, or crushed its face on the floor of the cage. Having no experience of mother love themselves they were unable to give it.

Feminism and psychology

It is always risky to extrapolate from animals, even from the higher primates, to humans, but if humans have a maternal instinct it is likely to be weaker than that of other species - all our 'instincts' are weaker. 'Baby bashing' is a phenomenon difficult to reconcile with universal mother love: every year in the United States alone some 250,000 children suffer serious physical abuse from their parents. Some feminists suggest that society has a heavy investment in the notion of a maternal instinct; it is, they suggest, a mechanism to keep women in subjugation.

David McClelland, b. 1917

McClelland, David The greatest formative influence on American psychologist David McClelland was Henry Murray and his theory that needs (for dominance, achievement, autonomy, aggression, sexual activity) are the major motivating forces in human behaviour. McClelland concentrated on studying just one major need, the need for achievement, and was responsible for much of the initial work on finding ways of measuring it - he developed a technique for reliably scoring it in 1951.

McClelland's method of setting a value on achievement need was to show his subjects a set of four pictures and then ask them to write a brief story about each (a modification of Murray's TAT technique). He then scored each story-statement according to the degree to which the writer seemed to be attempting to excel or compete with some standard of excellence. In later work he concentrated on studying the characteristics of high-achievers using fantasy techniques.

Achievement

In 1961 McClelland published *The Achieving Society*, in which he analysed the nature of achievement in social rather than individual terms. He argued that achieving societies are not necessarily those most naturally advantaged; what distinguishes them is a strong entrepreneurial spirit, and emphasis on educational achievement.

McClelland was born at Mt Vernon in New York in 1917 and became professor of psychology in the Department of Social Relations at Harvard in 1956. He stands in opposition to the dominant trend in psychology in arguing that motives develop from feeling and emotion, not vice versa.

Medical model The assumption that mental disturbances are analogous to physical diseases in the sense that leprosy or cirrhosis of the liver are diseases, with 'symptoms', 'treatments', 'etiologies', etc; the traditional viewpoint of Western psychiatry.

Meditation Bodily relaxation and mental concentration on an unchanging source of stimulation (an object, a candle flame, a riddle or 'koan', a string of words or 'mantra'). Meditative states are characterised by alpha brain wave activity and subjective feelings of deep passivity and intense but unfocused awareness of one's internal world. Meditation is increasingly used as an antidote to stress rather than as an Open Sesame! to mysticism. It also has applications in medicine (control of post-operative pain, hypertension, tension headaches), in industry (boosting concentration, productivity and ability to work under pressure) and in assertion training, desensitisation and personal growth programmes.

Megalomania A psychic condition involving delusions of grandeur (gross over-confidence in and overestimation of powers and abilities).

The Maharishi, bringer of Transcendental Meditation to the beat generation of the 1960s

Memory *Alan Baddeley*

Memory is the capacity for storing and retrieving information. Without it we would be intellectually dead. Although one occasionally reads newspaper reports about people 'losing their memory', such people are by no means totally incapacitated or intellectually dead. This is because human memory is not a single unitary system but many systems. Broadly there are three categories of memory: sensory memory, short-term memory and long-term memory.

Sensory memory The ears and eyes of an alert human being receive a continuous and changing stream of information. As we look at a landscape we perceive a single picture, rather than unrelated separate components like fields and hedges. For this to happen, information about hedges and fields must be recorded and fitted together with previous and subsequent information. This means that at some stage the information needs to be stored, briefly. This is precisely the function of the sensory memory. It is our brief visual memory which allows us to watch a film and perceive the actors as moving continuously; what we really see of course is a series of stills alternating with a blank screen. It is almost certainly the case that our visual system employs not just one brief memory system but several.

In the case of hearing, the importance of temporary storage is even clearer. Without some form of brief auditory memory system we would never be able to understand words or sentences; by the time the end of the word or sentence had been heard, we would have forgotten the beginning! As in the case of vision, auditory perception almost certainly involves several storage processes. Other sensory systems such as movement probably also rely on some form of sensory memory.

Short-term memory Suppose I ask you to do some simple mental arithmetic, like multiplying 23 by 7. How do you do it? There are a number of possible ways, but virtually all of them involve temporarily storing some of the information being processed. Such temporary storage is usually termed *short-term memory*, or sometimes *working memory*.

Once again we are probably not dealing with a simple unitary system. Perhaps the most thoroughly explored component of the system is 'inner speech' - indeed a fair proportion of short-term memory appears to be speech-based. Suppose I were to give you a telephone number and ask you to make a call from a telephone in another room. You would probably help yourself remember the number by 'rehearsing' it under your breath while you went to the telephone. This is a common strategy for a wide range of situations involving the temporary storage of material that can be verbally coded. It is as if an item unrehearsed gradually fades away, but that each time we say it the memory trace of the item is revived and therefore remains accessible.

*

We also appear to have a visuo-spatial imagery system for short term use. If you trace along the outline of the letter E opposite, starting at the asterisk, you'll find that some of the corners face outwards and some face inwards. Look away from the page and decide whether the seventh corner in the outline is an outward or inward one. To do this you probably had to hold the image of the E in your mind's eye. Had you tried to do some spatial task at the same time, such as driving a car, you would have found the task much more difficult. This suggests that the 'mind's eye' uses part of the system we normally use for spatially orienting ourselves in the world.

There are probably other temporary storage systems, besides the visuo-spatial and speech-based, which form part of short-term or working memory.

Long-term memory Obviously it would be highly inconvenient if we only had a short-term memory, which spontaneously faded all the time. In order to learn to talk, find our way about, or recognise a friend we need some more permanent record. This is the role of long-term memory, which can be split into two components, *episodic memory* and *semantic memory*. Episodic memory records specific, personally experienced events, like what you had for breakfast, semantic memory represents our accumulated knowledge of useful, and useless, facts.

Episodic memory is the most thoroughly studied aspect of human memory. Herman Ebbinghaus, the father of memory research, who published the first experimental research on memory in 1885, showed that the relationship between practice and learning was a very simple one: if you double the amount of time spent in learning, you double the amount learnt. He showed that rate of forgetting was slightly less straightforward, being rapid initially and then slowing down, a function that is linear if plotted on a logarithmic scale. To make investigation easier he attempted to simplify learning and memory tasks by using pronounceable but meaningless syllables (wux, jek, fij). This led to strong criticism on the grounds that by excluding meaning he left out the most important factor in most learning and remembering situations.

This point was most forcefully made by Sir Frederick Bartlett, who in 1935 published his classic book *Remembering*, based largely on the recall of pictures and stories. Bartlett emphasised the role of 'effort after meaning' in learning, and argued that all new learning builds on existing knowledge. Sorting items to be remembered into categories, or linking them together by means of a story or a series of mental images have a beneficial effect on learning.

Semantic memory What is the capital of France? What is Oliver Cromwell's telephone number? I suspect you gave a rapid and correct answer to the first question. A computer could easily be programmed to provide the same information. The second question you probably ruled out of court as silly: Oliver Cromwell died long before the telephone was invented, so he hasn't got a telephone number. But unless it were very sophisticated, a computer would not have done that. It would have scanned all the C telephone numbers in its 'memory' and concluded that Cromwell was not on the telephone!

The human semantic memory system is able not only to locate stored information correctly, but cross-connect it as well, evaluating two apparently diverse or conflicting pieces of information and come up with an answer to a question not previously encountered. Our semantic memory system is vastly more flexible, rapid and capacious than any existing computer memory.

Menopause The 'change of life' between 45 and 55, when the hormone system prepares for the end of fertility, the cessation of ovulation and menstruation. Many women experience

Middle age

the menopause without problems or regrets; a few find it extremely trying, either psychologically or physically (hot flushes, dizziness, dry skin, aches and pains and occasionally discomfort during menstruation as the vaginal lining becomes drier). Hormone replacement therapy is widely available to help with menopausal and post-menopausal problems. The 'male menopause' is not the functional equivalent of the female menopause; loss of libido and erectile difficulties in the late 40s and 50s may have many non-hormonal causes (stress, overwork, depression about coming retirement). Male sexual function declines very gradually, some men remain active into their 80s. The lesson seems to be 'those who don't use it, lose it'.

Hormones

The mental readjustments a woman has to make when her childbearing and childrearing years are over are fairly fundamental.

Menstruation The cyclic breakdown of the endometrium (lining of the uterus) and its discharge through the vagina along with blood from tiny uterine blood vessels; this happens each time there is no egg to implant itself in the womb.

In many cultures there is intense anxiety about menstrual blood; menstruating women are considered unclean or taboo, and may even be barred from normal activities of all kinds. There are no medical or hygienic reasons for abstaining from intercourse during menstruation – some couples find coitus at this time particularly exciting, others find it distasteful.

Mental age A person's degree of intellectual development as measured against standardised norms established by intelligence tests (see Intelligence, IQ).

Mental illness
A term derived from the medical model of mental disorder, and used to describe a variety of behaviour patterns which disrupt the smooth and orderly conduct of life. The term is a catch-all for pathological (medical) conditions; for problems arising from social maladjustment; for personal emotional and motivational problems; and for exceedingly rare psycho-

logical disturbances (abnormal psychology). Unfortunately the average person equates the entire discipline of psychology with the study of mental illness. The pity of labelling someone 'mentally ill' is that she or he is feared, shunned, and occasionally shut away, by the rest of society.

Paradigms of mental disorder Gerald C. Davison
The axiom that there are countless ways of viewing the world applies just as much to science as to art. Every scientist operates within a particular paradigm, a set of assumptions about what data are significant and how they should be collected. Every scientist has a predisposition or readiness to see certain things and not to see others. This selective awareness/blindness appears to be an inherent feature of human as well as animal perception.

In the field of psychopathology, the study of mental disorders, so little is known for certain that it is especially important to be aware of the paradigms being used. It is proposed here that the most important paradigms in contemporary psychopathology are (1) statistical, (2) physiological, (3) psychoanalytic, (4) learning (or behavioural), and (5) humanistic. Except for the statistical, each paradigm of disorder has an associated paradigm of treatment.

In the statistical paradigm, it is assumed that people who diverge from the majority are 'abnormal'. For example, if we measure a sample of people and find that most cluster around the middle of a distribution of scores, the individuals at either end will be defined as 'deviant'. The measurement of IQ is a prime example of this approach, though one might want to argue how useful it is to regard people with uncommonly high IQs as abnormal. Note, however, that the statistical paradigm says nothing about which characteristics should be measured.

Psychotherapy

In the physiological paradigm the assumption is that mental disorder is at least in part due to some organic or physiological defect. In other words, psychopathological states can be likened to medical 'diseases', and like diseases they manifest themselves as sets of signs and symptoms, are amenable to a diagnosis, and follow a predictable course. This paradigm has led to important advances, such as the discovery that general paresis (a serious neurological disease) is caused by uncontrolled syphilitic infection and that a predisposition to schizophrenia is probably genetically transmitted. Therapies associated with this paradigm sometimes, though rarely, entail biological intervention into the presumed physical cause of the mental disorder; a case in point would be the special diets prescribed to prevent some of the ravages of phenylketonuria, a severe form of mental retardation. In most instances, however, intervention takes the form of drugs or electroconvulsive shock therapy, with varying degrees of effectiveness; such interventions are not necessarily related to the actual causes of the problem.

149

The psychoanalytic paradigm is a very prevalent one. Its basic assumption is that mental disorder arises from repressed and unresolved conflicts in childhood. Underlying this paradigm is the classic psychoanalytic theory that we all pass through four psychosexual stages (oral, anal, phallic and genital) in childhood, in which a different part of the body is particularly sensitive to erotic gratification. The manner in which the developing human being deals with the Id's desire for instant gratification and copes with social and other constraints on such gratification has a big influence on the development of his/her personality. The seeds of mental disorder are sown when these inevitable conflicts are not resolved.

The learning or behavioural paradigm holds that abnormal behaviour develops in the same way as normal behaviour, and that it is only the judgement of society at a given time which determines whether certain behaviours are deviant or not. Principles and data from classical conditioning, operant conditioning, modelling, and cognitive psychology are used to explain how behaviour develops. It would be fair to say that overall this paradigm tries to use the methods and findings of experimental psychology to enhance our understanding of behaviour deemed abnormal. Behaviour therapy, the treatment approach based on this paradigm, is discussed in its own right on page 36.

Finally, there is the humanistic paradigm, sometimes called 'the third force' in psychology to point up its dissensions from psychoanalysis and behaviourism. The humanistic paradigm holds that within each human being there is an innate drive for fulfilment and growth, that Man's basic nature is good and beautiful, that human suffering develops when people deny this basic goodness in order to meet the approval and standards of others, and that therefore therapy should encourage people to get in touch with their own inner goodness and express themselves creatively and responsibly. These are some of the assumptions behind client-centred therapy.

Each of these paradigms has its uses. All of them contribute something to our understanding of mental disorder and how to prevent and treat it. It is probably good that there are these different points of view, given the rudimentary nature of our knowledge. However, the adoption of a particular paradigm simultaneously sensitises investigators to making certain discoveries and blinds them to information outside its purview. Fortunately, as far as treatment is concerned, most practitioners are eclectic: there are behaviour therapists who interpret their clients' dreams, and there are psychoanalysts who employ systematic desensitisation.

Mental illness: a myth? Thomas S. Szasz
The premise underlying theology is the existence of God. Theologians can neither define God nor demonstrate his existence; for them and their followers the existence of God is

obvious, beyond need of demonstration. Those who deny the existence of God are mistaken, misguided or worse. The burden of proof is on the non-believer to prove the non-existence of God.

Now the premise underlying psychiatry is the existence of mental illness. Psychiatrists can neither define mental illness nor demonstrate its existence; for them and their followers the existence of mental illness is obvious, beyond need of demonstration. Those who deny the existence of mental illness are mistaken, misguided or worse. The burden of proof is on the critic of psychiatry to prove the non-existence of mental illness.

Psychiatry: a pseudo-science   The proposition that mental illness is a myth – which I first advanced in a paper in 1960 and developed more fully in a book published a year later – is expressly intended to sap the pseudo-scientific ground on which psychiatry rests. It insinuates the idea that just as God exists only for those who believe in imaginary beings or 'powers' (religion), so mental illness exists only for those who believe in imaginary illnesses or 'causes' (psychiatry).

Why is the subject matter of psychiatry believed to be mental illness? The idea of mental illness receives its main support from such phenomena as neurosyphilis (syphilis of the nervous system) and traumatic or senile dementia (degeneration of the brain). These are conditions in which disorders of behaviour, or so-called psychiatric symptoms are caused by a demonstrable disease, a 'pathology'. However, correctly speaking, these are diseases of the brain, not of the mind. They are diseases in the same sense that arteriosclerosis or arthritis are diseases. They are diseases of a part of the body, the brain. In short, they are literal diseases. According to most contemporary psychiatrists all mental diseases are of this type.

Brain damage

Where the medical model fails   Revealingly, psychiatrists often speak of "medical diseases *underlying* psychiatric symptoms" – specialists in diseases of the heart, lungs, or stomach do not speak of "medical diseases underlying cardiac, pulmonary, or gastroenterological symptoms". Psychiatrists thus assume that a disease or defect of the nervous system, perhaps a very subtle one, will one day be discovered to be the cause and hence the explanation of all so-called mental diseases.

This view implies that the human problems now classified as mental diseases are *not* the consequences of conflicting personal aspirations, *not* the outcome of moral values, social controls, and similar individual or cultural factors. Instead such problems are attributed to physiological or chemical processes yet to be discovered, and hopefully remedied, by medical scientists. In short, mental illnesses are regarded as basically similar to bodily diseases, the only difference being that the latter affect the heart, lungs and other organs, and manifest themselves as symptoms which can be directly traced to these organs, whereas the former affect the brain and manifest

151

themselves as 'mental' or 'psychiatric' symptoms, symptoms which can be directly traced to the brain.

This view rests on two fundamental errors. First, to be at all analogous to a disease of the heart or kidney, a disease of the brain would have to manifest itself by neurological signs, not psychiatric symptoms; that is, it would have to be something like impaired gait or vision rather than something like depression or paranoia. Secondly, if psychiatrists believe or 'know' that so-called mental patients suffer from diseases of the brain, then for the sake of clarity and honesty they ought to say that and not something else.

Calling a spade a spade There are some psychiatrists, now in the minority, who believe that mental illnesses exist, but who do not consider them to be simply the symptoms of brain disease. They correctly observe that a diseased brain does not 'secrete' confused speech like a diseased kidney secretes albumen-rich urine. They see mental illnesses as abnormalities or deformities of the 'personality' which a person acquires or develops in a variety of ways (not necessarily through brain disease). They consider mental illness to be both a cause and a consequence of interpersonal and social conflict.

My objection to this 'psychosocial' model of mental illness is again twofold. First, it implies that countless personal, religious, legal, political and social problems can be classified as 'diseases', and that life would be meaningful and peaceful if these problems were prevented or cured. This view simply replaces a biological oversimplification with a psychosocial oversimplification.

Second, whereas the advocates of the biological view classify certain brain diseases as 'mental diseases', the advocates of the psychosocial view use the term 'mental disease' metaphorically but nevertheless insist that it is a literal disease. Put differently, the organic psychiatrist claims that mental illness *is* a disease and then names the wrong organ as the seat of the malady ('mind' rather than brain), but the psychosocial psychiatrist claims that mental illness is a disease *like* other diseases, which conveniently obscures the differences between deviance and disease.

Towards greater integrity and responsibility In pointing out the mythical nature of mental illness I am pointing out that psychiatrists have a vested interest in manufacturing and maintaining their mythology. I am attempting, if you like, to destroy their pretensions and privileges.

Mental illnesses do not exist; indeed, they cannot exist, because the mind is not a body part or bodily organ.

Inevitably the idea of illness, whether of the mind or the body, implies deviation from a norm. In the case of physical illness, the norm is the structural and functional integrity of the human body or some part of it. In the case of mental illness, it is impossible to name a single norm which is not stated in psychological, social, moral, or legal terms – all typical psychiatric symptoms or diseases, from agoraphobia to sexual intercourse with animals, conform to and illustrate this principle.

In asserting that mental illness is a myth, I am not asserting (as some of my critics have claimed) that certain distressing phenomena do not exist. On the contrary, it is belief in the existence of mental illness that prevents us grasping and accepting the truth about behaviours labelled 'mentally diseased'. In other words, just as disbelief in God does not imply disbelief in his alleged creations, so disbelief in mental illness does not imply disbelief in the myriad phenomena we now label mental illness. Personal misery and social unrest, aggression and suffering quite unavoidably exist. But they are not diseases. We categorise them as diseases at great peril to our integrity, responsibility and liberty.

Mental retardation A synonym for mental deficiency. There are degrees of mental retardation, borderline retardation being an IQ in the range 68-83, mild retardation 52-67, moderate retardation 36-51 and severe retardation 20-35. Most mongols come into the last category. Retardation represents a slight or large gap between mental age and chronological age, and is an enormous problem for society.

IQ

In America alone there are an estimated 6 million mentally retarded children and adults, cancer, arthritis, heart disease and mental illness being more prevalent. There are many causes of serious retardation, such as mongolism (Down's syndrome) or PKU (phenylketonuria), which are chromosomal and metabolic disorders respectively. But retardation may also be due to pre-natal damage (caused by German measles, exposure to radiation, various drugs, physical accident), to brain damage caused during delivery (prolonged delivery, inappropriately administered anaesthetics, lack of oxygen, physical damage from instruments used in delivery), or to hereditary defects.

Retardates with an IQ of less than 35 require constant care and supervision, but those with IQs between 35-51 are able to look after themselves to some extent and do useful work, though usually in an institutional setting. Retarded children and adults are, despite their handicaps, emotionally sensitive, and just as prone to love and anger as the rest of us. With care and support those only mildly or moderately handicapped become well-adjusted members of society.

Metabolism The sum total of chemical reactions which take place in the body. Metabolic reactions occur in thousands of small steps, each step made possible by organic catalysts called enzymes. Metabolic rate can be speeded up or slowed down by heat or cold, by exercise or lack of it, by a lot of or a little oxygen, by hormones, and by psychological processes. Yogis, for example, can drastically slow their

Homeostasis

Yoga

metabolic rate during *samadhi*, the deepest stage of trance, and quite ordinary people can be trained to do the same, though to a lesser extent, by biofeedback methods.

Middle age   *Marjorie Fiske*

Until recently, this rich period of the human lifespan was largely ignored by social and behavioural scientists, including psychologists. Freud's message (only slightly exaggerated) was that once the oedipal period ended at the age of 7 or 8, one's personality, problems, conflicts and adaptation were more or less set for the duration of life. Today the media, research studies and parents and grandparents (many of whom, perhaps the majority, now consider themselves middle-aged), are all eagerly convincing themselves that important changes take place in adult life.

Mothers, fathers and the 'empty nest' Many older people, when they look back on their life, recall that some of the events they anticipated with apprehension or anxiety caused a not unpleasant sense of release when they actually happened. This is especially true of such expected 'losses' as children leaving home, or retiring from work. Less predictable events, such as death, setbacks at work, divorce, even suddenly having to move house, make a greater impact because they call for major reorientation without advance warning.

The majority of men apparently do not anticipate the 'empty nest' stage, when the children have left home, as posing any problem at all. However, the mood of many women facing the 'empty nest' stage seems to be one of quiet desperation. Women who pass through the 'empty nest' crisis generally find one of two very different solutions. Some settle down to unequivocal resignation, having lost their former symptoms of agitation. Others make important changes in their lives, ranging from divorce or beginning a new career to redecorating their homes, and are, in their own terms, well satisfied, often happy. As always, it seems to be those who have the courage to take control over their lives who 'grow'.

The departure of the last child from under the family roof often coincides with the menopause. Do hormonal changes compound the problems of 'empty nest' women? Since today's middle-aged women are less susceptible to old wives' tales than their mothers were, the answer is probably no. For a few, however, psychological problems appear to exacerbate the physical discomforts. Women whose purpose, conscious or otherwise, is to dominate their children, and through them their husbands, are likely to have more troublesome menopausal symptoms. Mind and matter conspire to deepen the 'empty nest' crisis.

The ease with which women pass through the menopause and 'empty nest' phase also seems to be related to social class. Lower class women are unlikely to get much sympathy or understanding from their husbands or their children, but

The 50s and 60s: time to do those things that took a back seat when family and career came first?

Menopause

more privileged women by and large feel supported by their families. Discussion of personal problems, at least within the family, and usually with friends as well, is taken for granted among most liberal, articulate adults. By contrast, women of a more conservative and traditional stamp have few outlets for anxiety and fewer resources for coping.

"So we had the roof repaired, and a new extension at the front ..."

Maturity or passivity? Most people like to believe that sometime between 40 and 60 most of our potential has ripened and become reality. Jung's idea that the older we grow the more 'individuated' or like ourselves we become is wonderful in theory, but there is evidence to support the thesis that there are now, in the United States especially, fewer autonomous, self-generating, self-realising people in all walks of life than there were several decades ago. It is as if the uncommitted of all ages seem to want to be told what they 'should' want, know, feel and believe.

We are in a period of staggering and unprecedented social change. It is now obvious that the latter half of life involves confronting 'identity crises' every bit as serious as those at one time associated primarily with adolescence. Too often we seek out passive solutions or escapes. Middle age should really be the prime of life, the time when we most truly become ourselves, when we do and think things we would never have dared do or think in our youth.

Migraine Recurrent headaches usually confined to one side of the head and often accompanied by visual disturbances, nausea and vomiting; incidence is much higher in women than men and also in city-dwellers; can be controlled by taking ergot derivatives as soon as one experiences the visual disturbances which usually herald an attack. The one-sided nature of migraine headaches and their accompanying symptoms distinguish them from tension headaches which occasionally afflict perhaps one person in ten. Both migraine and tension headaches can be brought on by anxiety and a habit of fearing the worst. Meditation and relaxation techniques help many sufferers.

Mind A philosophical rather than a psychological concept meaning the organised totality of one's thought processes, conscious as well as unconscious, as well as their products; the opposite of matter or body, and possibly existing independently of them. Wilder Penfield, the Canadian neurologist, called the mind "the part of the brain we don't understand".

Memory

Mnemonics Most of us use little mnemonic strategies ("I before E except after C" for spelling, and "Every Good Boy Deserves Favours" for reading music) to help us remember things. Chunking is another mnemonic device. A *mnemonist* is someone who has brought the art of remembering to a high pitch by using such strategies.

The famous Russian mnemonist Shereshevskii relied heavily on mental imagery for organising material he was asked to remember; he tackled recall of a very complex and meaningless formula, which began

$$N.\sqrt{d^2.x\frac{85}{vx}}.\sqrt{\frac{276^2.86x}{n^2v}.\frac{1}{\pi264}}.n^2b, \quad \text{etc.},$$

by creating a story which went something like this: "Neiman (*N*) came out and poked with his stick (.). He looked at a dried-up tree which reminded him of a root ($\sqrt{\ }$) and he thought: 'It's no wonder that this tree withered and that its roots were laid bare, seeing that it was already standing when I built these houses, these two here (d^2)' and again he poked with his stick (.). He then said 'The houses are old, so a cross (×) should be placed on them.' This gives a great return on his original capital, 85,000 roubles ... " and so on.

Soldiers, policemen, nurses and doctors – people in uniform generally – are easily identifiable models for most young children. To copy them is to share their power and status.

Personality

Minnesota multiphasic personality inventory (MMPI) A personality inventory constructed of 550 questions or statements to which the subject responds True, False or Can't Say. The tester draws inferences about the subject's traits, interests, relationship, attitudes, values, etc. from the overall profile of the answers given. One of the first inventories to include a 'lie score' checking for inconsistencies between responses.

Social learning theory

Modelling A key concept in social learning theory; Bandura and other social learning theorists emphasise the role of modelling or imitation in the learning of complex behaviours. We do not always learn by directly experiencing reward or punishment; instead we imitate the actions we see others rewarded for, or refrain from those which are punished or disapproved of. We also imitate people we perceive as powerful and attractive. Modelling is therefore synonymous with observational or vicarious learning.

Social skills training

Mongolism (see Down's syndrome)

Mother–child relationship *Martin Richards*

A relatively new phenomenon in the history of the family which some psychologists have taken for granted and seen as a necessary and essential basis for child development. John Bowlby, for example, has argued that an unbroken relationship with a mother or permanent mother-figure is essential for adult health.

Current evidence, however, supports the view that children are most likely to develop satisfactorily if they grow up with several strong and close relationships and that there are disadvantages in spending a high proportion of time with a single person. Not only do different relationships have different things to offer an infant, but moving from one known person to another is in itself a valuable learning experience. An exclusive relationship with one parent can create a 'fish in a tank' situation: the fish never realises there is a whole world outside the tank.

It has been suggested that children who grow up in the more or less exclusive care of their mothers become very dependent adults who seek to form suffocatingly close and exclusive adult relationships which in turn perpetuate the narrow nuclear family situation into the next generation, and the next and the next.

Few mothers find the exclusive company of infants satisfying. But for fear of damaging infants by leaving them with other people they seldom seek adult company. The care of an infant really needs to be shared between the parents, and between them and other adults. Parents need their own social life and 'time off' from their children. We need to be less anxious about creating long-term psychological problems for our children and more concerned with providing a satisfactory life for all family members in the short-term.

Motivation The 'whys' and 'wherefores' behind our actions. Some of the whys are physiological (the need for food, sexual activity), others psychological (from lower-order needs such as safety, security and companionship to higher-order needs such as love, self-esteem and personal growth). Some theorists regard pleasure-seeking as the driving force of human behaviour (hedonistic theory of motivation); others give instincts pride of place (instinct theory of motivation); and others assume that in all behaviour we exercise choice and free-will (cognitive theory of motivation). Abraham Maslow's 'pyramid' of human needs integrates all these theories; when lower levels of need are satisfied, our motives switch to achieving higher needs. Thus when we have satisfied hunger and thirst, we make safety and security our goal; when these are achieved our goal becomes love, then self-esteem, and finally self-actualisation.

Multiple personality A rare hysterical dissociative reaction

A man in search of admiration? Our need for security is often satisfied by the esteem of others.

in which two or more distinct personalities vie for expression. One of the best known cases of multiple personality is that described in the book and the movie *Three Faces of Eve*, the story of a woman with three personalities. Originally Eve had two distinct personalities, Eve White who was modest, gentle, hardworking and kind, and Eve Black who was irresponsible, flashy and selfish; Eve Black was aware of Eve White but the reverse was not the case. During treatment a third, much more balanced personality emerged, Jane, who was aware of both Eves and eventually succeeded in producing a stable amalgam of the two. Multiple personality should not be confused with 'split personality', which is a somewhat misleading synonym for advanced schizophrenia. Our understanding of the mechanisms underlying multiple personality is poor. Freud maintained that hysterical symptoms represent the symbolic fulfilment of a half expressed sexual wish.

Dissociative reaction

Hysteria

Murphy, Gardner Gardner Murphy coined the adjective 'biosocial' to describe his approach to psychology. Many of his peers describe him as an 'eclectic' psychologist. Whichever term is used, the viewpoints he forged incorporate elements from almost every major branch of psychology.

Two of Murphy's most important concepts are *sensory needs* and *activity needs*. Our senses (sight, touch, hearing, taste, smell) need stimulation for organic as well as aesthetic reasons; our muscles, joints and tendons need to be active because exercise is pleasurable. *Canalisation* is the name Murphy gave to the process which strengthens the link between these needs and the behaviours which satisfy them. Each time we act out a need, the deeper the channel becomes between need and act.

Murphy also argues that perceptual habits (habitual ways of looking at and interpreting the external world) serve to give meaning and stability to the individual. Despite the stabilising effect of perceptual habits, however, Murphy believes that situations are equally powerful determinants of behaviour. When a situation changes, a person's behaviour changes too.

Murphy was born in Ohio, USA, in 1895, studied at Yale, Harvard, and Columbia, and served with the American Expeditionary Forces in World War I. The zenith of his career came in 1972 when the American Psychological Foundation awarded him its Gold Medal with the following citation: "A peerless teacher, a felicitous writer, an eclectic psychologist of limitless range, he seeks to bring the whole of human experience to bear in understanding behaviour."

Gardner Murphy, b. 1895

Henry Murray, b. 1893

Murray, Henry The study of personality owes to Henry Murray a widely used projective psychological test called the *Thematic Apperception Test*, TAT for short. This is a projective test, based on psychoanalytic theories, which purports to identify and measure a number of basic motivating needs.

Murray was born in New York City in 1893, and proceeded towards psychology by a somewhat roundabout route (history at Harvard, medicine and biology at Columbia and biochemistry at Cambridge, England). His interest in psychology blossomed in the mid-20s partly through reading Jung. For many years he was director of the Harvard Psychological Clinic, his most influential book, *Explorations in Personality* (1938), being the outcome of research at the Clinic. He also taught psychology at Harvard until his retirement in 1962.

TAT projective tests

Murray's research with a great number of healthy, well-adjusted subjects led him to suggest that everyone has certain basic psychological *needs*, including the need for *achievement*, *affiliation*, *deference*, and so on. The test consists of a series of black and white pictures, around each of which the subject is asked to construct a story. The assumption is that the stories give some insight into the subject's motivation, because feelings, thoughts and fears are projected into them.

Murray's achievement was that he made psychoanalytic theories respectable in academic psychology. The TAT is, in effect, an important attempt to make the psychoanalytic concept of need amenable to measurement.

Narcotic analgesics A group of drugs, including opium, heroin and morphine, used therapeutically to ease pain; they act on the central and autonomic nervous systems, producing a general state of euphoria; it is for their euphoric effects of course that they are abused; side effects are nausea and vomiting, depression of breathing and, with prolonged use, tolerance and physical dependence.

Nature–nurture controversy Shorthand for the continuing battle between hereditarians and environmentalists in psychology and the social sciences; the former maintain that genetic factors are the most powerful determinants of behaviour and personality, the latter that environmental and social factors are more influential. Members of both camps recognise that both influences are at work, but disagree as to their relative importance.

Need An important concept in the psychology of motivation. Needs can be physiological (for food, air, sex, etc.) or psychological (for affection, achievement, autonomy, etc.). Erich Fromm identified five uniquely human needs (relatedness, transcendence, rootedness, identity, frame of orientation). Henry Murray listed more than 20 needs, most of them social, including the need to be free of restraint (autonomy), to defer to authority (deference), to give support and sympathy (nurturance), to entertain and fascinate others (exhibition), to have fun for fun's sake (play), to attain a standard of excellence (achievement). Achievement-need in particular has been extensively researched. Rogers, Goldstein and Maslow identified other needs, which if achieved, added up to the overall need for self-fulfilment.

"Brother, can you spare more than dimes and dollars?"

Negative reinforcement Reinforcement, whether positive or negative, is used to increase the probability of a response; so negative reinforcement means removal of something (like a loud noise or an electric shock) in order to strengthen a response. Negative reinforcement should not be confused with punishment. Punishment is not reinforcing, its purpose being to decrease a response.

Neo-analytic Ideas based on the theories of Freud, but which de-emphasise the sexual determinants of behaviour and personality in favour of social and cultural factors. Alfred Adler, Erik Erikson and Gustav Jung were psychologists of the neo-analytical school.

Neocortex Literally 'new cortex'; that part of the brain

Diagram of a neuron
1 Incoming impulse
2 Main body of cell containing nucleus
3 Dendrite
4 Axon
5 Axon terminal synapsing with dendrite of next neuron

A synapse, showing sacs containing neurotransmitter substance
(6) releasing their contents into the synaptic cleft
(7), enabling the nerve impulse to cross it.

which evolved with the mammals (70-120 million years ago); distinct from the evolutionarily older palaeocortex, which is solely olfactory in function.

Nervous breakdown A popular blanket term for failing to cope. It is not an expression used by psychiatrists or psychologists and has no specific meaning within modern psychiatric medicine. Its sense could, in consequence, extend from mild anxiety at one extreme to severe psychosis at the other.

Nervous system

The nervous system is crudely analogous to a telephone network, a system for the rapid transmission of electrically coded messages between subscribers.

Nerve cells The basic unit of the nervous system is the *neuron* or nerve cell. Nerve cells have the same basic constituents as other cells but are specialised for conducting electrical impulses. Projecting from the main body of a neuron are fine filaments called *dendrites*, and a long extension called an *axon*, which eventually branches out into a number of *axon terminals*. The dendrites receive nerve impulses from receptor cells (in the skin, eyes, ears and other sense organs) or from other neurons, and the axons transmit them to other neurons. Between the dendrites of one cell and the axon terminals of another are junctions called *synapses*. Were it not for substances called *neurotransmitters*, stored in little sacs in the axon terminals and released into the synapse by the arrival of nerve impulses, communication between neurons would not take place.

Stimulus and response Nerve impulses begin when a collection of dendrites or a receptor cell in a body organ are stimulated by mechanical, thermal, chemical or electrical means. The receptors in the eye, for example, the rods and cones, contain pigments which react chemically to light energy. A nerve impulse can be generated only if the stimulus is of a certain minimum intensity.

Unlike electrical cables, the axons of nerve cells are active rather than passive transmitters of impulses. When not transmitting an impulse, a potential difference (a difference of electrical charge) exists between the outside and inside of the axon membrane: the outside is positively charged, and the inside negatively charged. When an impulse arrives this situation is momentarily reversed, which causes a wave of depolarisation (reversal of charge) to travel down the axon. Maintaining the necessary potential difference between the inside and outside of axon membranes is an energy-consuming process; positively charged sodium ions are actively pumped out of the axon to maintain the positive charge on the outside of the membrane.

Nerves A nerve is really a bundle of axons. Information from the eyes, ears, nose and tongue is transmitted directly to

161

the brain via the *cranial nerves*, of which there are 12. Information from other parts of the body goes into the spinal chord via one or other of 31 pairs of *spinal nerves*; these also provide a pathway for instructions going from the brain to various parts of the body, which is why they are known as *mixed nerves* - they contain *afferent* fibres (going into the spinal chord) and *efferent* fibres (coming from the spinal chord). Most sensory information sent to the spinal chord goes up to the brain for interpretation and processing; but a small proportion is dealt with in the spinal chord itself in what is known as a *reflex arc*; the 'knee jerk' reflex is an example of a 'brainless' response.

Command structure Though the nervous system is traditionally portrayed as two systems, evidence from biofeedback and other studies is beginning to blur this textbook distinction. The *central nervous system* or CNS consists of the *brain* and the *spinal chord* and participates in all 'voluntary' activities. Information is fed into the system and commands are sent out from it via the *peripheral nerves*, mentioned above.

The *autonomic nervous system* or ANS is the 'involuntary' part of the nervous system. Autonomic nerve impulses travel along nerve fibres (axons) which pass directly into and out of the brain or spinal chord. One of the cranial nerves referred to above, the *vagus nerve*, is also part of the autonomic system; it controls heart rate and respiration. The ANS operates on the brake–accelerator principle: one part of the system, the sympathetic system, reverses the effects of the other part, the parasympathetic system. In this way homeostasis, or a life-sustaining balance between all involuntary body functions, is continuously maintained.

Brain

Neurology Study of the brain and the nervous system, the branch of medicine which has contributed most to psychology; as a young doctor Freud specialised in the anatomy of the nervous system and in nervous diseases.

Neuron A nerve cell (see Nervous system).

Neurosis *Charles D. Spielberger*
The term 'neurosis' was originally used to describe a class of disorders presumed to be due to disturbances of the nervous system. With advances in scientific knowledge, it became apparent that neuroses were psychological rather than neurological in origin. It was in recognition of the important role of psychological stress and conflict in the development of neurotic symptoms that the term 'psychoneurosis' was coined.

While neurosis and psychoneurosis have essentially the same meaning, the former is now far more generally employed. It describes a class of disorders characterised by a wide range of physical and psychological signs and symptoms. Neurotic people display markedly inadequate emotional

Shutting out stress can be a healthy reaction to anxiety provided it is not taken to the extreme.

Social skills training

adjustment, feelings of inferiority, excessive worry, inability to adapt to everyday life, and numerous other psychological, somatic (physiological) and behavioural symptoms.

The give-aways The symptoms neurotics most commonly complain of are tension, irrational fears and anxiety, and a wide variety of vaguely defined discomforts like indigestion, headaches, insomnia, dizziness, shortness of breath, trembling and heart palpitations. Some forms of neurosis include obsessive and compulsive behaviour, depressive and dissociated states, conversion reactions, and paralyses and anaesthesia without any organic basis.

The personality of neurotic patients is generally characterised by feelings of inadequacy and insecurity, hypersensitivity to criticism and a strong need for affection and approval. Neurotics tend to worry over trivial things. They are often socially inadequate and indecisive. Sometimes they are so tense and nervous that they seldom get a good night's sleep. While some of these symptoms are not unknown to most of us at some time in our lives, in the neurotic individual they are relentless to the point of undermining efficiency and ability to adapt to the social environment.

The causes 'Psychosocial' stress, or stress occasioned by one's social environment, is generally considered to be an important contributor to neurotic symptoms. That said, similar stress situations may produce symptoms in some individuals but not in others. The adaptive style of the neurotic is not shaped by any single incident; it develops gradually as a consequence of emotional maladjustment to environmental stress and life circumstances. Studies of the onset of neurosis show that financial troubles, deaths in the family, sex and marital problems often precede an increase in neurotic symptoms.

There is little evidence that biological factors are critical in the development of neuroses, though it is possible that some people are genetically more vulnerable to the onset of neurosis than others. In its most serious forms, a neurosis reflects a mode of emotional adjustment which is maladaptive. Since maladjustment is often observable even in early childhood, we must assume that genetic predisposition plays some part in its development. However intelligence, education and cultural background may also be critical in determining the nature and form of neurotic reactions.

Approximately 15 per cent of the population of the United States and other Western industrial countries are believed to suffer from neurotic disorders. But the incidence may be even higher, depending on how neurosis is defined. For example, some physicians in general practice estimate that more than two-thirds of all patients who come to them with complaints of physical illness are neurotic individuals whose medical symptoms have no organic basis. The patients' somatic (bodily) symptoms in such cases are an expression of their neuroses.

Types of neurosis Although the pattern of symptoms in neurosis varies greatly from person to person, anxiety is always a pervasive underlying problem. Indeed most neurotic symptoms are either manifestations of anxiety or defences against anxiety. Neuroses are differentiated on the basis of their salient symptoms. 'Psychasthenia' was the term formerly used to describe patients with severe phobias, obsessions and compulsions, but it is rarely used today. 'Neurasthenia' refers to states of anxiety accompanied by restlessness, fatigue, and vague visceral sensations, but these now tend to be diagnosed as anxiety reactions.

Neurotic disorders are currently classified into five categories: anxiety reaction; phobic reaction; obsessive-compulsive reaction; hysterical reaction; and depressive reaction.

Anxiety

People with *anxiety reactions* report vague feelings of apprehension and impending disaster, and fears of dying, losing control or going to pieces. Anxiety neurotics are also insecure and inefficient in their work, frequently irritable and depressed, and likely to experience restlessness, forgetfulness, difficulty in concentrating, insomnia, recurring nightmares and fatigue.

Phobias

In *phobic reactions*, the most salient symptoms are intense irrational fears of specific objects or situations. By avoiding the feared object, the phobic person is prevented from discovering that it is in fact relatively harmless.

Obsessive-compulsive neuroses

Obsessions are irrational thoughts which repeatedly intrude into one's awareness and which one has great difficulty stopping or controlling. *Compulsions* are irrational actions that one feels compelled to perform, even though they serve no useful purpose. Most people who suffer from obsessive-compulsive neuroses are also indecisive, tightly controlled in their emotions, fussy about being neat and clean, and rigidly organised in their approach to work and leisure.

Hysteria refers to a group of neurotic conditions characterised by *conversion reactions* (the physical manifestation of repressions) or *dissociative reactions* (dramatic departures from normal states of consciousness). Conversion reactions can take the form of partial or complete paralyses of the arms, legs or other parts of the body; anaesthesias (loss of sensation); analgesias (insensitivity to pain); and disturbances in vision and hearing, which may include partial or complete blindness or deafness. In dissociative reactions, there may be amnesia, with partial or complete loss of memory of past events; sleepwalking; convulsions or fits which closely resemble epileptic seizures; and fugue (flight) states in which the individual escapes from a stressful situation by disappearing from his usual haunts and temporarily losing his memory.

Depression

The distinction between neurotic *depressive reactions* and psychotic depression is really one of degree and the extent to which depression can be blamed on environmental events. The symptoms of neurotic depression can include feelings of futility, irritability and sadness, loss of interest in one's job, family and friends, insomnia, loss of appetite, excessive worry about physical health, and bursting into tears. Neurotic depressions are sometimes referred to as 'reactive' to emphasise the importance of situational factors. The death of a parent, spouse, child or close friend, separation or divorce, or failure at school or at work are all common instigators of neurotic depressive reactions. While such events make most people feel at least mildly depressed, in neurotic depressive reactions the symptoms are more severe and tend to persist beyond a reasonable period of time.

Neurotransmitters Chemical substances stored in the terminals of nerve axons and released into the cleft between axon terminal and dendrite spine, making the dendrite more or less likely to pass on the impulse to its connected neuron.

Nightmares When extreme known as night terrors; the sleeper is propelled into wakefulness by the threatening nature of his dream; breathing and heart rate increase moderately in the case of nightmares, dramatically in the case of night terrors (64 heartbeats a minute to as high as 152). According to Freud, nightmares are 'failed' dreams; the tensions *Dreaming* they are supposed to relieve are too powerful to be dealt with unconsciously and so erupt into consciousness. Night terrors are usually interpreted as being massive anxiety attacks. Both nightmares and night terrors appear to be commoner in young people, presumably because their defences against anxiety are less efficient than those of older people.

Non-verbal communication *Michael Argyle*
The medium Non-verbal communication (NVC for short) is everything we communicate by means other than words. We convey these wordless messages by our facial expression, our gestures, by the movements, posture and orientation of our body, by physical distance or closeness, by gaze, touch, appearance and tone of voice. Some of these social signals are fairly slow or static, like body posture, clothes, or proximity to the other person; others are fast-moving, like gestures and *Blushing* facial expression, and are closely co-ordinated with speech.

All of us send and receive, encode and decode, NV signals. Sending is often unconscious and receiving conscious, but on *Subliminal perception* occasion both may be below the threshold of awareness. For example, pupil dilation is a signal of sexual attraction, but neither sender nor receiver is consciously aware of the signal. The signals we use to synchronise speech also operate at a subconscious level.

The message NVC can convey several different kinds of message. It is, for example, an extremely efficient way of indicating like and dislike; indeed it is our main way of telling other people what we think of them, and it does so more powerfully than words. NVC is also our main channel for expressing emotions, emotions we would often prefer to conceal, though our feelings sometimes 'leak' to less controllable areas of the body, like the voice or the feet.

If looks could kill and gestures speak ...   The face, in particular the brows/forehead, eyes/eyelids and mouth/jaw, is one of the main channels of NVC. Seven facial expressions are common to all cultures and are probably innate, as Ekman has shown: happy, sad, angry, surprised, excited, afraid/anxious and disgusted/contemptuous. There are of course finer shades of expression in between. In every culture there are certain 'display rules': for example, the Japanese rarely show negative facial expressions in the presence of others. Buck has shown that there are people who externalise their emotions, showing more than they feel, while internalisers do just the opposite.

Body movements, especially hand gestures, are another important channel of communication. Hand or hand-to-face signals with clear verbal equivalent (hitch-hike sign, beckoning) are referred to as 'emblems'. The Italians have a particularly extensive gesture language. But as Desmond Morris and his colleagues have shown, it is not safe to assume that signs have the same meaning in different countries.

Gaze is an important NV signal. During most social interactions there are periods of mutual gaze and wandering gaze. People look at each other to obtain information while listening, and to gauge reactions or feedback at the end of utterances. We also look more at people we like, and less at people a short distance away. Gaze is interpreted (correctly) as a sign of interest, the exact form of that interest (love, threat, cry for help) being provided by the context and the facial expression of the other person. Gaze acts as a signal for intimacy, together with such signals as proximity and smiling, which can substitute for each other.

NV vocal cues are next in importance to facial expression as indicators of emotions and attitudes to others. Anxiety is indicated by a breathy tone of voice, fast disjointed speech, and frequent errors (stammering, switching words, malapropisms). Accent, together with appearance, is one of the main cues for social class though it also reflects geographical origins. 'Prosodic' speech cues (pitch, stress and timing), add to the meaning of utterances, but are not strictly part of NVC.

Spatial behaviour includes putting oneself at a certain distance from the other person, and the way one moves in relation to them and the environment. Liking is expressed by proximity, co-operation by a side-by-side position, status by symbolic occupation of the most important place ... We all establish and define invisible personal territories (office space, tables in restaurants, seats on buses). Furniture and rooms are expressly designed and arranged to create private territories, status differences and various other conditions for interaction.

Appearance is an aspect of NVC that is often overlooked, but clothes, hair, skin condition, and body adornments all say something about personality, social status and group identity. Most people like to enhance their physical attractiveness and disguise their blemishes so that other people respond more favourably to them. Members of rebellious youth groups (punks, skinheads) use their appearance to proclaim their rejection of society.

Where words fail NVC is the only means of communication available to animals. We human animals continue to use it because it has a greater emotive impact than words, because words are sometimes inadequate or lacking, because our vocal channel is sometimes full, and because non-verbal signals are conveniently inexplicit. Some of the findings of NVC research have been applied to modifying the behaviour of mental patients and helping people who are lacking in social skills. Fascinating though NVC is, it has proved a poor tool for assessing personality; the links between a person's NVC behaviour and their personality, as measured by standard personality tests, are very weak.

Physiological arousal

Noradrenaline (Norepinephrine, USA) A hormone secreted by the adrenal medulla and also by the nerve endings of sympathetic nerve fibres; as a neurotransmitter, noradrenaline enables nerve impulses to pass across synapses; as a hormone it induces constriction of the blood vessels, and therefore a rise in blood pressure. High noradrenaline levels correlate with anger and aggression, low levels with depression.

Spot the norm

Norm A term widely used by social psychologists, meaning any behaviour, belief, attitude or value which is shared by the majority within a group and which constitutes a standard against which individual behaviour, etc., can be measured. Deviation from norms is often followed by some kind of sanction. Statistically speaking, a norm represents some kind of average of the data available. *A normative study* is one which seeks to establish norms.

Normal Moderate or high conformity to a specific norm or standard; extremes of deviation from the norm are then labelled subnormal or supernormal. Statistically the concept of normality has meaning; it is the value judgements attached to normality and abnormality which are questionable.

Authoritarian personality

Obedience Virtually all societies develop hierarchies in which certain people - parents, teachers, government officials - have authority over others. The wheels of society would grind to a halt if inferiors refused to obey superiors. But when does obedience become immoral and inhuman? 'I was only obeying orders' is an excuse which has worn a bit thin in the last century - it failed to save the perpetrators of the Holocaust when they came to trial at Nuremburg.

The psychologist most associated with research into obedience is American Stanley Milgram. In a series of experiments in which subjects were ordered to give electric shocks to helpless victims the following sobering facts emerged: the majority of people (possibly 65 per cent in American studies and up to 80 per cent in German studies) are prepared to administer lethal shocks, and presumably other fatal treatments, to their fellow citizens in obedience to a strong authority figure. This is not because they are sadists or psychopaths but because they abdicate responsibility, assume the 'helpless cog' mentality. Nevertheless obedience despite one's better nature causes acute inner conflict.

Obesity *Judith Rodin*

Obesity is usually defined as being at least 20 per cent above the weight norms established for one's sex, height and body build. Obesity is a complex disorder, brought about by a host of factors which interact with one another. Getting fat involves some combination of learned eating habits, not using up enough energy and having excess tissue in which fat can be stored. But the nature of the contribution of these three factors varies greatly from person to person. Eating 1000 calories a day may be a weight-maintaining diet for one person and a weight-gaining diet for another, the hidden factor being individual differences in constitutional make-up. Differences in genetic history, age, sex, or hormonal state affect metabolism (chemical processes within the body) and energy expenditure.

Apart from individual constitution, what other factors play a part in obesity? There is some evidence that genes are important. Fatness does tend to run in families. But families share environments as well as genes, so one cannot say 'Ah! yes, he or she is overweight because fatness runs in the family'. *Twins* Twin studies support the notion that a tendency towards fatness can be inherited, but that environment plays an important role as well. How genes affect fatness, however, is not yet understood. They may affect the number of fat cells we come into the world with, hence the number of storage places we have for excess calories, or they may affect the way hormones regulate digestion and fat storage.

O

Early life experiences are known to have a major effect on obesity. Overeating or overfeeding in childhood can irreversibly increase our complement of fat cells, and once developed fat cells do not disappear even with weight loss. Learning to eat in certain ways in infancy powerfully affects adult eating habits and tastes. Environmental food cues are yet another reason why some people gain weight. Some of us are especially responsive to the sight and smell of food. There are also important socio-economic factors related to the incidence of obesity. For instance, women in lower social class groups appear to be more prone to obesity than women in upper social class groups, possibly a reflection of differing attitudes to the cultural norms which emphasise thinness.

To summarise, we are what our genes, early learning history, responsiveness to external food cues, number of fat cells, individual metabolism, social class and culture ... make us.

This man has probably been ragged, bullied and insulted all his life. Fatness gets less sympathy than any other physical deformity.

Object constancy   Widely regarded by child psychologists as marking an important step in sensorimotor development. Piaget demonstrated object constancy by hiding toys his children were playing with under cushions; up until about seven months, they lost all interest in their toys as soon as they disappeared from view; but by the eighth month their behaviour was very different: they searched for their toys and eventually moved the cushions to find them.

Observational learning (see Modelling)

Repression

Obsession   An irrational thought which persistently intrudes into consciousness and cannot be willed away. The psychoanalytic view is that an obsession is a way of dealing with impulses which are repressed; the obsession relieves the hidden feelings but obviates the need for action.

Neurosis

Obsessive-compulsive neuroses   Repeated patterns of thought or behaviour stemming from feelings of guilt or from conflicts which have been repressed. Though obsessions and compulsions are separate types of reaction they occur together so frequently that clinically they are regarded as two sides of the same coin. An obsessive-compulsive neurosis can be grossly incapacitating: for example, an obsession with dirt and germs, translated into a bathing and handwashing compulsion, may take up many useful hours a day. Response-prevention is a behavioural technique occasionally used, with some success, to reduce compulsive behaviour.

Oedipus complex   According to Freud the powerful attraction a child develops for the parent of the opposite sex, accompanied by hostility towards the same-sex parent. This state of conflict begins around the age of 4. Resolution comes when the child begins to identify with the same-sex parent and develops strong positive feelings towards the other parent; this happens at about 6 or 7. In Freud's view failure to resolve the Oedipus complex can negatively affect personality growth. The Electra complex refers specifically to a girl's suppressed attraction for her father. (In Greek mythology Oedipus killed his father and married his mother, though he was unaware of his true relationship to them; Electra never recovered from her mother's murder of her hero father.)

Oestrogens   Female sex hormones produced mainly in the ovaries but also in the adrenal glands of both sexes and in small amounts in the male testes; responsible for creating female primary and secondary sexual characteristics and for maintaining the female sexual and reproductive system.

Olfactory   To do with the sense of smell; olfactory stimuli are received by special cells in the roof of the nasal cavity;

precisely which areas of the forebrain interpret olfactory signals is still something of a mystery.

Drug dependence

Opiates and opioids The pure drug which gives opium (the juice of the opium poppy *Papaver somniferum*) its characteristic effects is morphine; morphine and its many derivatives, which include heroin, are known as opiate drugs. Opioid drugs, on the other hand, refer to both opiates and to synthetic drugs which mimic their effects. The human nervous system is receptive to opioids because some neurons in the brain naturally secrete analogous substances known as enkephalins. The effects of opioids on mood and feelings depend on the taker's mental state and expectations, and on the method of administration (oral, inhaled, intravenous). On the whole, opioids are not as destructive to the organs of the body as alcohol.

Oral stage The first of Freud's psychosexual stages; in the first phase of the oral stage the infant derives oral-erotic satisfaction from sucking the breast or the bottle; in the second phase the infant derives oral-sadistic satisfaction from biting as well as sucking. Sucking and nibbling responses, initially associated with feeding, become associated with pleasure. Someone who becomes fixated at the oral stage continues to derive oral satisfaction from such activities as chewing gum, smoking, making sarcastic remarks ...

Organic psychosis Severe mental disturbance having an organic or pathological cause.

Orgasm In men, contraction of the whole sexual system, almost always followed by ejaculation and rhythmic throbbing of the penis. In women, involuntary rhythmic contractions of the outer third of the vagina, sometimes accompanied by contraction and movement of the uterus. In both sexes orgasm is the result of stimulation of erogenous zones, in men mainly the penis, in women mainly the clitoris but also the vagina, breasts and other parts of the body. However, a few women, and far fewer men, can think themselves to orgasm – as is often said, the most important sex organ is not between the legs but between the ears!

Fantasy

Female orgasm is strongly influenced by cultural expectations. Anthropologist Margaret Mead has suggested that the human female's capacity for orgasm should be viewed as "a *potentiality* that may or may not be developed by a given culture". Kinsey and others found that coital techniques had relatively little to do with whether a woman experiences orgasm. Masters and Johnson showed that simultaneous orgasm (when both partners 'come' together) is rare and not necessary for full sexual enjoyment; it is not, as is sometimes thought, a mark of superior sexual functioning.

Probably the majority of Western women do not regularly

O

Masturbation

Love

experience orgasm during intercourse, but the majority (according to the 1976 Hite Report) know very well how to have orgasms when they stimulate themselves. Among Polynesian peoples virtually all women experience orgasm. Interestingly they have few 'hang ups' about romantic love; sex is savoured as a full, physical experience not as an expression of mystical union or lifelong devotion.

Osgood, Charles Charles Egerton Osgood is unusual among prominent psychologists of his generation – he was born in 1916, in Somerville, Massachusetts – in that from the outset his discipline has been psychology. He is now professor of psychology at the University of Illinois.

Osgood's early research was in the field of visual perception but later he became known for inventing the technique known as the *semantic differential*. Using the statistical technique known as factor analysis, he and his associates isolated three basic factors or dimensions which can be used to measure the meanings people attach to specific words. These three dimensions are *evaluation, potency* and *activity*. Suppose you are presented with the word 'mother' and asked to rate it on a series of scales from 1 to 7 for each dimension. The opposites on the evaluation dimension scales might be good/bad, beautiful/ugly; on the potency scales they may be weak/strong or big/small; on the activity scales slow/fast or active/passive. You might rate 'mother' as 2 on the good/bad scale, 2 on the beautiful/ugly scale, 3 on the weak/strong scale, and so on. A profile can then be drawn up which reflects the overall meaning you attach to the word or concept 'mother'. Osgood even suggested compiling a dictionary of typical ratings to help authors and writers choose words with the exact shade of meaning for their purpose!

Charles Osgood, b. 1916

Altered state of consciousness

Parapsychology

Out-of-body experience Question: what is an OOBE? Answer: an out-of-body experience, a special state of consciousness experienced in dreams or illness in which a person has the sensation of floating above and looking down on their body. Classing such experiences as hallucinations or as body image distortions does little to explain them. Mediums claim to be able to travel non-corporeally outside their body, but this is disputed even by parapsychologists.

172

Pain *Christopher Macy, Frank Falkner*

Rapid technological advances in psychosomatics and psycho-physiology have made it possible to examine in great detail the links between the chemistry of the brain and the body's reaction to pain. But what most interests psychologists is not the physical side of pain but the way in which it is interpreted and experienced.

It seems possible that all the time our bodies are registering something - perhaps we could call it subliminal pain - which in the normal course of events we do not feel or notice. The level at which these unconscious warning signals become consciously interpreted as pain or some other sensation varies widely from culture to culture and from individual to individual. In one experiment, levels of heat stimulation which Northern Europeans experienced as 'warm' produced pain in persons of Mediterranean origin. At a more dramatic level, well-documented reports from societies all over the world describe people in religious ecstasies or 'rites of passage' inflicting serious wounds on themselves without apparent feelings of pain.

Shutting out and letting in To explain these phenomena Robert Melzack and Patrick Wall produced their 'gate' control theory of pain. They suggest that there is a nervous mechanism which opens or closes a 'gate' controlling how much input from pain receptors reaches the brain. The operation of this gate can be affected by psychological processes. Anxiety can increase pain, and a person's attitudes to events can determine whether or not they feel pain.

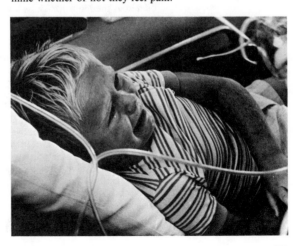

Few defences against pain except the comfort and reassurances of adults

If pain is anticipated, anxiety levels rise and the experience of pain increases. However, it is not the anticipation of pain which itself leads to pain. If it were, the most effective way of avoiding pain would be to deny that it exists. The real culprits are fear and ignorance. It has been clearly established for example that when a patient has some knowledge of a surgical operation and its aftermath, when he is told roughly how much pain and what kind of pain he can anticipate, then the experience of pain and the stress he suffers is also reduced.

A number of experiments have investigated the effect of psychoprophylactic techniques (psychological techniques for preventing pain, PPM for short) used in childbirth and other kinds of pain. The news is, they work. Two PPM techniques which have been investigated to compare their effectiveness are general relaxation and 'cognitive rehearsal' (carefully going over something in your mind before it happens). Both techniques appear to increase pain tolerance, although relaxation is generally more effective.

Paranoia   A psychiatric term used to describe the condition in which a person persistently has delusions that he or she is being persecuted. These delusions tend to be systematic and occasionally accompanied by hallucinations. From the point of view of the person concerned these delusions may be perfectly consistent and justified. The word paranoid is often misapplied in common parlance; what it usually describes is any bizarre or unsystematic behaviour arising from feelings of persecution rather than the clinical condition itself.

Schizophrenia

Parapsychology   *Hans Eysenck*

Parapsychology (lit. 'beyond psychology') deals with certain phenomena for which no natural science explanation can be offered at the moment. These phenomena fall into two main categories: cognitive and physical. Clairvoyance, telepathy, precognition and prophesy are all cognitive; they refer to a person's supposed ability to acquire knowledge of facts, of other people's thoughts, or of future events, without using ordinary sensory channels. Extrasensory perception (ESP) is the term most often used to label such phenomena. Other parapsychological phenomena may be physical in character; the fall of dice or the dealing of cards are thought to be influenced by a person's 'willing' them to fall or be dealt in a certain way; or objects are moved, often in a violent fashion, by 'poltergeists'. These and other physical phenomena come under the heading of psychokinesis (PK). Lately the general and very convenient term *psi* has become established to denote all kinds of parapsychological phenomena.

Both believers and non-believers in *psi* base their arguments on what they consider to be the scientific evidence, on their personal experiences, or on some larger system of attitudes and values into which ESP and PK do or do not fit. When such extreme and flatly contradictory views are widely held, one can be fairly certain of two things: that the evidence is not conclusive either way, and that confident conclusions are unlikely to be supported by a survey of all the known facts.

Investigating ESP Although ESP seems to be not one but several phenomena, the distinctions between these phenomena are difficult to maintain experimentally – in any actual investigation they tend to blend into each other. Clairvoyance is, allegedly, the perception of objects and events by paranormal means, telepathy the perception of the thoughts and mental states of another person by paranormal means, and precognition the perception of future events, including acts, thoughts, and emotions.

Arranging experimental conditions so that proof for or against ESP can be obtained is difficult. The best known and most foolproof procedures in this respect were those elaborated by the late J. B. Rhine, an American biologist, and his many collaborators and students. Much of this work was done with Zener cards. These cards bear one of five symbols (cross, star, circle, wave, rectangle), and there are 25 in a pack. The experimenter may shuffle a pack and put it on the table, hidden from the subject, and then ask the subject to guess the order of the cards (clairvoyance); alternatively the experimenter may look at each card in turn and ask the subject to guess which card he is looking at (telepathy, or possibly a mixture of telepathy and clairvoyance). There are many ways of varying this procedure, and millions upon millions of guesses or calls have been made in many different countries, and by many different people. The advantage of this procedure is twofold: first, a perfectly foolproof experimental design can be formulated that excludes completely the possibility of sensory knowledge of the cards and which is repeatable by other experimenters; second, the probability of any particular score (number of correct matchings of cards and calls) can be calculated and evaluated according to standard statistical formulae.

There have been a number of Zener card studies in which the probability of achieving the reported match rate by guesswork alone is so small that it can be ruled out. Typically these studies have either been ones in which isolated individuals have scored so highly that coincidence has been ruled out, or ones in which groups of individuals have been tested and no-one has done much better than chance, but in which on balance there has been a slightly higher match rate than chance. The most likely value in calling through a pack is 5.0; this represents complete chance. If a talented person consistently scores around 15, he only has to call through three or four packs to make chance an unlikely explanation of his performance. If 100 people are tested and each person averages 5.5 correct calls, this means little in terms of each person, but the excess over the chance value of 5.0 is most unlikely, and most interesting. Occasionally subjects persistently 'recognise' not the card presented but the one to be presented after it; this may be evidence of precognition. Sometimes believers in ESP ('sheep') score positively, and disbelievers ('goats') negatively; when the scores are averaged they do not depart from chance, but when they are separated according to the subjects' prior belief or disbelief in the existence of ESP, one finds that sheep score significantly higher than chance and goats lower.

There has been much argument about the design of experimental methods for investigating ESP and about the statistical treatment of the data. While early experiments can be criticised, it would be difficult to fault either the experimental design or the statistical treatment of studies done in the last 20 years. The former has been investigated by the American Psychological Society, the latter by the American Statistical Society, and neither body made any adverse criticisms. The possibility of cheating must of course be considered, but it is unlikely that a large number of academics would all cheat.

New research methods Recent work on *psi* has departed rather drastically from reliance on card sorting. Several very innovative methods have been introduced, one of which uses the random emission of particles from radioactive substances and requires the subject to predict which of several equally likely 'gates' a particle will enter. Some subjects appear to be capable of either indicating or avoiding the correct 'gate', a result which, if verified, would be of importance for physics, as the emission of particles in this way is considered impossible to predict on physical grounds. Other investigators have used shielded cages in order to test the hypothesis that electromagnetic fields are involved; hypnosis has also been used; in other experiments the subject is required to draw or recognise pictures or designs seen or drawn by the experimenter, who is a considerable distance away. Other experiments have been concerned with the personality of successful and unsuccessful *psi* subjects; there is good evidence that extraverts are more successful than introverts, and also more likely to be 'sheep' than 'goats'.

An evaluation of the total literature suggests thaat we are dealing here with some real but inexplicable phenomena but no foolproof and repeatable method of demonstrating ESP or PK has yet been devised that would satisfy all critics.

Pathology The scientific study of diseases. A psychological disorder may or may not have a pathological explanation; senile dementia apparently does, paranoia apparently doesn't. The implication behind the word *pathological*, as used in lay terms like pathological liar, is that the person 'can't help it', which is seldom the case.

Ivan Pavlov, 1849–1936

Pavlov, Ivan The pioneering research of Russian physiologist Ivan Pavlov into 'learned responses' exerted a profound influence on psychological theories of learning and behaviour.

During the experiments on digestion which earned him a Nobel Prize in 1904 Pavlov observed that the dogs he was using sometimes salivated in *anticipation* of receiving food. He called these 'psychic' secretions to distinguish them from the responses of the digestive organs once food is actually in the mouth. Intrigued by this phenomenon, he began systematically to investigate the process of *learned, or conditioned, responses.*

Pavlov summarised his experimental findings in the form of five 'laws' which together constitute what became known as *classical conditioning* theory. The *law of acquisition* describes the process by which a conditioned response is acquired. Pavlov found that if he paired an arbitrary stimulus (the sound of a bell or buzzer) with an unconditioned stimulus (offering meat powder for example), the result was the unconditioned response of salivation. But after repeated pairings, salivation could be produced by the bell or buzzer alone; in other words salivation had become a conditioned response. The *law of experimental extinction* refers to the fact that a conditioned response like salivating to a buzzer weakens and eventually disappears altogether if the unconditioned stimulus (in this case food) is removed. The *law of generalisation* states that once an arbitrary stimulus is regularly responded to, a similar stimulus will also produce the response: if one substitutes a low tone signal for a buzzer, for example, the conditioned response will be the same. The *law of selective conditioning*, on the other hand, allows for the fact that an animal has the ability to distinguish between two similar stimuli. Pavlov found that if two tones of different pitch were established as arbitrary stimuli, and only one of them was reinforced by presenting food, response to the lesser-used one faded and eventually ceased. The *law of higher-order conditioning* introduces the notion that a secondary reinforcer may be adequate to produce a conditioned response. Pavlov proved the point by pairing an initial stimulus, a bell, with a secondary stimulus, a flashing light. After a few trials the light alone produced the conditioned response.

More surprise and embarrassment than envy

Breast envy

Penis envy According to Freud the sense of deprivation suffered by girls when they discover they don't possess a penis. Psychoanalysts regard penis envy as a normal part of early psychosexual development, but the concept is by no means accepted by or acceptable to all psychologists. Along with many other sexual assumptions it has become a target for Feminist criticisms. No one, for example, has seriously suggested that boys experience the functional equivalent of penis envy, i.e. vagina or womb envy, rather than breast envy.

Percentile A statistic mainly used to indicate performance in attainment or intelligence tests. If your test score is in the 80th percentile, only 20 per cent of the other people tested scored higher than you; or to look at it the other way round, you did better than 80 per cent of the others in your group.

Perception

Perception is a psychological function which enables us to receive and process information about our environment. It is not the same as *sensation*, which refers to the simple registration of stimuli by our sense organs (eyes, ears, nose). Perception is a higher level process by which our brain makes sense of our sensations as well as receiving them.

The correspondence between objective reality, the world 'out there', and our perception of it, is by no means a direct and simple one. This is because perception is not a passive process. It is active and constructive. What we actually see, hear, smell or feel depends not only on external stimuli but on our past experiences, our personality and our current needs. All these factors influence the picture 'seen' by the inner eye.

Perceptual constancy

Visual illusions and *perceptual constancy* provide the clearest examples of 'non-veridical' (objectively inaccurate) perception. The famous Müller-Lyer effect, in which the lengths of two objectively identical lines appear unequal because of the way the arrowheads are drawn, is an illusion experienced by virtually all members of Western civilised society. Yet there is no law of human nature, nor anything in the structure of the brain or the eye, which requires that this illusion be experienced. Indeed members of certain more primitive cultures have been shown not to experience it. Another example of how cultural background can influence perception comes from the study of language. Apparently our ability to recognise different shades of colour may depend on the number of words we have in our vocabulary to describe them. English-speakers appear able to discriminate rather better between certain close shades of blue and green than other language groups which have only one word to describe the two colours.

Eye

Ear

The fluctuating state of our needs and drives can affect the readiness with which we attend to particular stimuli. A hungry tramp will more readily detect the delicious aroma of baking bread than a businessman who has just had lunch. Yet the effect of our needs on our *percepts* may be more pervasive than is generally realised. In one study for example it was found that childrens' estimates of the size of different coins was related to their economic backgrounds; children from poorer homes generally gave overestimates.

Hallucination

Hallucinations are perhaps the most extreme examples of psychological states affecting perception. Hallucinatory experiences may be artificially induced by drugs, but in certain psychiatric illnesses, notably schizophrenia, they may occur spontaneously. Clinicians often maintain that the contents of a patient's hallucinations betray much about fears and conflicts which are normally unconscious.

Perceptual defence is another phenomenon which illustrates how much our perceptual systems are coloured by unconscious feelings. It appears that the meaning we attach to a word can affect its *recognition threshold*, the speed with which we recognise it when it is displayed briefly on a screen. Emotionally charged words often have different recognition thresholds from ones with neutral connotations. In one study the word 'cancer' was shown to have a surprisingly high threshold (hard to recognise) for most subjects. The paradox of this effect is that in order to regulate their own threshold for identifying the word 'cancer' the subjects must already have been responding to it at some level, i.e. unconsciously. Sometimes however a contrary effect is found; emotionally loaded words are more quickly identified than neutral ones. 'Repressors' are people who generally put up perceptual defences (raise their recognition thresholds) against anxiety-provoking thoughts or events, while 'sensitisers' are people who do the opposite. In other words, differences in personality affect our perceptual processes.

Quirks of perception

Faces or candlestick? Which is figure and which is ground?

Necker cube: creating three dimensions from two, but which face is nearest?

Müller-Lyer illusion: which line is longer?

These squares stimulate the retina in such a way that grey spots appear to dance about in the crossroads between them.

The mysterious three-bar figure: only possible in two dimensions

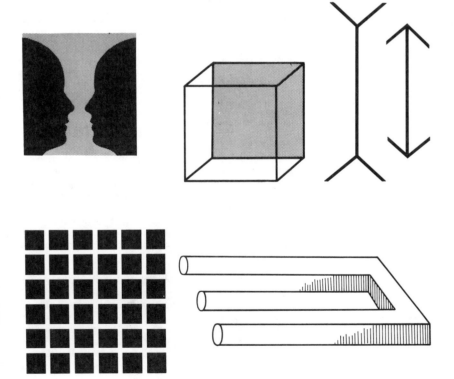

Ambiguous figures

A number of psychologists have argued that it should be possible to assess an individual's personality by looking at the way he or she perceives *ambiguous figures*, objects whose objective reality is indeterminate, offering scope for imaginative interpretation. The Rorschach inkblot test is a classic example. The testee's description of each inkblot is believed to reveal important aspects of his or her personality. Thus someone who gives a very detailed and longwinded account of one tiny fraction of a total design might be considered obsessional. The Rorschach is one of a number of *projective tests*, so-called because testees are believed to project their own beliefs and feelings onto stimuli which are ambiguous. Though projective tests use perception to investigate other psychological processes, their reliability and diagnostic validity have been shown to be poor.

Projective tests

Perception therefore is more than simple information reception. We create our percepts actively so that our image of the outside world reflects not only objective reality but our knowledge, thoughts and feelings as well. Although most of the examples given above involve the visual system, similar principles apply in other sensory modalities.

Perceptual constancy We perceive objects as themselves even if we see them from different angles and in different colours; a car is still a car whether we are behind it, overtaking it, or looking down on city traffic from a high building. In other words we impose *shape constancy* and *size constancy* on what we see. Try holding a pencil 12 in away from you and then at arm's length; at arm's length the size of the retinal image is reduced by a half; but the pencil does not look noticeably smaller.

To impose these constancies on raw sensations the brain makes use of a wealth of stored experience. We are also very fast at learning to impose consistency on our sensations. One psychologist tried wearing distorting spectacles for a few days; these turned his perception of the world upside down and changed everything from right to left. Within a very short time his brain was adapting to these novel sensations, and he began to see 'normally' again, even to the extent of being able to ride his bicycle safely down the high street! Interestingly, it took him much longer to adapt back to interpreting non-inverted retinal images.

Perceptual set Your perceptual set determines the level of detail you impose on things in order to maintain perceptual constancy. Most of the time whole objects, or groups of events, or patterns of stimuli, are what we see and make sense of. But it is possible to change the level of detail at which we make sense of the world, to change perceptual set. Some jobs (winetaster, quality control inspector, proofreader) depend on unusually detailed perceptual sets. Changing perceptual

Functional fixedness

set can also help in problem-solving. Camouflage, used for military purposes, exploits the perceptual set of enemy observers – the tanks cannot be seen for the bushes!

Persona A Greek word meaning 'mask', denoting the part of our personality we habitually show to others and which often conceals our true thoughts and feelings. In Jungian psychology the persona is that part of the psyche which bows to social convention.

Personal construct theory A theory of personality developed by American psychologist George Kelly. All of us develop personal constructs, habitual ways of construing the world, which are based not on facts but on hypotheses. Our constructs help us to categorise and make sense of our lives, and are based on past experience. No two people put the same construction on the same event: an election victory might be construed by some as 'a backlash against weak leadership', by others as 'wheeling and dealing behind the scenes' or 'victory for the moderate majority'. Kelly applied his theory in a new therapy technique, 'fixed role' therapy, in which clients are asked to play a fixed role for a specific period (someone whose main problem is shyness might be asked to be assertive for two or three days). The therapist's task is to convince the client that his habitual role is self-imposed and exchangeable for a more satisfying one. Methods of analysing personal constructs, which Kelly thought of as constituting personal 'psychological space', have proved useful with many patient groups, including smokers, sexual offenders and schizophrenics.

Personality *Hans Eysenck*

Essentially personality consists of those permanent or semi-permanent modes of behaviour which characterise an individual and make him or her different from other people. These individual differences are called 'traits' – sociability, persistence, impulsiveness, suggestibility, pride and humility are all traits. Much work has gone into measuring a wide range of traits, using ratings, self-rating questionnaires, observation and experiment.

Eysenck Personality Inventory

Methods of measurement Clearly it is not difficult to rate someone else, particularly someone one knows well, for such traits as sociability, persistence, impulsiveness, etc. Usually more than one rater is used, and the extent to which they agree is taken to be a measure of the reliability of their findings, high agreement signifying high reliability. Raters find some traits much easier to rate than others, probably because some are more observable than others; sociability is easy to rate, anxiety much less so.

Cattell 16 PF

Self-rating, usually by means of specially designed questionnaires, is something most people find fairly easy. Self-ratings tend to agree with other objective indices under ordinary experimental conditions, but they can be faked when there is the motivation to do so, as in the case of job or university interviews. Lie scales, designed to find out the less than truthful, only partly sidestep the difficulty.

'Miniature life situations' and other types of objective test, including observational ones, are clearly more reliable. But they are also more time-consuming and more expensive. A miniature life situation is a replica of a real life situation in which subjects are likely to display the trait the experimenter is interested in. Observation of the trait in question can be made more objective by precisely defining the actions to be classed as aggressive, compassionate, sociable, and so on. Time-sampling, which ensures that equal attention is paid to each subject in a complex interaction, is a frequently used method of observation. Observation of aggressive play among children in a school playground would clearly be most objective if each child was watched for exactly one minute on a random or sequential basis.

Types and traits Certain personality traits usually correlate with others. We know for example that people who are sociable are often impulsive, venturesome, physically active and talkative as well. These relationships between traits give rise to the higher-order concept of personality 'types'. The word 'type' in connection with personality originated with the Ancient Greeks; they believed there were four personality types (melancholic, phlegmatic, sanguinic, and choleric). We now think of people as occupying certain fairly constant positions along 'continua' or infinitely graded progressions of traits belonging to the same type-dimension. One such type-dimension is extraversion/introversion, with extreme extraverts characterised by sociability, impulsiveness, venturesomeness, physical activity and talkativeness; introverts are the exact opposite. Another dimension, quite unrelated, is that of emotionality/neuroticism-stability. The number of major type-dimensions is quite small, compared to the very large number of traits.

Biological bases? Personality traits and types are strongly determined by genetic factors. This has been shown many times by studying identical twins separated early in life, comparing identical and fraternal twins, and studying adopted children and family resemblances. The relative importance of heredity and environment is, in my view, very approximately two parts heredity to one part environment. Follow-up studies of infants in adulthood certainly verify the fact that adult personality is clearly foreshadowed at a very tender age. There may indeed be permanent or semi-permanent structures of personality.

The strong influence of genetic factors on personality suggests that personality may have a biological basis. Habitual differences in the level of activity in the cortex of the brain seem to be largely responsible for the patterns of behaviour we

A sharing situation. A major debate in social psychology today is whether personality or situation is the stronger influence on behaviour.

Genetic factors

Brain

182

label as extravert and introvert. Differences in emotionality-stability seem to be related to activity of the limbic system of the brain. Hormones too are intimately linked with personality, but in ways too complex to describe here.

Who does what Certain personality types and certain types of social behaviour go together in ways clearly predicted by various physiological and psychological theories. For example, extraverts have been found to differ from introverts in their sexual behaviour: they have intercourse earlier, in more different positions and with more partners; they also divorce more frequently, indulge more frequently in unusual practices, and have more pre-marital and extra-marital affairs. Emotionally unstable people experience more sexual problems that stable people, and are generally less happy in their marriages. Anti-social behaviour is more frequent in extraverts, neurotic behaviour more frequent in introverts; both types of conduct are more frequent in emotionally unstable people. Introverts do much better than extraverts in secondary school and at university, and emotionally unstable people are strongly handicapped in higher education.

Intelligence Intelligence is an area of personality usually treated apart from other aspects of personality, although of course it interacts closely with the personality traits and types considered here. A very intelligent extravert, for example, is very different from a very dull extravert.

Personality disorder A term used by psychiatrists to describe behaviour which does not neatly fit any of the usual pigeon-holes for mental illness, for example extreme callousness, self-centredness, frequent cheating, lying or stealing and a whole 'rag bag' of other unattractive behaviours; use of the term is strongly influenced by social and ideological assumptions about what is normal.

Personality inventory Personality inventories have been used in various forms since R. S. Woodworth developed the Personal Data Sheet to save time in processing military recruits during World War I. Usually personality inventories consist of a standardised printed sheet with a large number of questions or statements to which subjects answer Yes or No. Sets of questions are scored together to give a measure of different dimensions or traits of personality. Two personality inventories widely used today are the Cattell 16PF and the Eysenck Personality Inventory, which are cheap and easy to administer to large samples of people. Their value in clinical work is limited because they fail to take account of patients' individual circumstances.

Personal orientation inventory Really an inventory of mental health rather than mental illness, designed to show to what extent a person is self-actualising, or fulfilling his or her potential; consists of 150 pairs of statements, subjects saying which of each pair more truly reflects their attitudes.

Personal space We each have a kind of personal space around us into which only certain people are allowed. Only spouses, lovers, children and close family are permitted within eighteen inches – the intimate space. Friends we allow within between eighteen inches and four feet – the personal space. Most of our social relationships are conducted at a distance of between four and nine feet. At this distance we cannot touch or smell each other and cannot see the give-away details of appearance. Distances greater than this are regarded as public and completely impersonal. When obliged to crowd together in trains and public places our personal space is invaded and we studiously avoid any exchanges of social signals.

The use of space varies according to different cultures. Arabs and Latin Americans like to stand directly facing each other and closer than North Americans or Europeans. Black Americans prefer even more space between them. In parts of India, different castes traditionally kept a prescribed distance away from each other; the recommended distance between Brahmins (highest caste) and Nayadis (lowest caste) was 198 ft.

Non-verbal communication

Left: elbow length, the ideal distance for dealing on the Stock Exchange
Right: sorry we're full!

Personal unconscious In Jungian psychology that part of the unconscious which is a repository for forgotten or repressed personal experiences, as distinct from the collective unconscious, which consists of inherited racial memories.

Phallic stage The third stage of psychosexual development postulated by Freud, beginning around the age of 5, when the child begins to derive pleasure from handling and stimulating his or her genitals. At this stage boys direct their erotic feelings towards their mother, and girls towards their father, and for a brief period, the Oedipal period, feel hostility towards the same-sex parent. The Oedipal period ends when boys identify with their father and girls with their mother.

Phenotype A person's observable characteristics rather than those contained in their genes, which may not be expressed.

Phenylketonuria (PKU) A metabolic disorder characterised by a gross imbalance of acids in the body; if untreated, infants so affected grow up mentally retarded; the condition is thought to be hereditary.

Phobias *Charles Spielberger*

The term 'phobia' (from the Greek *phobos* meaning fear or dread) refers to intense fear reactions and avoidance behaviours provoked by objects or situations which are relatively harmless. When confronted with the thing he or she fears, the phobic individual experiences a sudden increase in state anxiety (see Anxiety) and takes elaborate avoiding action. Since this intense anxiety is a reaction to stimuli commonly perceived as fairly innocuous, phobias are clearly 'irrational' exaggerated responses.

How phobias develop In phobias the dread which becomes attached to a specific object or situation is the result of learning. For example, a small child who gets locked in a cupboard by a playmate and doesn't get found until hours later, is likely to experience intense fear. Terrifying memories of the experience are likely to flood back when encountering cues associated with small enclosed places. Thus, cupboards, elevators, and even cars, may subsequently trigger strong state anxiety reactions and avoidance behaviour.

Anxiety

Phobias are common in childhood, especially between the ages of four and seven. The prospect of starting school can be a source of intense fear, which can develop into a 'school phobia', especially in children who are extremely insecure and dependent on their mothers. Two symptoms of school phobia might be waking up in the morning complaining of pain and nausea, and refusing to remain at school without the constant presence of the mother. Primarily these are reactions related to a fear of leaving familiar surroundings, but they may also become attached to teachers, other children, the school building, or almost any aspect of school life.

Reinforcement

Phobias persist mainly because phobics invest such a lot of effort in avoiding the objects or situations they fear. By repeatedly avoiding the situation which originally caused the fear, they never discover that the situation is relatively harmless. Moreover, each time the phobic object is successfully avoided, anxiety is reduced, thus rewarding and reinforcing their determination to avoid the feared situation again the next time it occurs.

Things that crawl... Many adults have irrational fears of objects or situations they are unlikely to meet or be harmed by. In one study, for example, a fear of snakes was admitted by nearly half the interviewees and nearly a third reported being afraid of high places. Phobic reactions seem to occur almost twice as often in women as in men, but there appears to be no relationship between phobias and religion, race, intelligence or socio-economic status.

185

Specific phobias are identified by attaching a Greek prefix to the word 'phobia', as in claustrophobia (fear of closed or constricted spaces), haematophobia (fear of the sight of blood) and xenophobia (fear of strangers). Other common phobias are: acrophobia (fear of high places), agoraphobia (crowded public places), algophobia (pain), astraphobia (thunder and lightning), hydrophobia (water), mysophobia (dirt, contamination), necrophobia (dead bodies), nyctophobia (darkness, night), pathophobia (disease, suffering), phonophobia (speaking aloud), photophobia (strong light), sitophobia (eating), thanatophobia (death), toxophobia (being poisoned), zoophobia (animals).

Psychoanalysis

Psychoanalysts suggest that phobias are produced by internal conflict, often in childhood, in which unacceptable sexual and aggressive impulses and the anticipation of severe punishment arouse intense anxiety. The phobia begins when this anxiety is projected outwards and attached to a particular object. By avoiding the object, the anxiety is reduced to a tolerable level.

Behaviour therapy

Behaviour therapy techniques such as desensitisation and implosion therapy have proved very effective in treating phobias.

Physiological arousal The tell-tale signs of physical excitement are increased blood pressure, faster heart rate and breathing, clammy skin and quicker brain waves (in β frequency band). At one time all these responses were thought to be autonomic, outside our voluntary control, but biofeedback and stress management techniques have shown that with practise, we can exercise control over them. Attempts to match distinct patterns of physiological arousal with specific emotions such as fear, anger, love, and so on, have been largely fruitless. More progress has been made studying the different speeds at which individuals become aroused. Hans Eysenck has suggested that introverts and extraverts differ in their habitual level of cortical arousal (activity in the brain cortex), introverts having high and extraverts low levels of cortical arousal, prompting the latter to seek stimulation and the former to avoid it.

Emotions

Piaget, Jean Jean Piaget, born in Neuchatel, Switzerland, in 1896, was and still is one of the world's most-quoted psychologists on matters of educational and child psychology. His ruling interest was the development of the human intellect especially in childhood and adolescence (his own two daughters and grandchildren must rank among the most studied children in history).

Piaget published his first scientific paper at the age of 10, and gained his PhD, for a dissertation on molluscs, at the age of 21. He then switched from zoology to psychology, became director of studies at the Institut J.-J. Rousseau in Geneva,

Jean Piaget, 1896–1980

and professor of child psychology at the University of Geneva and the Sorbonne in Paris. Piaget actively pursued his research, and a taxing schedule of writing, lecturing and consultancy, until his death in November 1980.

The two major concepts we owe to Piaget are *functional invariants* and *structures.* He theorised that certain modes of interacting with the environment are functionally invariant, that is universal, inherited and independent of age. We come into the world equipped to organise and absorb incoming information, and adapt our behaviour accordingly. But as we grow up the way in which we do this changes; we slot incoming data into a succession of subtly different structures or frameworks of thought.

Child psychology

Piaget identified four major stages of development, each characterised by several distinct structures of thought. During the first stage, the *sensorimotor period* (birth to age 2), the infant learns to co-ordinate his body reactions. Next comes the *pre-operational period* (age 2 to 6), when the child begins to think of himself as separate from the rest of the world; he also builds up mental pictures of objects, and learns how to think abstractly, how to manipulate these pictures or symbols rather than the objects themselves. Then comes the *concrete operational period* (age 6 to 11), when the child begins to perceive categories and patterns. In the course of the last stage, the *formal operations period* (age 11 to 15), the child/ adolescent becomes capable of forward planning, of making predictions and hypotheses and testing them.

At present Piaget's theories are under intense debate, many critics arguing that he failed to take account of the social world of the infant. Nevertheless Piaget's great virtue is that he drew attention to the positive role children themselves play in both their own development and that of their contemporaries.

Hormones

Pituitary The 'master gland' of the endocrine system, situated at the base of the brain and receiving instructions from the hypothalamus via a thin stalk known as the infundibulum. The anterior part of the pituitary secretes at least six different hormones, most of them trophic or concerned with activating other endocrine glands. The posterior part secretes at least three other hormones, incuding vasopressin, which constricts blood vessels and sharpens the memory.

Placebo A substance or treatment of no known efficacy which has a beneficial effect because the recipient believes it to be efficacious. An innocuous pill and a hefty doctor's bill can sometimes work wonders! Investigating the *placebo effect* New York psychiatrist Samuel W. Perry found that placebos not only make patients feel better, but in some cases actually promote healing. Far from being occult, however, placebo responses are thought to have a basis in the chemistry of the brain. The brain secretes powerful natural analgesics (pain killers) called endorphins, particularly in the area associated with strong emotion. Could these be part of the explanation of the placebo effect?

Hedonism

Pleasure principle In psychoanalysis the principle on which the impulses and instincts of the Id operate, demanding immediate gratification; pleasure is the final aim, and therefore the motivation, of the individual. The reality principle on which the Ego operates is sometimes contrasted with the pleasure principle, but as Freud observed even reality is subservient to pleasure in that the Ego is capable of vetoing immediate pleasure in the expectation of greater pleasure to come.

Lying

Polygraph A multi-recording device for measuring physiological arousal, incorporating all the necessary bioelectronic equipment for measuring heart rate (electrocardiograph), brain waves (electroencephalograph), changes in the electrical conductivity of the skin (galvanic skin resistor), electrical activity in muscles (electromyograph) and blood volume in any part of the body (plethysmograph). Thanks to microprocessor technology the recording devices placed on the body are now extremely small. Perhaps the best known form of polygraph is the 'lie detector', which picks up the minute changes in physiological activity caused by the anxiety associated with lying.

Stereotype

Prejudice A combination of beliefs or attitudes based on incomplete or inaccurate information; a set of prejudices, when generalised to a group (women, blacks, policemen), constitutes a stereotype. Prejudices and stereotypes blind us to individual qualities and differences. Often prejudices develop not from firsthand experience but from hearsay; they also thrive on hostility between groups but wilt where there is cooperation. Strong ideological commitment is often accompanied by prejudice.

Pre-operational stage The second of the four major developmental stages proposed by Piaget. Between the age of two and six children gradually realise that they are separate from the surrounding world. This is because they have arrived at the stage of imagining objects and events, and manipulating them in their head. At the beginning of this stage, at about the age of two, a child's understanding of what is going on is marked by glaring contradictions. The toddler will say, for example, that her elder sister doesn't have a sister, or that mummy is mummy, not a lady. The child cannot, in other words, imagine situations from several angles at once. By the end of the pre-operational stage, however, some ability to do this becomes apparent. A seven- or eight-year-old (already well into the concrete operational stage) will be able to reshape a ball of plasticine into a snake, and then into a horse, and back into a ball again, and will take it for granted that the same amount of plasticine is there, but a pre-operational child thinks that the amount of plasticine depends on the shape made.

Prevalence The frequency with which a characteristic or event occurs among a given number of people. For example, the prevalence of fraternal (non-identical) twins is 1 birth in 70. Birth rate and death rate are statistics of prevalence, expressed as so many births or deaths per thousand of the population. Incidence, on the other hand, is a statistic of frequency in a given period of time.

Primal therapy A new form of therapy pioneered by Arthur Janoy and based on the idea that maladaptive behaviour is the result of bottling up the pains and tensions caused by early-life or 'primal' frustrations. The rationale of primal therapy is that re-experiencing these frustrations unbottles them, enabling the client to express and handle them more effectively. As yet there is little independent evidence that primal therapy works.

Forgetting

Proactive interference Loss of efficiency in learning a second task immediately after learning the first, most marked when the tasks are similar. The opposite phenomenon is called *retroactive interference*.

Projection In Freudian psychology a defence mechanism by which unacceptable impulses and feelings are attributed to an external object or to another person. For example, someone who persistently criticises others for being rude, stubborn or stingy might be getting rid of his anxiety about being rude, stubborn and stingy himself. We project our own fear of death and illness onto those who are terminally ill by avoiding frank discussion with them. We project our own likes and dislikes onto the gifts we give others ...

Ambiguous figures

Projective tests Two of the best known projective tests are the Thematic Apperception Test, designed by Henry Murray, and the Rorschach Inkblot Test, both of which provide ambiguous, neutral pictures around which subjects imagine a story or say what they are reminded of. The assumption is that aspects of the personality not normally accessible project themselves onto unstructured stimuli. Test conditions, materials and interpretation are standardised, nevertheless many clinical psychologists dismiss projective testing as fairly unhelpful in diagnosing personality disturbances.

Psyche From the Greek, meaning 'breath', 'soul', 'mind'; Jung's term for the whole personality, including all psychological states and processes whether conscious or unconscious.

Psychedelic drugs Literally 'mind-clearing' drugs (see Hallucinogens).

Mental illness

Psychiatry The treatment of mental disorders on the premiss that they have a pathological basis. A psychiatrist has a medical degree and can prescribe drugs – a psychologist doesn't and can't. Whereas a psychiatrist is strictly concerned with mental ill-health, a psychologist is concerned with *all* mental functions (normal and abnormal, healthy and unhealthy).

Psychoanalysis *Gerald C. Davison*

Freud

There can be no question about the enduring importance and influence of the writings of Sigmund Freud on the thinking and methods of mental health professionals today, indeed on the art, drama and folklore of modern Western civilisation. Many changes have taken place in psychoanalysis over the past few decades, but there are certain features shared by all types of psychoanalytic treatment.

The central assumption of psychoanalysis is that much human functioning is to be explained by the operation of forces buried in our unconscious selves. A slip of the tongue, being late for an appointment – these and other apparent trivialities have their causes, asserted Freud, in pressure from the Id to express itself in hostile or sexual ways. Classical psychoanalytic theory supposes that people shut away conflicts in their lives, especially childhood conflicts, because they are unbearably painful. Conflicts arise because the primarily sexual and aggressive instincts of the Id are incompatible with the reality-oriented, plan-making, rather serious activities of the Ego. Problems of anxiety and depression in adulthood are assumed to be traceable to such conflicts which lie buried and unresolved in the psyche. Psychoanalytic treatment aims to help a person to uncover these deep-frozen childhood dilemmas and examine them in light of adult reality.

Let us take as an example a young woman who says she is terrified of lifts. Through careful questioning within an analytic framework, her therapist might come to believe that her fears are really centred on how she might behave towards members of the opposite sex if she was trapped in a lift with them. Her lift phobia, then, would be symbolic of repressed fear of her own sexual impulses, a conflict she is totally unaware of. So how do analysts help people to gain insight into problems locked out of reach of their consciousness, sometimes for many years?

The techniques of psychoanalysis Analysts have a number of techniques which they use to bring repressed conflicts into the light of day, the theory being that once conflicts have been exposed they can be resolved. One of these techniques is *free association*, in which the patient is asked to give free rein to his thoughts and feelings as he talks, to say whatever comes into his mind. First, of course, he makes himself comfortable on the analyst's couch or easy-chair. Considerable practice and trust in the analyst are required before a patient can free associate revealingly. According to analytic theory, blocks or defences can gradually be bypassed through free association, especially if the analyst applies other psychoanalytic techniques as well, such as dream analysis and analysis of a person's defences.

Dreaming

Dream analysis rests on the assumption that, during sleep, the watchdog functions of the Ego and Superego are relaxed, allowing previously repressed material to emerge into consciousness. Most of the material which emerges in the dream state is threatening and heavily camouflaged in symbols. For example, the woman who was phobic about lifts might also report dreaming about being chased by men carrying spears; putting this information together with material gleaned from other sources, the analyst might infer that she was excessively afraid of sexual advances, equating spears with penises.

Defence mechanism

Another technique used in analytic sessions is analysis of a person's *defences*. Defences are mechanisms of the Ego which we unconsciously use to protect ourselves from anxiety. Take, for example, a client who changes the subject, steering the conversation in another direction, whenever the therapist refers to his father. If it is pointed out to him that he is avoiding painful emotional or 'affect-laden' memories, he may initially deny that he is doing so. To the therapist this might suggest that he is being defensive. However, the skilful analyst is very cautious about making such interpretations, and only does so in the context of other information obtained over many sessions with the client.

A final concept which deserves discussion is *transference*. Analysts attach special significance to the dependent love-hate relationship which often develops between themselves and their clients. Freud believed that the way in which his clients acted and felt towards him had nothing to do with him as an individual; rather they seemed to look on him as a representative of one or both of their parents. Unless a client is encouraged to act out infantile wishes and fears in the presence of an analyst, much of the point of an analytic session is lost. Transference provided a unique opportunity for both client and analyst to examine conflicts long hidden by the client's adult Ego.

Classical psychoanalysis, as described above, is an arduous and time-consuming enterprise, involving many sessions each week, possibly continuing for several years. Modifications in analytic theory, and perhaps economic realities too, have spawned variants that take less time and concentrate more on helping the client achieve control over the present rather than digging into the past for presumed causes. *Ego analysis*, as this development is often termed, still shares with Freudian analysis an abiding belief that human suffering arises from the repression of conflict, and that greater awareness of true motives can improve the way we function.

Psychokinesis (PK) As demonstrated by Uri Geller and 'physical' mediums, the apparent power to influence physical objects by sheer strength of will. The best known producer of PK effects was the nineteenth-century Scottish medium D. D. Home: in his presence people and objects flew and spirits 'rapped', and so on, and in 30 years of mediumship he was never once accused of fraud; he generally worked under good lighting conditions, often in other people's homes, and never received payment for his seances.

Psycholinguistics A relatively new branch of science and psychology concerned with the development and structure of language. How, for example, it is possible for human beings to learn so many different words, create new words for new situations, and manipulate them to produce the infinite variety of meaningful sentences we use in everyday conversations? The magnitude of this learning process is staggering – the number of possible word combinations in the English language is around 10^{20} (10 followed by nineteen zeros). Clearly learning each combination by simple conditioning would take far too long.

Language Learning

Noam Chomsky, the doyen of psycholinguistics, has suggested that humans have an innate capacity for grammatical construction, that there are 'deep structures' for language. If this is true, we do not have to learn all the possible combinations of words. Support for this theory comes from the fact that the grammatical structures we develop as children are not only quite different from the actual grammar we use in our respective languages as adults, but also remarkably similar throughout the world. In short, children appear to speak according to fairly universal grammatical rules of their own, and only later learn the formal rules of their parents' language. This theory has been strongly decried by many psychologists, in particular the behaviourists and B. F. Skinner on the grounds that it is 'mentalistic', in other words not amenable to direct or inferential measurement.

Psychopath, psychopathic personality Someone who is free of the more obvious symptoms of psychoticism but who is emotionally unstable to the point of being unable to learn from experience or form meaningful emotional relationships; a psychopath never learns the social and moral lessons which inhibit ordinary people from being impulsively violent and destructive. The majority of recidivists convicted of vandalism or assault can be classified as psychopaths. A predisposition to violence may be inherited, but environmentalists argue that psychopathic tendencies are aggravated by emotional deprivation and lax or inconsistent discipline within the family. Mental illness, alcoholism and criminality are usually present in the family background of most psychopaths.

Psychopharmacology The study of the psychological effect of drugs, chiefly of those which come into the antidepressant, sedative-hypnotic, anti-epileptic, antipsychotic, and hallucinogenic categories.

Psychophysiology The study of the biological basis of psychology, in particular the links between the central and autonomic nervous system and cognitive and emotional behaviour, the links between the sensory organs and sensory perceptions, and the effect of hormones on cognitive, emotional and sexual behaviour and orientation. Psychophysiologists use a battery of bio-electronic tools (electroencephalograph, electrocardiograph, electromyograph, galvanic skin resistor, plethysmograph, electrical stimulation of the brain), biomedical techniques (radio-immune assay), drugs and surgical procedures in their research. Experimental subjects are often animals.

The electroencephalograph: reaches parts which questionnaires cannot reach

Psychosexual development For Freud, the adult personality is the outcome of a five-stage process of sexual and emotional development spanning the period from birth to adolescence. Psychosexual development begins with the oral stage (infancy); then comes the anal stage (early childhood), the phallic stage (age 5 to 7), the latency stage (age 7 to puberty) and finally the genital stage (puberty onwards). Freud assumed that the conflicts created either by excessive gratification or excessive frustration of erotic impulses at each stage of development, especially during the first three, express themselves as adult neuroses and colour all adult relationships. Research has failed to confirm that Freud's psychosexual stages are universal or that adult personality characteristics closely or reliably reflect childhood sexual experiences. Nevertheless Freud's ideas have had an immense impact on the way children are reared in the West and on social work and psychiatric practice.

Schizophrenia
Paranoia
Depression

Psychosis A severe psychological disorder, characterised by loss of contact with reality; psychotic symptoms include complete social withdrawal, profound apathy, delusions, hallucinations and other sensory distortions, and wildly inappropriate speech, behaviour, thoughts and feelings. There are four major categories of psychosis: *organic psychoses* (due to brain damage through injury, poisoning or disease); *schizophrenia*; *paranoia*; and *manic-depressive (affective) psychosis*. There is much heated debate about the causes of non-organic psychoses, with explanations ranging from the genetic and biochemical at one extreme, to the environmental and frankly existential at the other. Antipsychotic drugs (phenothiazine derivatives and others) are useful in that they alleviate some of the symptoms of non-organic psychoses (without sedation) while other forms of therapy are tried.

Drugs and mental disorder

Voodoo, making contact with another reality. Existentially-minded psychiatrists believe that what society calls sanity is a form of estrangement from the inner self.

Diathesis-stress hypothesis

Psychosomatic In common parlance, any physical complaint (migraine, aches and pains, colds) which is caused or aggravated by mental stress. *Psychosomatics* is in fact the study of the correlations that exist between psychological phenomena and abnormal and pathological (diseased) body states. New psychophysiological and biomedical techniques have identified many such correlations but without pinpointing the mechanisms responsible.

Psychosurgery Any surgical procedure involving the cutting, removal or lesioning of brain tissue. Less radical treatments for mental illness are now preferred, and in any case legal constraints on the use of brain surgery are now more stringent. Nevertheless brain surgery is still carried out on a small scale. The three most common operations in the past have been prefrontal lobotomy (cutting certain fibres connecting the frontal lobes to other parts of the brain), amygdalotomy (lesioning the amygdala, the part of the limbic system assumed to be responsible for rage and aggression), and the split-brain operation (cutting the corpus callosum, the bridge of nerve tissue connecting the two cerebral hemispheres). Prefrontal lobotomy was used to alleviate obsession and mania, amygdalotomy to pacify violent criminals, and the split-brain operation to prevent epileptic convulsions. Needless to say all these procedures were tried on animals first, and all have at some time been the subject of public scandal, either because they were used in ways which grossly infringed the rights of the individual or because they had tragic side effects. More recently procedures have been developed for implanting electrodes in the brain to control persistent pain or forestall epileptic seizures.

Lobotomy

Split brain

Psychotherapy Literally 'mind treatment'; any treatment based on psychological principles designed to alleviate emotional distress, social difficulties or behavioural disorders. A psychotherapist can be a trained psychiatrist, psychoanalyst, psychologist or psychiatric social worker, and clients can attend therapy sessions individually or in groups. There are dozens of different forms of psychotherapy, but most can be grouped under one of the following headings: *psychoanalysis* and derivative therapies such as Transactional Analysis, all designed to achieve catharsis, the release of pent-up conflicts; *behaviour therapy*, in which problem behaviours are unlearned; and *humanistic therapy*, which includes client-centred therapy and Gestalt therapy, and has self-knowledge, self-acceptance and personal growth as its goal.

Quality Important in all relationships and experiences but not directly measurable. 'Quality of life', for example, is one of the *cris de guerre* of behavioural medicine, encounter groups and Gestalt.

Questionnaire Any list of questions or statements used to assess aptitudes, attitudes or personality traits; usually cheap and easy to administer and so widely used in research (to standardise sample groups) and in personnel selection. In clinical work questionnaires are usually combined with other diagnostic tests. Most questionnaires include several response sets which are separately scored so as to throw light on particular skills or attitudes. The drawback of self-rating questionnaires is that subjects sometimes try to 'fake good' or 'fake bad'; this is why most well designed questionnaires incorporate a 'lie scale'.

Quiescence The opposite of excitement. According to early German psychologist Wilhelm Wundt quiescence-excitement was one of the three dimensions of feeling.

Getting the best of both
worlds, quality and quantity

Threat
Anxiety

Rational-emotive therapy (RET) A psychotherapy developed by American psychologist Albert Ellis which seeks to alter the way people think about stressful events in their lives and so reduce anxiety. Between an event and its effect on the individual a process of appraisal or interpretation takes place; it is this middle link in the stress–appraisal–anxiety chain which rational emotive therapy seeks to change. Anxiety is not the direct result of stress, but of exaggerated, irrational or unrealistic appraisals of the threat the stress poses.

Rationalisation Finding a 'good reason' for doing or not doing something because one would rather not face up to the real reason – a very common defence mechanism. In a 'boy jilts girl' situation the girl might defend herself against the uncomfortable knowledge that she is boring or over-demanding by telling everyone that her boyfriend had some very weird habits and so it was she who broke off the relationship.

Reaction formation Developing tendencies that are the polar opposite of tendencies we dislike in ourselves, a rather subtle defence mechanism in that unacceptable feelings are first repressed and then externalised in a form which makes them unrecognisable to the conscious self. Many extreme forms of behaviour are the outcome of reaction formation: over-protective mothers may feel intense anger towards their children deep down; pacificism may disguise powerful aggressive drives.

Pleasure principle

Reality principle The principle which guides the conscious aims of the Ego; initially the pleasure-seeking aims of the Id rule our lives, but slowly, as we realise that wishing and acting are not the same thing, the pleasure principle is tempered by the reality principle. Appreciation of reality serves the final aim of pleasure, in that it is directed towards avoiding unpleasure and sometimes towards deferring immediate pleasure in anticipation of greater pleasure to come.

Nervous system

Receptors Special cells in the skin, sensory and other organs which respond to thermal, electrical, mechanical and chemical stimuli and so initiate nerve impulses in adjacent neurons. We have heat- and pressure-sensitive receptors all over our skin.

Psychopath

Recidivism Reverting to old, usually undesirable, behaviours after a period of therapy, medication or corrective detention; implies that treatment has failed to bring about a permanent change or cure.

Nervous system

Reflex An automatic unlearned response co-ordinated by the spinal chord rather than the brain; the knee-jerk reflex (get someone to tap you just below the knee and see what happens), drawing your hand away from a flame and jumping when you hear a sudden loud noise, are all reflex responses.

Regression Freud likened regression to a retreat to a safe psychological 'base camp' in the face of an advancing enemy (psychic conflict). In this sense, regression is a defence mechanism enabling the Ego to feel secure and in control. Regression to earlier behaviour patterns sometimes fuels creativity, intuition and imagination. *Age regression* is a specific technique in hypnosis: by reliving traumatic episodes under hypnosis problems can be dissolved more quickly.

Quick reflexes, but of the learned kind

Reinforcement Anything which increases the frequency of a particular behaviour or strengthens the link between a stimulus and a response – a key concept in operant conditioning. The man who most extensively explored the effects of various patterns of reinforcement, *schedules* or *contingencies of reinforcement* as he called them, was American psychologist B. F. Skinner. He found that reinforcement at intervals led to longer-lasting behaviours than continuous reinforcement. Reinforcement is often a synonym for reward; but reinforcement can be negative as well as positive.

Conditioning

Skinner

REM (rapid eye movement) sleep Dreaming sleep; most people dream about two hours a night on average. The eyes dart and roll about under the eyelids (presumably because the dreamer is 'looking' at dream events), blood pressure, pulse rate and breathing increase slightly, and brain-wave patterns increase in amplitude and frequency. Most people have their first REM period about an hour after falling asleep; this usually lasts for 5 to 10 minutes; later in the night REM

Dreaming

episodes are longer, up to 25 or 30 minutes. If wakened during REM episodes, people remember their dreams; dreams are rarely reported on waking from non-REM sleep.

Remission Improvement or recovery during the course of an illness, occurring spontaneously or as the result of treatment, the implication being that improvement or recovery may not be permanent.

Research design

Replication The acid test of experimental findings: can they be replicated (reproduced) by another team of researchers under the same experimental conditions? If findings cannot be replicated doubt is cast on the experimental design or on the probity of the original researcher. Replication is really a term borrowed from biology: DNA in the cell nucleus is said to replicate (double in quantity) prior to cell division.

Suppression

Repression The most powerful of all defence mechanisms; the Ego simply banishes anxiety-making feelings, thoughts and memories to the unconscious. Repression can be as trivial as forgetting a dental appointment or the name of the bully who used to push you around at school, or as major as being unable to recall events leading up to a dreadful accident. If repression were like locking a safe and throwing away the combination it would be highly effective and protective. But most repression is partial; cues distantly or closely related to repressed material may trip the lock causing free-floating anxiety, phobic reactions or massive anxiety attacks.

Research design Fundamentally a set of instructions developed by the principal of a research project and adhered to by research colleagues and subordinates; the data to be gathered are specified, as are the conditions under which they are to be gathered, the various stages of data gathering are planned, and methods of analysis are also clearly laid down. The aim of careful planning is to eliminate error, variance and wasting time and resources. Good research design usually ensures that findings can be replicated.

The first stage of any research must be to formulate a hypothesis, a conjecture about the relationship between two or more variables, which must be practically testable. The second stage is to devise some means of controlling 'variance'; in other words, variation in the dependent variable being studied must be the consequence of manipulating known independent variables. To control unwanted or extraneous variables the researcher vets his experimental subjects, making sure they all have certain personality traits, physical characteristics, backgrounds or experiences in common. Thirdly, variance in measuring the dependent variable must be minimised by experimenting in rigidly controlled conditions.

Freud

Resistance Forces in the personality which actively maintain repression and interfere with the progress of analysis. Freud claimed that the examination of a person's resistances and transferences is what psychoanalysis is all about. If a resistance can be overcome, repressed material achieves catharsis.

Retroactive interference Recently learned material adversely affecting one's ability to recall previously learned material. Demonstrate this for yourself by trying the memory experiment on page 146.

Conditioning
Social learning theory

Reward and punishment Why do we behave as we do? Because we learn that some behaviours are rewarded and others punished. A child who throws temper tantrums experimentally to begin with may continue to behave outrageously if her parents give in to her (reward her) for the sake of peace. Our behaviour is overwhelmingly shaped by the approval and disapproval of others, and also by seeing other people rewarded or punished. Rewards can range from love and admiration to money and possessions. Punishments can range from dislike or being ignored to imprisonment or fines.

Carl Rogers, b. 1902

Client-centred therapy

Rogers, Carl Carl Ransom Rogers, born in 1902, was the man who pioneered the now very popular *client-centred* approach to psychotherapy. This requires the therapist to adopt a non-judgemental, empathic and positive attitude towards clients and their problems; in other words clients are gently prompted towards deciding what their real needs are, and how to set about satisfying them.

After several false starts, studying agriculture, then theology, then history, Rogers decided to make clinical and educational psychology his career. In 1939, while a lecturer at Rochester University, he published *The Clinical Treatment of the Problem Child*, based on his work with troubled children.

In the 1930s Rogers began to question the traditional psychoanalytical approach to psychotherapy. In 1940, in an article entitled *Newer Concepts of Psychotherapy*, he dared to suggest that clients might derive more benefit from therapy if they were allowed more say in the way it is conducted. Clients, in his view, are most likely to get the help necessary to rebuild their confidence from an understanding and accepting therapist, rather than from an aloof and analytical one. The proof of the pudding, so to speak, came during his term as professor of psychology at the University of Chicago (1945-57). Sixty per cent of the clients who attended a counselling centre set up by Rogers and his colleagues showed a marked improvement, and about half of the remainder showed some improvement. These encouraging results were published in *Psychotherapy and Personality Change* (1954), buttressing the theories he had put forward earlier in *Client-Centred Therapy* (1951).

Rogers remains firmly convinced that anybody, however disturbed, can develop in a positive direction and gain emotional maturity. His book *Carl Rogers on Encounter Groups* (1970), arguing that encounter groups deserved to be taken more seriously, gave a powerful push to the encounter movement in the USA.

Encounter groups

Roles The behaviour associated with and required of occupants of defined positions in society; in hospitals the roles of patient, nurse, doctor, visitor; in court the roles of judge, jury, defendant, accused. Specific clothing and behaviour distinguish different roles. Some latitude is allowed within roles, particularly in those which carry power or high status. Sometimes a role may require one to suppress one's usual style or at least learn to express it within the confines of that role, a possible source of conflict. Roles prescribe interactions between people in some detail - for example, a conversation between a customer and waiter, will tend to follow a rather standardised course.

Social skills training

Rorschach test A projective test developed by Hermann Rorschach in 1921; the testee is shown ten different inkblots printed on cards and asked to place an interpretation on each of them; five of the inkblots are black, two are a mixture of red and black, and three are multicoloured. The Rorschach is usually used as one of a battery of personality maladjustment tests. Responses to each blot are scored in five categories, each category representing a specific area of personality.

Projective tests

A source of hypotheses to be checked against other data. Bats, witches and bits of human anatomy are common responses to Rorschach blots.

Sadism Deriving erotic enjoyment from inflicting pain and humiliation on others, whether in a sexual context or not; often co-exists with masochism, hence sadomasochism. The 'Marquis' de Sade's sexually explicit novel *Justine*, written at the turn of the eighteenth century, remains a pinnacle of sadistic fiction. Some psychologists have pointed out that there is aggression and pain in the courtship of many animals, and that sadism is merely an extension of the scratching, biting and rough handling that some lovers find enjoyable. Another view is that fear of aggression from the opposite sex leads to sadism as a 'safe' form of sexual expression – if you do to others what you feel they will do to you, you no longer have to be afraid. Sadism represents 5 per cent of treated sexual disorders, presumably because occasional acts of sadism are by mutual consent.

Sanity or insanity?

In a notable challenge to the conventional diagnosis and treatment of mental illness in 1973, psychologist David Rosenhan and 7 colleagues used false identities and had themselves 'committed' to various mental hospitals in America. They falsified certain information about their supposed complaints ('I hear voices, unclean voices . . .'), but everything else about their past histories and current circumstances was truthfully reported.

Schizophrenia

At 11 out of 12 hospitals, the would-be patients were diagnosed as 'schizophrenic' and committed to psychiatric wards on the strength of their simulated 'abnormalities'. Once inside, however, Rosenhan and his colleagues stopped simulating psychiatric symptoms – each behaved as normally as possible in every way. Yet despite their public 'show' of sanity, the pseudo-patients remained undetected. Each was eventually

Remission

discharged with a diagnosis of 'schizophrenia in remission' after having been hospitalised for an average of 19 days. At no time did any hospital staff member realise that an admissions error had been made or that a perfectly normal person was being kept in an asylum for the insane. It was left to husbands, wives and colleagues to secure their release.

The staff of one American hospital which heard about Rosenhan's study staunchly professed that such errors of judgement could not have happened at their establishment. Rosenhan put their claims to the test by stating that one or more 'impostors' would apply for admission to their hospital during the following three months. Each of the 193 patients admitted during this period was systematically rated by the staff, and 19 were classified by both a psychiatrist and a staff member as fakes. A total of 41 patients were judged to be 'pseudo' by at least one staff member. The number of actual pseudo-patients sent to the hospital by Rosenhan was ... nil.

This is undoubtedly (unless you are cynical enough to think Rosenhan's group was, indeed, mad) a most shocking indictment of certain 'medical model' techniques of hospital admission and diagnosis. But, reassuringly, there has been a major change of ideas within psychology and psychiatry about concepts such as 'normality' and 'insanity' even in the last five years or so.

Mental illness

Schizophrenia

A major category of psychiatric illness comprising the most severe of the *psychoses*, in which the sufferer is considered to be quite out of touch with normal reality. One person in every hundred can expect to suffer from a schizophrenic episode at some time in their life and a substantial proportion of all mental hospital beds are occupied by such patients.

Psychosis

The word schizophrenic is derived from two Greek roots, 'schiz-' meaning 'split' and 'phren-' meaning 'soul' or 'mind'. For this reason the term schizophrenic is often erroneously applied to cases of split, double or multiple personality (the Jekyll and Hyde phenomenon), which are hysterical illnesses. Properly speaking the split involved in schizophrenia is a disintegration of the personality rather than the splitting of a person's mind into two complete personalities.

The symptoms of schizophrenia are highly variable. Those described here are some of the common ones.

Thought disorder This may range from a woolly vagueness in thinking to a total fragmentation of mental processes. Patients may experience both thought blacking and pressure of thought. A number of sufferers report that at times they feel utterly overwhelmed and bombarded by sensations, images and thoughts. Not surprisingly thought disorder often shows itself in bizarre, illogical language which is sometimes little more than a 'word salad'.

Word salad

Disturbance of emotion This can manifest itself as a general flattening of emotional experience and as inappropriateness of emotional response or 'incongruity of affect' (like giggling on hearing of a close relative's death).

Delusions These are beliefs which are patently untrue and yet held with illogical tenacity. Delusions may be of a grandiose or paranoid nature. The sufferer may believe that he is the rightful King of England and that he is being persecuted by enemies who wish to keep him off the throne. Delusions of control are not uncommon among schizophrenics: a patient may believe, for instance, that his thoughts are being influenced by messages from another planet being transmitted through the electric power points. Such delusional beliefs often entirely dominate the patient's life.

Delusions

Hallucinations

Hallucinations These may be auditory or, more rarely, visual. Auditory hallucinations often take the form of voices, and the patient may hear these voices talking about him all day long. At times he will feel compelled to reply to them, thus appearing, to everyone else, to be talking to himself.

In the past a number of distinct forms of schizophrenia have been recognised. The best known of these are: *paranoid schizophrenia* in which delusions of persecution and grandeur are predominant; *hebephrenic schizophrenia* in which the patient engages in incomprehensibly silly behaviour and speech; *catatonic schizophrenia* characterised by stuporous and unresponsive immobility and occasional bursts of wildly excited behaviour; and *simple schizophrenia* in which the main features are gradual social withdrawal and a slowing up and general disorganisation of thinking.

Despite these sub-classifications it is quite rare to find pure 'textbook' cases of them. Very often the symptoms manifested by any one patient overlap several categories. For this reason simpler forms of classification have been developed in recent years. In one such system a distinction is made quite simply between *acute schizophrenia*, in which the patient's symptoms are bizarre and 'florid', and *chronic schizophrenia*, in which withdrawal, apathy and incompetence are more apparent.

The cause of schizophrenia is unknown. A number of psychiatrists believe that it is the result of a biochemical abnormality of the brain, in other words that the chemicals responsible for transmitting nerve impulses are in some way at fault. Despite years of research, however, conclusive evidence for this view is still lacking. Genetic factors appear to play a major role in predisposing a person to become schizophrenic under stress. Nonetheless many psychiatrists, and the generality of psychologists too, believe that non-constitutional environmental influences are the most potent determinants of schizophrenia. Indeed a small number of investigators actually believe that schizophrenic symptoms represent a perfectly sane reaction to a very abnormal upbringing.

It was once believed that schizophrenia was a degenerative condition for which there was no cure. Nevertheless a few patients experience complete remission with no subsequent

Drugs and mental disorder

recurrence of the symptoms. Drugs, especially the phenothiazines, constitute the main treatment at the moment. A major problem facing contemporary psychiatry is that of rehabilitating the large numbers of hospitalised schizophrenics who are now symptom-free but who have become dependent on the institutions they live in. Clinical psychologists have made a valuable contribution in this sphere by developing and im-

Token economy

plementing token economies, which promote a gradual return to independence and responsibility.

Sedation The act or process of calming. Tranquillisers are widely administered for this purpose, the minor tranquillisers such as Valium being prescribed by general practitioners and psychiatrists for a variety of anxiety-related complaints (e.g.

Drugs and mental disorder

agoraphobia). The major tranquillisers include the phenothiazines, used in the treatment of schizophrenia. In addition to having a calming effect tranquillisers are believed to have a specifically anti-psychotic action. One effect of sedation is to reduce the patient's responsiveness to his or her surroundings. It has sometimes been argued that sedation is nothing more than the physical strait-jacket of the bad old days in pharmacological guise - a strait-jacket which restrains the mind rather than the body. The ethics of sedation become most acute when admission to psychiatric institution is involuntary. Nevertheless it is generally accepted that the gains achieved by sedatives in reducing personal distress far outweigh doubts about their over-zealous use.

Self-actualisation The process of achieving one's full potential in all spheres of life; the goal of humanistic psychotherapy (client-centred, Gestalt). To achieve self-actualisation, all facets of the self, both desirable and undesirable, must be accepted, and full responsibility taken for one's decisions and actions. The concept of self-actualisation was developed by Jung and Goldstein, and most fully by Maslow.

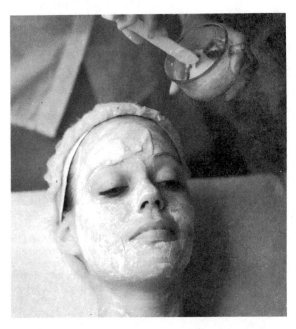

Balm to the tottering self-concept

Self-concept In the words of Carl Rogers, the "organised conceptual gestalt [pattern] composed of perceptions of the characteristics of the 'I' or 'me' and the perceptions of the

205

relationships of the 'I' or 'me' to others and to various aspects of life, together with the values attached to these perceptions". It includes perception of one's basic roles, traits and body image. A sense of self develops gradually throughout childhood, and is the framework into which all experiences are integrated. A threat is really an experience which is inconsistent with one's self-concept.

Semantic differential (see Osgood)

Senility *Robert Kastenbaum*

What are the characteristics of the kind of old person whom most clinicians would consider 'senile'? The most obvious of them are not physical but cognitive. Someone who is senile tends to repeat the same statements over and over again; this is known as 'perseveration', and is closely related to several other cognitive problems, such as a lack of ideas, a sloweddown tempo of thought, and sometimes an inability to grasp abstractions ... to see the forest as well as the trees.

Someone who is senile thinks concretely. In other words, they miss the relationships and implications which give richer meaning to experience and help to solve problems. Senility may also bring serious difficulties with memory, with impairment being greatest for recent events. Yesterday may draw a blank. Even something that happened ten minutes ago may

Memory

be completely erased. Problems with memory are not confined to the senile of course, but memory loss is more radical and extensive in senility.

The alertness and concentration needed to register new experience may also be missing or undependable. The senile individual may also withdraw from interaction with others, have difficulty in keeping himself clean and groomed, suffer accidents related to forgetfulness or misunderstanding, and so on.

Body changes The process of senility can begin as early as the age of 50 though it is more likely to be detected in the mid-60s or beyond. It is caused by physical changes in the central nervous system, which in turn are caused by the hard-

Brain damage

ening and narrowing of the blood vessels which serve the brain (cerebral arteriosclerosis). Those brain cells which are starved of blood and oxygen atrophy and die, but the pattern of deterioration is fitful and episodic.

There is another common pattern of deterioration associated with old age, *senile dementia*, but here there is widespread wasting away of cells in the cerebral cortex independent of change in the blood vessels, and deterioration is usually steady and gradual.

Unfortunately, these two general types of brain damage are progressive and, at present, not much can be done in terms of treatment or cure.

Label with care Far too often the label 'senile' is carelessly and ignorantly applied. Diagnosing a person as 'senile' is accurate only when we mean the pattern of progressively deteriorating thought and behaviour associated with irreversible brain damage. There may be many alternative explanations for confused thinking and memory lapses after the age of 60 – illness, fatigue, anxiety, malnutrition, hypothermia, the effects of hospitalisation or institutionalisation, depression, grief reactions, culture shock...

Understanding and helping The comfort and well-being of someone who is properly diagnosed as 'senile' can be improved, even though the disease process is progressive. Damaged brain cells cannot be repaired, but the individual becomes motivated to make better use of his or her remaining functions. Good nutrition and careful use of medication and exercise can also dramatically improve the condition of those with degenerative brain disease.

We must also understand the continual effort of a jeopardised and stressed old person to cope with his difficulties and to make the best he can of the situation. Even when senile-type behaviour appears quite bizarre and ineffective, it often has the same goals as our own behaviour: to understand, to relieve anxiety, to achieve safety, to feel like a person.

Waning faculties, distressing to the old person, and to friends, relatives and care givers

Sensorimotor period The first of Piaget's four stages of intellectual development in childhood, the period from birth until roughly 18 months during which children gradually develop a sense of physical distinctiveness from the surrounding environment, and begin to appreciate that objects do not simply cease to exist when they cannot be seen or touched (object constancy).

Sensory deprivation Withdrawal of all forms of stimulation – light, sound, taste, touch, smell. The subjective experience of sensory deprivation includes boredom, restlessness, irritability, an inability to concentrate or think clearly, depression, unrealistic fears, and sometimes hallucinations. 'Stayers' in sensory deprivation experiments appear to be less influenced by their environment and less in need of stimulation in general than 'drop-outs'. In controlled laboratory conditions subjects might be confined to bed for several days in an otherwise empty soundproof room, or wear earphones and a blindfold and be suspended in a tank of warm water. All subjects are provided with a 'panic' button. Sensory deprivation is one of the techniques of brainwashing.

Brainwashing

Sexual difficulties   *Leonore Tiefer*
Difficulties associated with frigidity and impotence are discussed on pages 100 or 122. Here we will briefly describe problems which most sex therapists in Western societies would regard as requiring some treatment. Most therapists stress, however, that it is for people themselves to judge

whether they are happy with their sexual functioning; sexual activity is not something that can be 'objectively' valued.

Problems with arousal Many men and women report that although they feel desire and look forward to sexual pleasure, as the action begins they do not find themselves experiencing increasing arousal. Often, they feel pleasure, and yet excitement is not reflected physiologically by erection or vaginal lubrication. The result is sometimes impatience, self-consciousness, annoyance or embarrassment – negative feelings which actually prevent increasing arousal. It would be more to the point to appreciate whatever pleasurable sensations are occurring, hoping that nature will eventually take its course!

Orgasm

Problems with orgasm Both men and women report two kinds of problem with orgasm. Either it is absent and sexual arousal builds up but does not culminate in the type of explosive few seconds that are expected, or else it comes too soon, before the individual is ready. Both problems occur in both sexes, although the former is reported more by women, and the latter more by men.

In recent years, the definition of 'premature ejaculation' has changed. The definition now most widely used says that a man ejaculates prematurely when he 'comes' before he wants to, or feels that he has no control over timing. Treatment of the problem teaches men to focus on their sensations immediately before orgasm. Gradually, they become able to delay orgasm longer and longer. Sensate focus exercises can also help women to reach orgasm more reliably.

Not experiencing orgasm has only recently been defined as a sexual problem in Western society. The pressure to 'achieve' orgasm has diminished the focus on enjoyment and turned many sexual encounters into task-oriented activities. Now, for the first time, many women are able to empathise with the apprehension some men feel about whether they will be able to 'perform' adequately.

Sex therapy *Leonore Tiefer*

Therapists regard and treat non-medical sexual problems as long-standing habits, which, like any habit, are difficult to break. The goal of therapy is to create an atmosphere where the natural processes of arousal and orgasm can occur unimpeded by anxiety. Contemporary sex therapists do not focus on creating sexual arousal or orgasm in situations where these responses are absent. Rather, and this comes as a surprise to most clients, they focus on breaking down the blocks to sexual responsiveness. Once the blocks of anxiety, inhibition or fear are removed, it is assumed that natural sexual responsiveness will emerge.

Anxiety
Inhibition

The goal of treatment is for the individual or couple to have one successful experience as a result of improved technique, understanding, trust and communication. Once the goal (firm erection, presence of pleasure, orgasm, etc.) is attained, the individual or couple is encouraged to identify the factors that contributed to their success, and make them part of their future lovemaking. Therapy ends when the individual or couple is confident that the new patterns are well-established. Follow-up research suggests that the level of performance which marks the end of therapy is not usually maintained; nevertheless the ultimate level of performance and satisfaction is usually significantly better than the pre-treatment level.

Correcting sexual misinformation Many problems stem from misunderstanding the processes of sexual response and the range of individual differences. Education is an important, some would say the most important, ingredient in easing sexual problems.

For example, girls are usually given inadequate information about their genitals and their different functions. Information about the role of the clitoris, for example, often leads to satisfying changes in technique and more relaxed attitude towards oral or manual caresses.

Many men worry that their penis is too small. But such worries usually vanish when they learn that the range of penis size is less in the erect than in the relaxed state, and that more women report discomfort from an overly large penis than dissatisfaction with a small one.

Another major source of misinformation has to do with what is considered 'normal', in terms of frequency of sexual activity, techniques, fantasy, differences between men and women, unconventional practices such as anal intercourse, making love in funny places, and so on.

Revealing the mechanisms of anxiety During therapy each individual must come to understand both in a general and a personal way how anxiety diminishes sexual response.

Therapy almost always includes 'homework' assignments carried out between sessions with the therapist. The first assignment often requires each partner to take turns in caressing the entire body of the other, excluding the genitals, and telling each other what is most and least pleasant. The purpose of this assignment is to diminish the pressure to perform, and with it anxiety. In fact many couples fail to comply with their assignments most of the time, and it is the discussion of their failure and their resistance to breaking down established habits which provides most of the substance of sex therapy.

Specific techniques Masters and Johnson and other sex therapists have identified several techniques, besides improving communication and increasing experimentation, which can help with specific sex problems. For example, erection can be prolonged, preventing premature ejaculation, by the 'squeeze technique' (applied by the woman when the man feels he is close to coming) or by the woman ceasing to stimulate the man, thus allowing his erection to subside for the space of a few seconds.

Another useful technique was developed for women who

experience orgasm during masturbation but not during intercourse. First, the woman teaches her partner how she stimulates her vulva to produce intense excitement and orgasm. Then either she or he provides manual stimulation during intercourse. After a number of repetitions manual stimulation is gradually decreased. It is quite normal for a woman not to be able to achieve orgasm during thrusting activity alone.

Another technical suggestion is often given to the man with erectile difficulty. First, the couple is forbidden to have intercourse and encouraged to engage in frequent erotic caressing. Usually, the man will begin to have erections during this activity, although if he thinks about intercourse the erection subsides. However, he learns the important message that erections come and go, and that should one begin to lose an erection during sexplay, there is no need to panic. This increased confidence will usually allow the man to achieve entry into his partner.

The existence of specific treatments for sexual problems dates only from the last decade, and we can expect much change in how such problems are viewed and treated in the next ten years.

Shadowing A technique for studying shifts in attention (see Dichotic listening).

Shaping Shaping is a procedure in operant conditioning whereby the experimental animal is rewarded for successively more accurate approximations to a desired response. In attempting to teach a rat to press a lever, for example, it may be necessary at first to reward it with food simply for going near the lever, then to give a reward only when it touches the lever, and finally to reward only when it actually presses the lever. Similar principles apply when teaching a pet to perform tricks. Shaping is sometimes used to train mentally retarded children and adults to perform simple day-to-day activities.

Sheldon, William William Herbert Sheldon's legacy to psychology was the link he established between physique and personality, a branch of psychology known as *constitutional psychology*.

Sheldon was a doctor twice over, in psychology and medicine. After two years of psychiatric study in Europe, mainly with Carl Jung, he became professor of psychology at Chicago and Harvard, and director of the Constitution Laboratory. He retired from the University of Oregon Medical School in 1970, aged 72.

From his extensive study of the links between personality traits and general body build, Sheldon concluded that the human physique could be split into three primary components: *endomorphy*, *ectomorphy* and *mesomorphy*. These correspond, respectively, to general stoutness and prominence of

Masturbation

Two messages on non-conflicting channels, on the screen and through earphones. With practice both can be attended to efficiently.

William Sheldon, 1898–1970

210

the abdomen; general slenderness and relatively long limbs; and a general build somewhere between the extremes of stout and slender. Anyone can be rated on a seven-point scale for each of these components; their overall rating represents their body type or *somatotype*.

Sheldon measured temperament in a similar way. His three temperament components are *viscerotonia* (love of comfort and sociability), *somatotonia* (love of physical adventure) and *cerebrotonia* (restraint, inhibition and concealment). Each of these components can be rated on a 1 to 7 scale, and the scores combined to give a *temperamental type*.

Sibling rivalry Rivalry between children of the same family competing for affection and reinforcing attention from parents and adults; can be overt (one four-year-old child, having just heard how infectious diseases can spread, started coughing in her baby brother's face), or covert (stealing or mutilating dolls and toys belonging to another child). Rivalry is commoner between two boys, or between a boy and a girl, than between sisters and between siblings of similar age.

The only effective way of managing sibling rivalry appears to be to make each child feel fully loved, and to encourage each to develop his or her own interests. Rivalry is most intense where affection is ,a scarce resource. Punishment of aggressive acts and the encouragement of 'brotherly love' appear to be rather inadequate remedies.

Open rivalry for a favourite toy

Situational analysis *Michael Argyle*

Situational analysis really has three purposes: to instruct and train people who find certain social situations difficult, to modify troublesome situations, and to create new situations to meet new contingencies. The assumption underlying situational analysis is that our behaviour varies greatly in different situations.

M. Wish has found that people interpret social situations as belonging to certain categories: cooperative-competitive, equal-unequal, work-social, intense-superfical, formal-informal. These are useful categories, but they do not analyse situations in sufficient detail to be of practical help to people with social difficulties. A rather more helpful approach is to *Games* analyse situations rather as if they were games, in terms of 'goals', 'rules', 'repertoire' and so on.

Common types of social situation like meals, parties, committee meetings and so on, exist because they enable people to *Social interaction* attain certain *goals* which somehow satisfy other needs or drives. The goals of a situation may serve bodily needs, social needs, or the need to earn a livelihood. Members of a given culture know the goals which can be attained in different situations, and they enter situations with certain goals either at the back or the front of their mind.

All situations have *rules*, often unwritten, which reflect generally shared opinions about what should or should not be done. Rules are functional in that they develop to co-ordinate behaviour so that situational goals can be met. There are certain universal rules such as 'be polite', and rules like 'tell the truth' when visiting the doctor, 'don't interrupt' in class, and 'be cheerful' at parties. Each particular situation has rules which guard against temptations and difficulties likely to frustrate its goals. Rule-breaking can occur for various reasons - ignorance of the rules, taking selfish short-cuts, accidents, trying to be funny or original.

Most situations have a definite *repertoire* or range of social acts which are meaningful and relevant. The analogy here is with the moves in a game like chess or tennis. These moves are functional, providing the steps towards the goals of the situation.

Most social situations have recognised *environmental settings*, such as committee rooms, classrooms, bars, dining rooms. These settings are not at all random - they are usually consciously chosen or created to make it easier to attain certain goals. The environment may contain special equipment, such as a blackboard and slide projector; or it may be conducive to certain social relationships or patterns of interaction and not others, by the design and placing of furniture.

Social situations can also be analysed for other features *Roles* such as *role-structure*, *use of language* and *shared concepts*. A pattern of roles arises from the pursuit of different goals (waiter and diner), division of labour (waiter and cook), or the need for someone to be in charge (waiter and manager). Special use of language is a particularly fascinating aspect of interaction; all crafts and professions have their technical vocabularies: we may even use different languages for work and worship.

Social situations which cause the most trouble are those which require assertiveness, performance in public, conflict with others, or intimacy. People can be helped over such difficulties either by social skills training, which enables them to handle the situation better, or by behaviour therapy which reduces their anxiety.

Social skills training

There are two main areas in which situational analysis is of practical value. The first is *social skills training*, in which problem situations are analysed to enable trainees to deal with them better. Trainees can be taught the goals, rules and repertoire of situations which they find difficult and then trained in the patterns of social behaviour which research has found to be most effective. The other area in which situational analysis is effective is in redesigning situations to make them less troublesome. Shoplifting can be reduced by installing closed-circuit television surveillance and making goods less accessible; the social climate of mental hospitals and old people's homes has been improved by better arrangement of the furniture. Situational analysis has also been used to create totally new situations (encounter groups, brainstorming) for specific purposes.

Skinner, B. F. Skinner is one of the best-known and most controversial psychologists of our time. He has applied his ultra-objective behaviourist approach to a bewildering range of topics - learning, teaching machines, verbal behaviour, behaviour therapy, raising babies in 'baby boxes', guiding missiles by pigeon, and so on. In his novel *Walden Two* (1948) he even proposed a design for society in which people's behaviour would be 'shaped' and controlled by deliberately planned systems of rewards.

Burrhus Frederic Skinner was born in Pennsylvania in 1904. His early interest in writing was displaced by an even greater interest in the mechanisms of human and animal behaviour. His first and probably most influential book, *The Behaviour of Organisms*, was published in 1938. He went to Harvard in 1948 and is still one of the university's most illustrious figures.

B. F. Skinner, b. 1904

Conditioning

The concepts advanced by Skinner have their roots in the work of Pavlov, Watson and Thorndike. However, Skinner distinguishes between two types of behaviour, *respondent* and *operant*. Respondent behaviour is simply the response of an organism to a stimulus, but operant behaviour, of much more interest to Skinner, is any behaviour which in some way operates on, or changes, the environment and does not appear to be connected to any identifiable stimulus. Operant behaviour is therefore goal-directed, which is why it is sometimes referred to as 'instrumental' behaviour. Skinner designed a special box, a 'Skinner box', to investigate the effects of rewards,

Reinforcement

or *schedules of reinforcement* as he called them on operant behaviour. In a typical experiment, a hungry pigeon receives a food pellet after accidentally pressing a lever in the box; after a while it presses the lever when it wants food; pressing the lever is the *operant response*.

From this and many similar experiments Skinner concluded that an animal's behaviour can be 'shaped' in a desired direction by a system of rewards. The inevitable inference from this is that reinforcement might also explain the development of behaviour in human beings; any action, thought or feeling which is reinforced will tend to be repeated. Skinner discovered that the rate at which his animals made operant responses, and the length of time these responses persisted when reinforcement was discontinued, depended closely on the schedules of reinforcement he used. The simplest schedule of reinforcement, for example, would be when every response gets a reinforcer.

The concept of reinforcement as an explanation of human behaviour is not in itself particularly controversial. But Skinner's suggestion that the rather haphazard schedules of reinforcement that characterise everyday life should be planned and managed has aroused intense indignation.

Doing the delta rhythm

Brain waves

Sleep Researches have identified several stages of sleep involving changes in muscle tone, blood pressure, heart rate, eye movements and so on, as well as changes in brain activity.

There are considered to be five basic stages of sleep, as measured by electroencephalograph. At rest, with eyes closed, our brain indulges in 'alpha' activity. In the first stage of sleep, alpha activity disappears, to be replaced by low voltage mixed frequency waves. Muscles begin to relax and the sleeper becomes unaware of external stimuli. The second stage, which lasts for about half the night, is characterised by the appearance of 'sleep spindles' on the EEG record. In stage three the spindles give way to longer, slower waves, and in stage four, the stage of deepest sleep, the waves become slower still, the 'delta' rhythm. In stages three and four the sleeper may dream but will be unlikely to remember much.

Dreaming

Dreams, characterised by rapid eye movement (REM), are most readily recalled from the final stages of sleep, immediately before waking, but they occur cyclically throughout all stages of sleep. The EEG record during REM indicates that cortical activity is high. Although the sleeper may twitch during REM episodes (men not uncommonly experience erections) the muscles are almost completely relaxed; sleepwalking, which comes under the heading of a dissociative reaction, cannot therefore occur at such times.

The value of sleep is not an issue many people dispute, but its true function is not at all clear. One recent suggestion has been, quite simply, that sleep keeps organisms out of harm's way, giving them respite from the hazards of activity.

Sleep deprivation   *Robert Wilkinson*

Ask most people what happens when they lose sleep and they will tell you "I feel tired". We know what they mean from personal experience, but 'feeling tired' explains nothing. Experiments on sleep deprivation have been going on for the last 100 years, and in some respects the deeper we probe the deeper the mystery.

Short sleepers   The record for doing without sleep now stands at 264 hours (11 days). It has never been established, using the appropriate scientific criteria, that anyone can do without sleep indefinitely. Nevertheless there are a few people who sleep remarkably little. Scientifically the best-documented case is that of a 70-year-old retired nurse, who claimed that she had not slept for more than an average of about one hour a night since childhood. A 24-hour watch was kept on her for a full five days, and every night her EEG was recorded to detect her periods of sleep. Her minutes of sleep during the five days were: 1, 82, 204 (a record she said), 19, and 29, giving an average of 67 minutes a day. By nature she was a cheerful and very industrious person and these qualities remained evident throughout the five-day period of observation, during which she showed no very obvious signs of sleep deprivation.

Though less well-documented, there are many other reports of very short sleepers. Interestingly, most of these people share certain features: they are usually in good physical health, athletic both in build and inclination and tend to fill their abnormally long waking hours with active pursuit of work and leisure, appearing not to have time for sleep. Unlike

Chukka fatigue

normal insomniacs, they rarely complain of being tired and find it difficult to understand why others need to sleep so long.

Short sleepers probably represent the extreme end of a spectrum which bulges in the middle to accommodate all those people who feel cheated if they don't get eight hours sleep a night and tapers off at the other extreme with people who need much more than eight hours. The data currently available, obtained by self-completion questionnaires, reveal· a broad distribution of the number of hours people say they sleep, with the mean around $7\frac{1}{2}$ hours.

Pinpointing the effects of sleep loss Unfortunately the vast majority of us become very tired if we have to do without sleep altogether or even restrict it to one or two hours a night. Why? Attempts to discover how loss of sleep affects the body, by measuring various physiological parameters, have *not* produced evidence of important changes, at least not in people deprived of sleep for up to 100 hours ... and arguably much longer perhaps.

Yet effects there must be, somewhere. We know for certain that behaviour and performance are affected. In the 30 years since the advent of sophisticated methods of measuring performance, largely pioneered by the Medical Research Council in Cambridge, England, and by the Walter Reed Army Institute of Research, USA, it has been repeatedly demonstrated that lack of sleep impairs performance. The nature of this impairment has been well described by the Walter Reed group as one of 'periodic lapses'. Performance declines, not steadily like a clockwork toy running down, but in fits and starts like a car running out of fuel. But there the car analogy ends - we humans never seem to run completely out of fuel. There are, for example, no well-documented cases of people dying from lack of sleep *per se*. And no one has yet demonstrated convincingly that one night's loss of sleep adversely affects any task which can be interpreted as exciting or intellectually demanding. The tasks most at risk, it seems, are those which lack interest, such as driving along a motorway.

It has been suggested that we have a 'drive' towards sleep, just as we have a drive towards food, sex and other basic requirements of life. Deprive the body of sleep and it will increase its drive towards sleep-attaining behaviour at the expense of all other forms of drive, the weaker drives going to the wall first. This is why uninteresting tasks fail first, and why the body seems remarkably able to withstand the effects of loss of sleep when there is a good enough incentive. The drive model of sleep is helpful in a general way, but it still leaves us in the dark about how this interactive system of drives works physiologically and how not sleeping differentially influences their relative strengths. Behavioural studies of sleep deprivation have established a working hypothesis for this general input–output relationship. We now have to use this hypothesis to guide us to the physiological mechanism.

Social interaction

Anything that happens between two or more people can be called 'social interaction'. Most interaction takes place on two levels verbal and non-verbal, with the spoken messages usually alternating and the non-spoken ones being sent and received at the same time. Social encounters can be divided into three kinds: the first is the 'one person in charge' encounter, as in teacher–pupil, interviewer–interviewee situations; the second is the 'two-sided' encounter, as in a discussion or negotiation where each side is pursuing certain goals; then there is the 'casual' encounter in which each person responds mainly to what happened last. Any of these encounters may be primarily social or primarily concerned with other activities, like work, sport, eating and drinking.

Non-verbal communication

Most socially skilled people perform unthinkingly what the socially inept usually fail to perform. They reward the other person, they initiate interaction, they have an accurate perception of the other person and an ability to see their point of view, they intuitively follow certain conversation sequences, and they are sensitive to the rules or other properties of a situation.

Social skills develop best among age mates and classmates. None of us is at our social best when feeling outnumbered, overawed or outclassed.

Socialisation The gradual process of learning the rules, the rights and wrongs, of a particular society or culture in order to be recognised and effective within it.

Social learning theory A theory developed by Albert Bandura and others and indebted to learning theory. The theory states that we learn correct social behaviour by observing the behaviour of others, imitating the actions we see rewarded and refraining from those we see punished. Because we too

Modelling

217

expect to be rewarded and punished for similar actions, the learning process is as often indirect as direct. For the social learning theorist, it is the sum total of learned behaviour which constitutes personality.

Social psychology The scope of social psychology is very wide – at its widest it embraces every possible relationship between individuals and their social environment. What distinguishes it from the other social sciences (sociology, anthropology) is its emphasis on the psychology of the individual in relation to social structures, how our thoughts and feelings affect and are affected by others, whether in simple friendship pairings or in large business organisations. Social behaviour can be studied in a variety of ways, ranging from experiments in the laboratory to research in completely natural settings. Each approach has its advantages. In the laboratory of course conditions can be controlled so that observed behaviour can be attributed to factors in the experimental setting and not to the many extraneous factors present in real-life settings.

As a field of enquiry, social psychology can be divided into a small number of major spheres of interest, three of which will be considered here.

Social influence processes Under this heading come all the processes involved in shaping behaviour in social situations. The study of attitude formation and attitude change, for example, is of intense interest and importance to advertisers, educators and political propagandists. One finding is that, under certain conditions, two-sided presentation of information, in which both the pros and cons of a particular view are set out, tends to be more effective at persuading people to change their minds, and keep them changed, than one-sided presentation. Party political broadcasts might be more effective opinion-changers if they allowed the other party a crumb of credit here and there!

The structure of groups Groups and their effects on the individual can be examined in many ways. The pressure to conform to group norms, for example, has been very thoroughly explored. In one classic experiment subjects were asked to take part in a study ostensibly concerned with judging the lengths of different lines; each subject was asked to sit at the end of a row of people who were in fact confederates of the experimenter and not fellow-subjects; several lines of different length were then projected onto a screen and each subject was asked to judge which lines were the same length as a standard line. For the first few judgements everyone agreed. Then, by prior arrangement, each of the confederates in turn made the same obviously wrong judgement. A surprisingly high proportion (50 per cent) of real subjects confirmed this warped judgement on at least two occasions. Clearly they were under very great pressure to disregard the evidence of their senses and conform. Those who resisted the pressure did so with some discomfort. But if the real subject has even one 'ally' who makes the correct judgement, the overall rate of conformity drops dramatically.

The individual in a social context It is difficult to imagine how 'personality' or 'individuality' could develop in the total absence of other human contact. Most of our learning is the result of observing the people around us, and many of our fundamental urges (sexual and creative activity) and beliefs (sense of right and wrong) would be meaningless without a human social context.

A debate of central concern to social psychologists in recent years is whether individual behaviour in different situations is more closely tied to personality or more dependent on context. We naturally tend to regard our personality as determining our behaviour, but social psychologists argue that it may often be the characteristics of the situation which are more important. Studies of moral behaviour provide good evidence for such an argument. In one study, in which large numbers of children were exposed to a variety of situations in which they could lie, steal or cheat, investigators found that moral behaviour was surprisingly situation-specific; it proved quite impossible to predict which children would cheat in any one situation on the basis of their behaviour in other situations. Similar results have been found with adults, and across a range of different behaviours.

Many other areas of investigation within the ambit of social psychological research have yielded findings which have been applied in the clinical, educational and industrial fields.

Social skills training (SST)   *Michael Argyle*
It has been estimated that at least one in ten 'normal' adults has a significant social behaviour problem, but until about 15 years ago the extent and influence of social skill deficits was largely unrecognised. The remedial methods collectively known as 'social skills training' or SST are now fairly widely applied. Since follow-up studies show that 'role-playing' is the most effective of the various SST methods currently in use, this is the one we will discuss first.

Role-playing consists of instruction and demonstration, followed by 7–15 minutes of role-play by the trainee, and then feedback in the form of verbal comments and video-tape playback. The whole process may then be repeated. Seeing desired behaviours 'modelled' (realistically demonstrated) live or on film is usually a great help to the trainee. So is feedback, but it must be unambiguous and tactful. Before the advent of video-tape technology instant visual feedback would have been impossible. A course of role-play training usually consists of six to ten 1½-hour sessions. Transferring new skills to real-life settings is accomplished by 'homework'; trainees are encouraged to try out their new skills between training sessions. Sessions are usually attended by about six trainees, though in the case of psychiatric patients some individual sessions are usually needed. One advantage of groups is that they provide a convenient source of role partners.

Role-playing can be supplemented by other special training techniques. Non-verbal communication, for example, can be improved by watching oneself in a mirror or listening to voice recordings. Sensitivity to other people's non-verbal signals can be improved by looking at photographs of facial expressions, gestures, postures ... Failure to plan or initiate interaction can be helped by practise in simple interviewing, where a plan of topics is prepared beforehand. Failure to keep a conversation going needs rather careful analysis before something can be done about it; one may not be handing the conversation over to the other person after replying to a question, for example. Situational analysis may also be necessary to guide role-play training for problem situations.

The more traditional method of SST training is *learning on the job*. Though it works for some people, it fails to help others and a few people find their difficulties actually increase. Success usually depends on there being an instructor who can comment on the trainee's performance and suggest better ways of doing things. The great advantage of learning on the job is that there is no problem transferring skills from the training situation to real life.

There are also *educational methods*, using reading, films and lectures. These make a valuable contribution to SST but they need to be combined with more active methods. Programmed texts have been quite successful for intercultural training (training for transferring from one culture to another). Group methods (T-groups and related procedures) have also been widely used in management training programmes.

Training targets Having outlined the main SST techniques, let us look at the people to whom they are applied. Social inadequacy and anxiety in social situations are typical of many psychiatric patients. SST by role-playing does help neurotics to improve their social behaviour and reduce anxiety, but it is not markedly more successful than desensitisation. Social inadequacy would therefore seem to have a strong anxiety ingredient. There is also such a thing as social phobia, but it overlaps to some extent with social inadequacy. Schizophrenia and other psychotic conditions can be improved by intensive individual SST lasting 30 hours or more. Successful results have also been obtained with prisoners, disturbed adolescents, and withdrawn or hostile children.

Many quite normal adults have social behaviour difficulties but SST is not always available. In North America the commonest form of SST is *assertion training*, a form of role-playing designed to train people to stand up for their rights, argue and disagree, ask for favours, etc. It is particularly popular with women as part of the Womens' Movement. There is also considerable demand for *heterosexual training* among young people. Follow-up studies have found that both assertion and heterosexual training are very successful.

Managers usually receive some SST in addition to their formal technical training. Sometimes this takes the form of generalised *sensitivity training* in groups, often on residential courses. More frequently offered nowadays is *training in specific managerial social skills* such as committee work, chairmanship, selection interviewing, supervision, negotiation and presenting. Most teacher training colleges provide *microteaching* opportunities, a form of role-playing in which a particular aspect of teaching is explained and demonstrated, and the trainee gives a short, prepared lesson to a class of about six children which is video-taped, followed by feedback and playback, and 'retaught'. Similar *vocational training* methods are coming into use for doctors, policemen and many other jobs where social skills are important. People about to go and work abroad for firms or governments are sometimes given *intercultural training*, the main features of which are language teaching, reading, lectures and films, role-playing in situations which typically cause the greatest problems; and interaction with members of the other culture.

Situational analysis

Sociogram A diagram of the social relationships between the members of a group; can be used to understand how a group functions or how function might be improved.

Specificity theory An approach to the study of psychosomatic illness, the idea being that a particular organic complaint is caused by a specific emotional conflict. It has been suggested, for instance, that high blood pressure is the result of repressed aggression. Despite its appeal, specificity theory is not generally supported by the available evidence.

Split-brain operation Originally used to reduce the frequency of severe convulsions in advanced epileptic patients. 'Split' brain is a slight misnomer, since the two cerebral hemispheres remain connected at a deeper level even when the corpus callosum connecting them has been surgically severed.

Psychosurgery

Brain

Split-brain patients, and more recent research involving brain-wave activity, have fairly conclusively shown that the left hemisphere is more involved in verbal skills and logical thinking, and that the right more active in spatial tasks and emotional experiences.

Schizophrenia

Split personality The non-technical term for schizophrenia, misleading because schizophrenia is a fragmentation or breakdown of personality, not a dissociative reaction.

Stammering Stammering or stuttering typically involves speech blocks, uncontrolled repetition of words and syllables, and prolongation of speech sounds. Nearly 1 per cent of children are noticeable and persistent stammerers, but only 0.5 per cent of these grow up to be adult stutterers.

The major contention in this field is whether stammering is the result of some organic impairment or whether it is caused by some psychological malfunction. The organic view is supported by the apparent heritability of the complaint – one certainly finds more speech problems in stammerers' families than in the normal population. There is also evidence that stammering is sex-linked – many more boys stammer than girls – and that it has little to do with the specific language one speaks – stammering is relatively evenly distributed across the world's cultures. The psychogenic view is that stuttering is either a symptom of underlying neurotic conflict or a learned maladaptive behaviour.

There is however a simpler explanation. It has been suggested that parents of stutterers may have responded to quite normal levels of early speech difficulties in their children with panic and so charged the idea of speaking with anxiety; stammerers begin to anticipate failure and the struggle not to fail blocks and embroils their speech. Reducing avoidance of speaking situations, which in turn reduces the anxiety felt in such situations, appears to be a crucial part of treatment for stammering.

Intelligence

Stanford–Binet test A popular intelligence test given to children. Test items are related to school activities: pre-school children are given objects to identify; primary school children have to say what words mean, make choices and decisions, and work out arithmetic problems; secondary school children are required to repeat sentences, draw designs from memory, find absurdities in sentences or pictures, find similarities and differences, and explain stories. Test performance is related to average performance of children of similar age.

Statistics in psychology *Brian Everitt*

It was Disraeli who said that there were lies damned lies, and statistics. Who, for example, has not heard the comment 'you can prove anything with statistics'? Perhaps we should begin by asking: what is a statistic? what does the subject of statistics concern itself with, and what are its aims?

To answer these questions we need first to be clear that there are, essentially, two branches of statistics, *descriptive* statistics and *inferential* statistics. It is the first of these that is most familiar to the general public since it is concerned, in essence, with statistics as pieces of numerical information. For example, each of the following statements is a *statistic*: the life expectancy of a male child in the USA is 67 years; 2 out of 5 marriages end in divorce. However, it is the inferential branch of statistics which is central in contemporary behavioural research, since it is intimately concerned with assessing whether particular theories are consistent with experimental findings, whether one treatment for a particular disorder is preferable to another and so on. But before we can discuss either of these two aspects of statistics in more detail we need to become acquainted with a number of terms and expressions in constant use in psychological research.

Useful terms The first of these is the term *variable*, which is essentially some property of an object or individual which can be measured. Height and weight are two obvious examples. Anxiety is perhaps a less well defined variable, but it is possible to imagine its measurement, say by assigning the value zero to an individual who is regarded as being not at all anxious, 1 to a person with a mild degree of anxiety and so on up to perhaps 5 implying high anxiety. As the name suggests a variable is a property which takes on different values for different individuals and it is often this *variation* which is of interest to the behavioural scientist.

The next term we need to consider is *population*. This is simply the complete set of objects or individuals under consideration. For example, all men over 6 feet high living in Finland might be regarded as a population for some particular reason. Let's assume that a researcher is interested in studying the variable intelligence for such a population. Obviously it would be impossible to record the intelligence scores of every member of the population, so the researcher is forced to study only a portion of the population, that is a *sample*. The set of intelligence scores he obtains for the sample would commonly be referred to as *data*.

The concept of *probability* also deserves consideration. Probability is a measure of the uncertainty that a particular event will happen, with a value of zero being used for an event that is impossible, and a value of 1 for an event that is certain. Intermediate values quantify the degree of uncertainty of the event. For example, in 1960 the number of babies born in Great Britain was 785,005; of these 404,150 were boys, so we would say that in that year the probability of a male child being born was 0.515 and of a girl 0.485. Having defined these technical terms, let us move on to consider in more detail the aims of the two branches of statistics mentioned above, beginning with descriptive statistics.

After measuring one or more variable values on a sample of individuals from some population of interest, the researcher looks for some way of processing that information so that it can be easily communicated to others. Now descriptive statistics provide a number of techniques for describing and summarising sets of data in a sensible manner. For example, nearly everybody is familiar with the concept of an *average* or *mean* value. Such values are often misunderstood (sometimes even ridiculed) because they do not apply to any particular person, or family or group. So are they really of any use? The answer is definitely yes, since such summary statistics enable one to make comparisons between different data sets very simply, and to do many other meaningful operations as well.

However, on its own an average is only a partial summary of a data set; consequently a further summary statistic which is often quoted by research workers is the *variance* or *standard deviation* of the data. These provide information as to how much the individual variable values spread out on either side of the average, with large values indicating that individual variable values may be quite different from the average, and small values indicating that individual values tend to be close to the average.

Answering questions Having summarised his data in some useful way the researcher may then want to use it to answer questions of special interest. For example, having measured intelligence scores on samples of men and women from a particular population, the investigator might address himself to answering the question: do men and women, on average, have different values for the variable intelligence? Questions such as this are generally termed *hypotheses*, and it is for the purpose of evaluating these that the scientist uses inferential statistics.

Although details of inferential methods are inappropriate in an article of this nature, they are in essence procedures for assessing the probability that observed data are compatible with a particular hypothesis. The important point to note here is that the concept of probability is involved, implying that we can never be completely certain about the truth or otherwise of a particular hypothesis. This is mainly because one is always dealing with samples rather than complete populations. So, for instance, in the example above we may sample 100 men and 100 women from our population, measure their intelligence values, and find that the average of the men is 95 and of the women 105, so in these particular samples women score higher. But in further samples of 100 men and 100 women, this situation could change; consequently we cannot argue directly that a sample difference implies a population difference. Instead, we use the methods of inferential statistics to determine the probability that an observed sample difference reflects a true difference in the population. If this probability is high, we draw the appropriate conclusion, namely that is it very likely that there is a difference in the intelligence scores of men and women in this particular population.

Statistical methods (and statisticians!) are frequently hissed and booed. Such accusations are based upon imperfect notions of the purposes and uses of statistics, which are not to reflect the idiosyncrasies of individuals but rather to help researchers in many fields understand what their data mean. Of course, statistical methods can be misused and inadequate data sets made to look more acceptable by a mass of inappropriate statistical operations and calculations. Yet statistics, in all its aspects, is an essential tool in modern behavioural research.

Stereotyping Blacks, Jews, WASPS, Gooks, cops, hippies, women's libbers – all these groups suffer from the stereotypes imposed on them. Stereotypes are really collections of prejudices and when they are not discriminatory or negatively used are a useful short-cut to 'getting on the same wavelength' as people we meet; it would be very tiresome and time-consuming if we had to start each interaction completely from scratch, without making any assumptions whatsoever.

S. S. Stevens, 1906–1973

Stevens, S. S. Born in Ogden, Utah, in 1906, Stanley Smith Stevens spent three years as a Mormon missionary in Europe before completing his higher education. He gained an AB from Stanford in 1931. He then enrolled at Harvard to read medicine but switched to psychology, receiving his PhD in 1933. Stevens stayed on at Harvard for the next 40 years until his death in 1973.

Stevens is noted for having revised Fechner's classical law of psychophysics. *Psychophysics* is that branch of psychology, founded by Fechner, which studies the relationship between the physical intensity of a stimulus – a noise, say – and its subjective magnitude – the sound heard. Fechner proposed a logarithmic relationship between stimulus and sensation which, when plotted on a graph, would produce a straight line. In other words, as a noise increases, he believed, its perceived loudness increased correspondingly.

A century after Fechner, in 1960, Stevens demonstrated that the sensation of a stimulus equals its intensity multiplied by a certain number or 'power'. This is known as the *power law*, which can be expressed mathematically as $x = y^n$, where x is the sensation, y the stimulus and n the exponential power. On a graph this yields a curve, not a straight line. The exponent n varies with the nature of the stimulus. With light it is 0.33, with electric shocks 3.5. This means that doubling the intensity of a light produces an increase in perceived brightness of only 30 per cent, but doubling an electric shock will make it feel more than ten times stronger.

Stevens also applied his power law to judgements in matters of social psychology. Thus for one watch to be perceived as worth double the price of another, it would have to be twice as desirable. But for a theft to be considered twice as serious as another, the amount of money stolen would have to be 60 times as great.

Stimulants Substances which produce a lift of mood, ranging from cosy pick-me-ups like tea and coffee, through the amphetamines and drugs like phenmetrazine and methylphenidate, to the ultimate high produced by cocaine.

Stimulus In conditioning theory, any change in the environment which elicits a response. Sometimes stimuli can become generalised, *stimulus generalisation*: one makes a simi-

Pavlov

lar response to stimuli only loosely related to the stimulus which caused the response initially. In a neurological context, a stimulus is a change in energy (pressure, light, temperature, chemical concentration) which excites a receptor cell or nerve ending; provided such an energy change is above a certain intensity, known as *stimulus threshold*, a nerve impulse is generated.

Nervous system

Stimulus–response psychology The view that all psychological phenomena can be explained in terms of stimuli and responses; essentially the view pioneered by J. B. Watson, the founder of behaviourism.

Stress *Donald Meichenbaum*
Stress can be thought of in various ways. One can talk of stress as a condition of the environment, something out there in the social and physical world which impinges unpleasantly on us. Using this model, external things like war, work, competition, heat and cold are viewed as stressing agents or 'stressors'. This is a concept borrowed from engineering – engineers are always calculating the strains which stresses exert on various objects.

The opposite view of stress is that it is subjective, an individual's response to threats and challenges in the environment. The individual is said to be 'under stress' or 'stressed'. Using this model, stress is an internal event, sometimes psychological, sometimes physiological, sometimes both.

The sources of stress This inside view of stress was put forward by Hans Selye, a major pioneer in the study of stress and the man responsible for making doctors aware of the role of stress in certain illnesses. In his recent book *Stress without distress* Selye distinguished between harmful kinds of stress or 'distress' (failure, frustration), and other kinds of stress, 'eustress', which may be benign or positively beneficial. It is the way we view events and how we cope with them that determines whether we are harmfully or beneficially stressed. Conflict, threat, anxiety, challenge, sexual arousal – all these events are stressful, but their potential to do harm or good depends on how we react to them.

The most common source of stress is what the Americans neatly call 'hassle' – the small conflicts which simmer and occasionally boil over during our daily dealings with children spouses, bosses, colleagues, even inanimate objects ... Hassle is insidious and cumulative, but most of us have strategems for coping.

Another potent source of stress is loss – the death of someone we love, the end of a love affair, a drastic reduction of income or prestige. Stress can also be the result of traumatic events – floods and earthquakes, or man-made disasters like war, plane crashes, car accidents, fires, muggings, rape ...

It is most important to realise that we are seldom 'victims' of stress. In fact we often behave in ways which actually create, maintain or increase the stress we feel. It is our lifestyle and pattern of behaviour, which in large measure we choose ourselves, which determine the degree of stress we feel. Another important aspect of stress is that it occurs mainly in situations in which outcome is felt to be highly significant but in some doubt or jeopardy. Failing in unimportant situations in which we have no personal stake is very seldom stressful.

The transactional view The currently accepted view of stress is that it is a *transaction between the individual and the environment*, not simply a set of circumstances which overwhelm or a set of psychological or physiological reactions which incapacitate. Every individual defines and creates stress in his or her own terms, and deals with it in a very personal way. Some of us, because of our lifestyles and personal values, experience stress more acutely than others.

Cognitive style

Personal construct theory

Are there biochemical events associated with the experience of stress? Laboratory studies show that body hormone and enzyme levels change with stress, and they change in order to help us combat stress. Over thirty different hormones enter the fray in moments of stress; by measuring their concentration doctors can assess the intensity of stress.

Hormones

A point worth making here is that these physiological happenings, do not in themselves constitute stress. Nor are their effects necessarily debilitating. It is not physiological arousal *per se* which causes stress, but the way in which threats or challenges are perceived. What may appear to be the same phenomena physiologically may be poles apart psychologically.

One factor which determines how we appraise both external stressors and internal reactions is whether we feel in control of our reactions or not. We are less likely to experience acute stress if we know, for example, that the stressful situation won't last long, or that we are fairly resilient.

Stress management Having explained the nature of stress let's turn our attention to the nature of coping. Coping is a concept which owes much to the writing and research of Richard Lazarus. It denotes all the mechanisms we use to neutralise threats to our psychological stability and enable us to function effectively. Sometimes *direct action* is an adequate coping response. We manage to change a situation for the better, or beat a quick retreat or maybe relinquish certain goals. Direct action means changing one's relationship to the environment. In practice it may mean readying oneself for the stressing event on the principle that forewarned is forearmed, or it may mean physically avoiding the stressor.

But not all situations can be altered or avoided, in which case we may have to resort to what Lazarus and Launier call *palliative* methods of coping, methods which make us feel better although they don't make the threat or the challenge go away. There are various palliative strategies, including denial (not thinking about it), intellectualisation (rationalising the threat or adopting a philosophical stance), detachment ('it has nothing to do with me') and self-deception.

So successful coping in a given situation does not always involve active mastery over one's environment. In some circumstances retreat, toleration or disengagement may be the healthiest possible response.

Subconscious A term used mainly by French psychopathologists to describe conscious processes which occur outside of personal awareness, and used in a similar sense in everyday speech. But the majority of psychologists prefer to divide psychological processes into conscious and unconscious.

Brain

Subcortex Sometimes called the 'old brain'; influences many of our basic behaviours, such as sleep, arousal, temperature control, eating, drinking, sexual activity, fear, etc. The main subcortical structures are the thalamus, hypothalamus, reticular activating system and the limbic system.

Sublimation Working off frustrated sexual desires in non-sexual, socially acceptable substitute activities; yet another defence mechanism, and a very important one.

A none too serious look at sublimation

Subliminal perception Perception of stimuli at a level below the threshold of conscious awareness; can be studied

Consumer psychology

systematically by presenting stimuli tachistoscopically. Despite the big outcry against subliminal advertising in the late 1950s and 1960s, there is little evidence that subliminal stimuli can be used to manipulate buying habits or any other form of behaviour for that matter.

Mental retardation

Subnormal Having a value substantially below average; an IQ of 83 is considered to be on the borderline between normal and subnormal.

Depression

Suicide In some cultures an acceptable, even heroic, method of dealing with defeat or dishonour; in others a criminal act or a mortal sin. People who work in suicide prevention argue that suicide is not an act of self-destruction but a 'cry for help'. Suicidal thoughts often accompany deep depression or loss. More men commit suicide than women, but the suicide rate is probably far higher than official statistics show. How many fatal car accidents are suicides, for example? And for every successful suicide there are probably ten attempts which fail. Suicide is less frequent among married people than among single, widowed or divorced people, which suggests that the lack of meaningful relationships may be an important trigger factor. Recent pressure groups for voluntary euthanasia have made the whole subject of suicide more than usually newsworthy.

Superego Loosely speaking, one's conscience; that part of the personality which operates according to a personal value system and moral attitudes absorbed from the society one grows up in; begins to develop around the age of 7 or 8 when we realise what is expected of us, strive to live up to expectation and develop an *Ego ideal*, an idea of the sort of person we would like to become.

Superordinate goals In Maslow's hierarchy of needs, the needs which rank highest, namely achievement of self-actualisation, complete emotional satisfaction. Superordinate goals cannot be achieved until subordinate goals like food or sex have been achieved. However, Maslow's views lack firm empirical support.

Repression

Suppression Unlike repression which is done unconsciously, suppression is done consciously, to push disturbing or unacceptable thoughts to the back of mind - we all have experiences we would prefer to forget. At one time suppression was thought unhealthy - far better the full and free expression of one's feelings, however destructive. It now seems, however, that the reverse is true: well adjusted individuals often make extensive use of suppression.

Symbolism The representation of one object by another.

The ability to use symbols is, as far as we know, unique to *Homo sapiens*. Psychologists normally distinguish two types of symbols. When one object clearly represents something else it is a *discursive symbol*. The colour red, for example, is accepted as a symbol of danger (traffic lights, brake lights, red alerts, panic buttons). But what if we are discussing the significance of a work of art or literature? Whole books have been written about the meaning of the Mona Lisa's smile, but for all that it is ambiguous – perhaps it symbolises ambiguity. Mysterious symbols are *propositional symbols*.

Psychoanalysis

Symbolism is of considerable significance to psychoanalysts. Freud pointed out that real objects or dream objects which arouse no particularly strong feelings may stand for other objects to which very powerful conflictual feelings are attached. A female patient, for example, reported dreaming that she took an extremely long bright red stick of rock out of her therapist's pocket and bit into it eagerly and hard only to find that her teeth crumbled in the process. A psychoanalytic interpretation of this fantasy might symbolically equate the rock with the therapist's penis and the crumbling of the patient's teeth with the guilt she unconsciously felt at wishing to destroy him sexually.

Jungian psychologists also make use of symbolic interpretation in their analysis of dreams and fantasies, but they usually give somewhat abstract, even mystical, meanings to them. Far from attaching phallic meaning to quite neutral objects the penis itself is seen as a symbol of virility and strength.

Taboos Acts outlawed by society; incest is one of the most universally encountered taboos. Strong Oedipal wishes (a boy saying 'I'm going to marry my mother', or a girl saying 'I'm going to live with Daddy all my life and take care of him') seem to suggest that there are no innate barriers to incest; the barriers are presumably learned, and founded on the fact that persistent inbreeding is bad sense biologically, liable to perpetuate undesirable traits. Most food taboos are founded on historically good reasons, although such avoidances today are purely formal.

Teasing A mildly aggressive form of social behaviour intended to provoke laughter, embarrassment, irritation or physical retaliation; among intimates teasing is usually playful, done within a context of affection; among children in a school playground teasing is usually malicious and hurtful.

Telepathy (see Parapsychology)

Temper tantrum A sometimes violent display of ill-temper, classed by child psychologists as a behaviour disorder; especially common in pre-school children and again at puberty. Girls appear to grow out of temper tantrums earlier than boys, perhaps because they are taught to internalise aggressive feelings more than boys. If a child learns that tantrums are productive, that parents give in, he or she is likely to use them over and over again. Adult tantrums are generally rare and much more violent.

Temporal lobes The lateral lobes of both cerebral hemispheres, situated roughly at eye level; primarily associated with hearing, but perhaps also having some importance in visual memory and discrimination.

Brain

Tension Measurable by recording brain-wave activity (electroencephalogram), electrical activity in muscles (electromyogram), blood pressure, and electroconductivity of the skin (galvanic skin resistor); can be reduced by relaxation exercises, meditation, biofeedback methods, or by drugs (alcohol, barbiturates, tranquillisers).

Variables

Test construction Test construction is the systematic development of scientific methods of measuring variables (intelligence, personality) so that tests can be widely used, by different testers, and their results be accepted as reliable and valid by the scientific community at large. All tests must attain certain standards and be subjected to certain validating statistical operations before their general use is permitted.

Obviously *test materials* and *test instructions* must be *standardised*; in other words their administration must be made identical for all testers. Instructions must be standardised so that a brisk unhelpful tester obtains the same results as a helpful kindly one, and test materials must be assessed for their objectivity, so that they have the same meaning for each person (a picture of a subway train will not have the same meaning to all children in a sample if some live in the city and some in the country).

The test must also be *reliable*, which means that it must produce the same result when administered two or three times – it would not be satisfactory for an intelligence test to indicate above-average performance one day and subnormality the next. All psychological tests must also be valid, in the sense that they must measure what they purport to measure. A test is said to have *face validity* if it looks as if it does this. However, this may not be enough. A test which supposedly measures creativity by requiring people to tell original stories may in fact be measuring memory for recent books or films! So face validity alone may not be sufficient. There are many other ways of validating a test, depending on its purpose. *Criterion validity* is widely used for diagnostic tests, which identify patients with particular psychological or neurological problems; for example, a test of brain damage would be given to a group of people with brain damage, and to a group without. The test would be said to have criterion validity when it successfully discriminated between the two groups.

The final stage of test construction is that of *calibration*. A large, random sample of the population is tested to establish a scale against which to measure testees. One can then identify whether someone's performance is above or below average, very uncommon, etc. For this exercise to be meaningful, the population upon which a test is calibrated should be identical with the one in which it is used. This requirement is not always observed. The most widely used intelligence test in Britain was standardised on an American sample!

Testosterone The 'male' sex hormone produced in the testes and also in smaller amounts in the adrenal glands of both sexes; responsible for libido and sexual performance in both men and women. Impotence is occasionally due to malfunction of the pituitary, which switches on testosterone production in the testes, but more frequently to psychological factors such as anxiety. To digress for a moment, the word 'testis' comes from the Latin word meaning 'witness'; no one lacking testicles could 'testify' in court!

T-Groups Also referred to as training groups, encounter groups or sensitivity groups. Pioneered by American psychol-

Halo effect

Experimenter effect

Statistics in psychology

Sexual dysfunction

Psychotherapy

ogist Kurt Lewin, and much in vogue in the late 1960s, the aim of T-groups is to heighten one's awareness of social relationships, and increase the satisfaction one derives from them, by dispensing with many of the conventional props and rules of social interaction. Although individuals with emotional problems are often attracted to T-groups, the function of T-groups is not so much to provide therapy as to build on existing social skills.

Nervous system

Thalamus The 'relay station' of the brain, plentifully connected to the cerebral hemispheres above it and to various subcortical structures and the spinal chord; its function is to sift through sensory messages coming from all parts of the body and route them to the appropriate areas of the cortex.

Eros

Thanatos Greek for 'death'; coined by Freud to refer to the 'death instinct', coeval with Eros, the life instinct, and driving us towards aggression, self-destruction and a return to the inorganic state. Eros and Thanatos fuse in varying combinations, of 'instinct fusions' as Freud called them; in aggressive instinct fusions, Thanatos predominates, in sexual instinct fusions Eros predominates. It is our attempt to gratify both the death and life instincts simultaneously which leads to neurotic conflict.

Projective tests

Rorschach test

Thematic apperception test (TAT) A projective personality test developed by Harvard psychologist Henry Murray in 1938; usually consists of about 20 pictures (of people or landscapes, more structured but also more ambiguous than inkblots) around which subjects are asked to construct stories, saying what is happening, what is being thought, what led up to the situation, what will be the outcome, etc. When analysed the themes of these stories reveal the tone of personal relationships, conscious and unconscious needs, perception of the environment, control over impulses and contact with reality.

Symbolism

Thinking Mental activity involving the manipulation of symbols, concepts, ideas, and mental images. Thinking is what frees *Homo sapiens* from an existence entirely dominated by internal needs and external events. It appears that most of our thinking involves putting sensations, events and objects into categories; this is *conceptual thinking*. When we make a sustained series of links between concepts we are indulging in reasoned or *rational thinking*. During our waking hours we spend far more time daydreaming, making casual associations between wishes, sensations, ideas and mental images, than thinking logically about practical matters. All thought processes make use of symbols – whether in the form of words or mental images. We can recreate sensory perceptions in thought – we talk of having a 'mind's eye' – but we also hear speech and music with an 'inner ear', and can vividly imagine sensations of taste, touch, movement, and so on. The psychologist who contributed most of our knowledge of how thinking abilities develop was undoubtedly Jean Piaget.

The power behind the throne

Edward Thorndike, 1874–1949

Thorndike, Edward Although Edward Lee Thorndike is chiefly remembered for his work on animal learning, he was an educational theorist of the most eclectic kind and the leading educational psychologist of his day. He designed widely used psychological tests, developed a theory of intelligence, studied sex differences, interests, attitudes and vocabulary, and wrote many influential textbooks.

Thorndike's early years in psychology were spent under the tutorship of William James at Harvard. Finding Harvard's research facilities too limited, he moved on to Columbia University, where he spent the rest of his long and productive career. By the time of his death, in 1949, he had produced a quantity of research and writing which no psychologist, except perhaps Piaget, has equalled since.

Thorndike's book *Animal Intelligence*, published in 1911, describes the experiments on trial and error learning which led up to his most famous formulation, the *law of effect*. Working with cats, who learned to escape from a locked cage by pulling on a rope, he demonstrated that it was possible for animals to select an appropriate response from a number of possibilities. By escaping from their cage his cats obtained food, and thus pleasure. Thorndike believed that by randomly discovering the correct response, in this case the pleasure-giving one of food, other unsuccessful responses were gradually 'stamped out'. Further work with chicks, monkeys and dogs produced similar results, enabling him to generalise his ideas.

Animal behaviour, Thorndike theorised, is not based on reasoning but on results, and on whether those results are pleasant or painful. The greater the pleasure or pain, the greater the strengthening or weakening of the bond between behaviour and result. Later work led to a refinement of the law of effect: the quicker a stimulus is followed by a result, the quicker the bond forms; Thorndike called this particular theory *belongingness*.

Threat *Shlomo Breznitz*

The ability to occasionally anticipate the future is one of our most cherished possessions. No longer bound to immediate sensory experiences we can plan ahead and prepare for things to come. This competence to leap beyond the here and now has its cost however. Our premonitions of the future are a threat to the present, a psychological threat.

Different scholars use different definitions for the concept of threat, but the basic idea they share is that threat is *a prior warning about some future negative event*. The impact of such a warning depends on the specific nature of the impending event, the quantity and quality of the information one has about it and one's physiological and psychological make-up.

There are some dangers one can prepare for in advance. Well organised communities usually receive early warnings about floods, hurricanes, fires, and so on, and use the warning time to take precautions. Science and technology are continuously trying to improve the accuracy and earliness of disaster forecasts.

Accurately forecasting unpleasant events is one thing, developing effective warning systems is another. One's psychological reaction to threatening information is very important. Protective behaviour may be the most appropriate reaction in the face of threat, but for purely psychological reasons one may do something quite different. Chief among inappropriate reactions to threat is defensive denial. "This can never happen to me" is a very common form of psychological protection against intolerable threats. While reasonably helpful when

Stress

Anxiety

235

painful information is presented for the first time, persistent denial can be quite harmful.

Another frequent reason for ignoring threat warnings is that they are assumed to be false alarms. Threats which never materialise cast substantial doubt on the forecaster, so like the boy who cried wolf in the fairy tale, professional doomsters tend to lose their credibility. To further complicate matters, it so happens that the more sensitive a warning system is the greater the likelihood of false alarms. Early warnings, based as they are on remote and weak signals, are less reliable than late warnings. One has a choice between warning time and accuracy.

Eliminating the threat of hijack involves some threat to personal dignity.

Threats are sometimes deliberately used in order to obviate the need for unpleasant direct action. As long as the desired behaviour is produced by the threat alone, its credibility is not put to test. The crunch comes when behaviour is not modified and the threat does not materialise. Thereafter the value of the threat is substantially reduced; threat ceases to become an effective weapon.

Another intriguing aspect of threat is the so-called 'incubation of threat' phenomenon; duration of anticipation of a frightening event has been found to increase the fear reaction to it. Fear is most intense when no active preparation is possible. Long, helpless waiting leads to especially high levels of fear and anxiety, to a form of 'psychological exhaustion'. It may be wise not to break certain kinds of news at the earliest opportunity, especially when the recipient has little direct experience of similar threats. Under the shadow of a powerful threat most of us tend to imagine things as very black.

Nervous system

Threshold The amount or intensity of stimulus required to produce a response, a useful concept in studying stimuli and responses; loosely used in phrases such as *pain threshold*, *anxiety threshold* or *laughter threshold*. Our thresholds for various stimuli can be raised or lowered by our physical or emotional state. Anxiety lowers one's pain threshold, for example; alcohol raises one's anxiety threshold. The phenomenon of tolerance in drug dependence is a threshold phenomenon; increasing doses of the drug increase the threshold at which one begins to experience euphoria.

Token economy A technique of behaviour therapy pioneered in the late 1960s, and mainly used in mental and rehabilitation institutions to mould behaviour in a desirable direction. Improved behaviour is rewarded with tokens which can be exchanged for 'privileges'. For instance when a patient feeds himself, or goes to the toilet by himself, he accumulates tokens, and when he has a certain number he is allowed to eat his favourite food, watch television or visit relatives over the weekend. Undesirable behaviours cost patients tokens. The main virtues of a token economy are that it sets clear goals and specific behaviour criteria to achieve those goals. The method has scored some notable successes in educational and industrial settings.

Edward Tolman, 1886–1959

Tolman, Edward As a neo-behaviourist, Tolman was concerned with hunting down the processes which intervene between stimuli and responses. Early behaviourists like Watson of course claimed that no such intervening variables existed, but for Tolman behaviour was far more complex than a straightforward sequence of causes and effects; it was instead a chain of goals, and actions which led towards *goal-objects*. In his own words, learning is "an affair of sign formation, refinement, selection and invention", a theory sometimes referred to as *purposive behaviourism*. Tolman insisted that all psychological concepts must be testable by "concrete, repeatable observations", a requirement he labelled *operationism*. His demand for rigorous experimental standards influenced a whole generation of American psychologists.

Tolman's theory concerning the intervening variables of behaviour was influenced as much by Gestalt psychology as by Watson's behaviourism. The Gestalt influence can be seen in the stress he laid on the wholeness of behaviour. He identi-

Variables

fied three types of variable: *independent, dependent* and *intervening*. Among the independent variables he grouped environmental stimuli, physiological drive and heredity. The dependent variables included the observable behaviour of any organism, which Tolman regarded as goal-directed. But the intervening variables, he believed, were the real determinants of behaviour. These included needs and motives, and what he described as 'behaviour spaces', situations in which some objects are seen as desirable and others repulsive.

Tolman spent the greater part of his distinguished academic career at the University of California at Berkeley. He died in 1959 at the age of 83.

Trait theories of personality In contrast to type theories, trait theories view people as possessing unique combinations of traits, both common and individual, rather than as typefy-

Personality

ing major categories of personality. Gordon Allport, a leading trait theorist, regarded traits like shyness or aggression as

Allport

common traits, and traits like sadism or meanness as individual traits.

Drugs and mental disorder

Tranquillisers The sedative-hypnotic class of drugs used to reduce anxiety; the main categories of tranquilliser used today are the benzodiazepines, which include Librium, Valium, Dalmare and Mogadon, and the barbiturates, which include Nembutal and Mandrax. Many mental health professionals consider tranquillisers to be the scourge of our times - they are a very temporary answer to life's problems.

Transactional analysis (TA) A method of group therapy originated by Eric Berne in 1964. TA applies various principles of psychoanalysis and social learning therapy to analysing social 'transactions', the trade-offs which take place during social interactions. The goal of TA is openness to one's own and others' feelings through becoming aware of the 'games' and 'roles' we all play. The transactional analyst assumes there are three ego states, Parent, Adult and Child (roughly analogous with the Superego, Ego and Id), within all of us. In some social situations the Child comes to the fore, in others the Adult; equally, the person we are interacting with shifts between the Parent, Adult or Child. The healthy personality is one in which the parent ego state is in control, but indulges the Child and keeps a tight reign on the Adult.

Transcendental meditation (TM) A popular modern form of meditation based on *Mantra yoga*, that is retaining certain Indian religious elements, but simplified for modern use. Its originator, the Maharishi Mahesh Yogi (of The Beatles fame), defined it as: "Turning the attention inwards towards subtler levels of thought until the mind transcends the experience of the subtlest state of thought and arrives at the source of the thought." The unchanging focus of attention in TM is a *mantra*, a special set of syllables, which is chanted over and over again. All in all TM appears to be of positive value in reducing aggression, hostility and anxiety, and increasing self-confidence, concentration and learning ability. It has been used effectively to aid therapeutic progress among mental patients, prisoners and drug addicts.

Transference In psychoanalysis, transferring the feelings one has about an important person in one's life to the analyst. According to Freud, it is transference which makes analysis possible. The task of the analyst is to discover the kind of wish, usually a sexual wish retained from the oral, anal or phallic stage, which is causing the transference.

Transsexualism A sometimes tragic problem of sexual identity; the male transsexual believes he is a woman trapped inside a man's body, and the rather rarer female transsexual that she is a man in a woman's body; usually involves no detectable disorder of the genes, gonads or sexualia. Sex change operations have been legal in the United States for 20 years. A large number of transsexuals seem intensely unhappy and disturbed; for many sex change surgery is a kinder option than years of suffering (not much alleviated by behaviour modification techniques), or self-mutilation or suicide.

Transvestism Cross-dressing or wearing the clothes of the opposite sex as a regular behaviour or as a condition of erotic satisfaction; even in these days of unisex dressing, a man is ridiculed for wearing a woman's clothes, but not vice versa. Some male transvestites are on the borders of transsexualism, but most do not doubt or question their masculine identity; many in fact are heterosexual. Women transvestites are rare. Male transvestites commonly speak of the advantages of being female, which has suggested to some researchers that cross-dressing is a way of asking for the love and security withheld in boyhood, and perhaps given to sisters instead.

Trauma A physical or psychological event which the individual cannot assimilate because it is drastically shocking,

Altered state of consciousness

Dressing up: for the majority of transvestites a guilty secret

T

Such stuff as dreams, bad dreams, are made of ...

horrifying or anxiety-arousing. The Ego deals with such events by denying or repressing them.

Trial and error A method of problem-solving, but a very hit-and-miss one; all possible alternatives are looked at in a random or systematic manner until one 'clicks'. One of the major explorers of trial and error learning was E. L. Thorndike, using cats as his experimental subjects.

Turner's syndrome About one in every 3000 female babies born with Turner's Syndrome (the combination XO in the 23rd chromosome) survive into childhood. In external appearance they are girls, but at puberty the ovaries degenerate and the breasts fail to develop. Secondary sex characteristics, and even menstruation, can be ensured by giving oestrogen, but there is no question of bearing children.

X chromosome

Twins Ready-made experiments for the biologist and psychologist. Monozygotic (identical) twins, which develop from the same zygote, have 100 per cent of their genetic material in common; it therefore follows that any differences between them arise because of different experiences and different environmental circumstances. This does indeed seem to be the case when twins reared apart are studied. With dizygotic (fra-

Behavioural genetics

240

ternal) twins, the amount of genetic material shared is no more and no less than that shared by other offspring of the same parents. So similarities between fraternal twins could be attributed to similar upbringing.

For many years twins have been the main battle ground for the genetic and environmental champions of psychological development. Both recognise that personality is the result of interaction between genetic and environmental factors, but viewed as a whole the literature seems to suggest that genetic factors are up to twice as important.

The Magnificent Two

Personality

Type theories of personality Typecasting people into conveniently broad personality categories. Current type theories view individuals as occupying positions along four major personality dimensions or continua, these dimensions are extraversion–introversion, neuroticism–emotional stability, intelligence, and psychoticism.

Client-centred therapy

Unconditional positive regard The attitude a client-centred therapist adopts towards clients – an update of the old adage 'the customer is right'. The therapist is warm, empathic, non-judgemental, and accepts what the client says as the objective reality of the situation. This is the climate in which clients most quickly discover their true wants and feelings.

A natural, unconditioned response to a sudden drenching

Pavlov

Unconditioned response A completely automatic, natural, non-interfered-with response to a natural stimulus – like blinking on emerging into bright sunlight, or stretching to relieve tension. A loud noise which makes you jump, onions which make you cry, or mustard which makes you go red in the face, are all unconditioned stimuli.

Freud

Unconscious At one time Freud was widely criticised for using the term unconscious in connection with mental phenomena, because all mental activity was thought to be conscious. Today we assume that the whole Id, part of the Ego

242

and a small part of the Superego are unconscious. Two kinds of unconscious are recognised: that part which is easily accessible, sometimes called the pre-conscious, and that part which isn't, or can only be accessed once the censorship separating it from the pre-conscious and conscious has been removed.

Unpleasure A heightening of tension, as distinct from a release of tension which gives a feeling of pleasure. Where a release of tension is anticipated, the feeling may be forepleasure rather than unpleasure, but when release appears to be obstructed unpleasure is experienced. Conversely, a very low state of tension may be experienced as unpleasant too.

Pleasure principle

Forepleasure

Vanity Misplaced reliance on appearances or abilities, often to compensate for feelings of inadequacy.

Hairdresser and client: the vanity business

Behavioural psychology

Test construction

Variable The aim of psychological research is to investigate a particular *dependent variable* by manipulating a number of *independent variables* and trying to exclude *extraneous variables* which might confuse the matter. An independent variable is a particular trait, attribute or set of circumstances which in some way determines behaviour in a given situation. Take achievement at school: high marks in class may be determined by intelligence, by the trait of persistence, by help and encouragement from parents, by a good teacher and by a host of other causes. These causes are all independent variables, independent in the sense that intelligence can contribute to high school achievement but not vice versa. In this example school achievement would be the dependent variable.

Voyeurism Compulsive and often planned peeping at other people's bodies and sexual activities; a substitute for sexual relationships in that most voyeurs ('Peeping Toms') feel sexually inadequate and inept at making or maintaining sexual friendships.

Watson, J. B. Although Watson's involvement with academic psychology lasted a mere 20 years – he was asked to resign from Johns Hopkins University in 1920 in consequence of a liaison which precipitated his divorce – his approach to psychology, known as *behaviourism*, is one of the pillars on which psychology stands today.

Watson rejected all 'mentalistic' concepts – theoretical constructs like consciousness, unconsciousness, sensation and will – and also introspection as a means of tracking them down. In their stead he proposed a *stimulus-response approach*, the idea that all behaviour can be broken down into, traced back to, controlled and predicted on the basis of responses to stimuli. A collection of stimuli constituted a *situation*, a collection of responses an *act*. In contrast to Pavlov and Thorndike, however, Watson proposed that the connection between a stimulus and a response is not maintained by reward or reinforcement, but by *frequency* and *recency*. The more frequently a response is made to a stimulus, the more powerful becomes the link between them; also the more recently a response is made the stronger the link. A reflex act like walking comes easily to us because it is characterised by both frequency and recency.

Four years after resigning from Johns Hopkins, Watson was appointed Vice-President of J. Walter Thompson, then as now the world's largest advertising agency. The practical intelligence he had devoted to studying the reactions of animals and children in the laboratory he devoted to manipulating, with great flair and success, the reactions of consumers. He died in 1958, aged 80.

J. B. Watson, 1878–1958

Behavioural psychology

Wechsler adult intelligence scale (WAIS) Introduced in 1955 by American psychologist David Wechsler as an intelligence test for all people over the age of 16. It consists of 11 parts arranged in ascending order of difficulty. The verbal section comprises a battery of tests of general information, comprehension, vocabulary, similarities between words, mathematics, and digit span. The performance section includes a block design test, picture arranging, picture completion and object assembly. The tester usually continues with each test until a certain number of items have been incorrectly answered or missed.

IQ

Word association test An early projective test developed by Jung and others and used to diagnose complexes. It began with the test administrator saying: "I am going to read you a series of words one by one. I want you to respond to each word with *one* other word. It doesn't matter what your word

Projective tests

245

is, as long as it is the *first* word that comes into your head after you hear my word." In the second part of the test the stimulus words - words which had homely, aggressive, phobic and various sexual connotations - were repeated and the subject was asked to reproduce his original responses. The test has now been replaced by the Sentence Completion Test, frequently used today in personnel selection.

Schizophrenia

Word salad Speech which is incongruous, irrelevant, illogical and disorganised to the point of being unintelligible; reflects the severely disordered thinking characteristic of advanced schizophrenia; to the schizophrenic such utterances may be very exactly and logically expressive of the conflicts he or she is trying to resolve.

Acting out

Working through In psychoanalysis, the overall process of free association, dream interpretation and overcoming of resistances which enables the analyst to draw out into the open the client's inner feelings and conflicts. This may take many weekly sessions because resistances are only gradually dissolved. Neurotic symptoms reduce or disappear once working through is complete.

X chromosome   One of two factors in the 23rd pair of chromosomes, the sex chromosomes; the mother always contributes X chromosomes to her offspring, but the father, who has an X and a Y chromosome, can contribute either. If the chromosome in the sperm which fuses with the ovum at conception is an X, the new being will be genetically female (XX); if the sperm contributes a Y, the embryo will be genetically male (XY). The X chromosome is enormous compared with the Y, and codes for many more characteristics than the Y, which codes for maleness only. This is why so many sex-linked abnormalities (haemophila and colour blindness, for instance) are carried by the female but expressed in the male.

Xenoglossia   Literally 'speaking foreign tongues'; reading, writing, speaking and understanding a real language which one cannot possibly know or have learnt; taken by some to be evidence of telepathy, but a phenomenon that has not attracted serious parapsychological investigation so far.

Xenophobia   Literally 'fear of foreigners'; being deeply apprehensive of people you don't know, or being afraid of meeting people.

XYY syndrome   A very rare form of trisomy in the 23rd pair of chromosomes, resulting in a very tall and aggressive male of below average intelligence. Serious scientific attempts have been made to associate the XYY configuration with criminal and psychopathic behaviour.

Psychopath

Yerkes–Dodson law States that there is an optimum level of arousal for the performance of any given task; as arousal builds towards the optimum, performance increases, but beyond a certain level of arousal performance suffers. The optimum level of arousal for tackling a difficult mathematical problem or for doing a complex jigsaw puzzle is much lower than that required for doing simple tasks well. This is why stress, which causes high levels of physical arousal, is so damaging to concentration and precision.

Yoga Several different systems of meditation of Indian and oriental origin based on body postures and breathing exercises, the aim of which is union of the individual self with the Universal Self. In the final stage of meditation – most systems have several graded steps ascending to this ultimate stage – a state of trance is reached, characterised by alpha brain waves and imperviousness to stress or pain. *Raja yoga* includes the following eight stages: self-control, *yama*; religious observances, *niyama*; physical postures, *asana*; regulation of breathing, *pranayama*; suppression of sense impressions of all external events and objects, *pratyahara*; concentration on a particular object, *dharana*; contemplation of a solitary object for long periods, *dyana*; losing consciousness of one's concentration and becoming totally absorbed in the trance state, *samadhi*.

Voyage to the centre of being

Zest General energy and *joie de vivre*, especially in a social context. What you put in you get out – zest is a good investment.

'Hallalujah!' Putting one's heart and soul into it, a gift that often goes with an extravert personality

Split brain

Z lens A sophisticated piece of apparatus developed by Roger Sperry and his associates in 1955 to enable them to project visual stimuli onto the retina of the eye so that they are interpreted either by the left or the right hemisphere of the brain, not by both at once. Sperry, pioneer of the split brain operation, used the Z lens to demonstrate that split brain patients had two separate visual inner worlds: if the picture of an object was presented to one hemisphere the patient recognised it when it was presented again to the same hemisphere; however if the same object was presented to the other half of the visual field so that it was projected to the opposite hemisphere, the patient had no recollection of having seen it before.

Credits

Our acknowledgement also to the following people who provided expert writing and research assistance: John Boddy, Ph.D., Department of Psychology, University of Manchester; Mary Boyle, B.A., B.Phil., Department of Psychology, North East London Polytechnic; Barrie J. Brown, Ph.D., M.Sc., Institute of Psychiatry, University of London; Peter Fonagy, B.Sc., Department of Psychology, University College, University of London; Sarah E. Hampson, Ph.D., Department of Psychology, Birkbeck College, University of London; Belinda Hollyer, B.A., Dip.Ed; Anne H. Richardson, B.Sc., M.Phil., Psychology Department, Goodmayes Hospital, Essex; Philip H. Richardson, B.Sc., M.Phil., Department of Psychology, University College, University of London; Sheila Stevens, B.Sc., Department of Psychiatry, Charing Cross Hospital Medical School.

Also for their meticulous checking and suggestions at final manuscript stage, our thanks go to Arthur Wingfield, D.Phil., The Psychological Laboratory, University of Cambridge, and to Gerald H. Fisher, Ph.D., M.Ed., Department of Psychology, University of Newcastle upon Tyne. Finally, for typing and photocopying their way through successive versions of the manuscript, we would like to thank Zahida Hirjee and Sue Morawski.